Hide Your
A$$ET$
and
Disappear

Hide Your A$$ET$ and Disappear

A Step-by-Step Guide to Vanishing Without a Trace

EDMUND J. PANKAU

ReganBooks

An Imprint of HarperCollinsPublishers

A hardcover edition of this book was published in 1999 by HarperCollins Publishers.

HarperCollins books may be purchased for educational, business, or sales promotional use. For information please write: Special Markets Department, HarperCollins Publishers Inc., 10 East 53rd Street, New York, NY 10022.

First paperback edition published 2000.

Designed by Ruth Lee

The Library of Congress has catalogued the hardcover edition as follows:

Pankau, Edmund J.
     Hide your assets (and disappear) : a step-by-step guide to vanishing without a trace / Edmund Pankau. —1st ed.
        p. cm.
     Includes bibliographical references and index.
     ISBN 0-06-018394-2
        1. Commercial crimes—United States. 2. Computer crimes—United States. 3. Finance, Personal—United States—Corrupt Practices. 4. Electronic fund transfers—United States—Corrupt practices. 5. Fraudulent conveyances—United States. I. Title. II. Title: Hide your assets.
     HV6769.P35 1999
     364.16'8—dc21   98-50354

ISBN 0-06-098750-2 (pbk.)

02 03 04 RRD/❖ 10 9 8 7 6 5 4

This book is dedicated to the man who taught me all about the real ways of life—my dad. As a young boy, I watched him beat the system every day of his life; he got around city officials, entertained the local police, conned the FBI, and beat the IRS like a drum (although they did nab him once for running booze from Canada).
He taught me that everything and everyone has a price. With some it was money, others it was sex, and once in a while, it was for love.
Working at my dad's bars, I learned more about life than any college or police agency could ever teach. That's what really made me a good investigator.
Thank you, Pop. If there is a devil, I suspect that you have conned him, too. I miss you more than I could ever say.

This book is for entertainment and informational purposes. It is not intended to offer or replace legal or investment advice. Readers should obtain such advice from licensed professionals.

It is the author's intention to provide suggestions for the creation and maintenance of legitimate strategies for asset protection. Please take note that great emphasis is placed on timing. Asset protection actions taken close to the time when an individual encounters credit or legal difficulties are often not effective, and may be illegal, depending on the intent of the parties at the time such actions are taken.

With the exception of the names of public figures and the names of people involved in widely publicized criminal and civil cases, all of the names of people described in anecdotes in the text have been changed and are not the real names of the people whose experiences are described.

CONTENTS

ACKNOWLEDGMENTS

This book could not have been possible without assistance or inspiration from the following people, wherever they may be.

The good . . .
Doug, my secret sailor, and the many clients whose stories contributed to this book
Ron Kaye and Connie Schmidt, my co-conspirators, researchers, and favorite cooks
Al Zuckerman, the best agent in the business, for believing in me
And most of all, my beautiful bride Lisa—I think I got it right this time

The bad . . .
Meyer Lansky, who gave me my first taste of organized crime and the ways of deceit
The Texas S & L Kingpin who inadvertently taught me the trade
Manuel Noriega, "mister money laundering" himself

And the ugly. . .
My several ex-wives, for the motivation they provided
Their attorneys, who are now scared to death of me
The miserable bastards who gave me grief and lived to regret it
And the government that over-charged us all!

FROM THE AUTHOR

To paraphrase the words of the immortal Colonel Kurtz, in the movie *Apocalypse Now*, "Sell the house, sell the car, ditch the dog, and give the kids to your mother."

The good colonel was so fed up with the system, betrayed by his superiors and berated by his peers, that he chucked it all and went back to Vietnam to fight the war his way.

If you have ever felt that way, if you are fed up with the lies, the scams, and the just plain old bullshit from your spouse, your friends, the government, and the people who claim to represent it, then this book's for you.

There is a revolution brewing, not only in the United States but also around the world. It's not politically or socially motivated, it's about the bucks that get taken from us every day in the name of what's good for us. It's about our having less and less control over our own lives, and less to say about what we can do and where we can do it.

Before you blow out your brains, or take it out on half the population of your neighborhood, consider just walking away and starting over. It's really there to be done, and you can live to enjoy it. Besides, you can think about those who caused you stress and laugh at them every day, because they are the ones left in the trap.

In the words of the Romans, "*Non corborundum illigitimi*"; don't let the bastards grind you down.

Did You Ever Just Want to Disappear?

As he walked out of divorce court, Brad made up his mind that his wife wasn't going to get away with it. He could still remember her mocking him as she sweetly and graphically described how she had bribed the judge sexually (giving him a "Slick Willie" special), right in his own chambers, in order to get the divorce settlement that now gave her almost all of Brad's money and worldly assets.

Perhaps worst of all, she was granted possession of Brad's prized 36-foot sailing yacht, a beautiful Hans Christian Sloop. The bitter taste in Brad's mouth, from picturing his wife engaged in that sexual act with the judge, made him want to go to the harbor and light a match to his favorite play toy.

What kept him from complete despair was his knowledge that, unbeknownst to his sweet spouse, Brad had already transferred all of the hundreds of thousands of dollars made in his last big business deal to a Bermuda corporation, which in turn had wired it to another trust headquartered on the Isle of Mann. Very simply, his wife would never be able to touch the money, as it was long gone from United States jurisdiction. Now all Brad had to do was disappear with his boat.

Although burning the yacht had seemed like a good idea at first, that would only rob him of the use and pleasure of his favorite toy, and then his wife would have the insurance money from its untimely demise. As a matter of fact, she'd enjoy that even more than watching the boat rot at the local harbor, which is exactly what would happen unless Brad could get it away from her and into a friendly foreign port.

So that night, he and one of his sailing buddies slipped the moorings and took the boat out on the tide to another marina 40 miles down the road. And as his wife and the process servers feverishly scoured the surrounding marinas the next day for signs of the yacht, Brad and his friend loaded water, food, supplies, and clothing for an extended trip far from the reach of U.S. laws.

Before his conniving spouse could even get the court documents prepared for the constable, and before her investigators had a chance to track down our boy in his boat, Brad had transferred its title to Panama Registry in another corporate name. Soon he was sailing south into the beautiful blue Caribbean.

These days, with dozens of islands to choose from between Puerto Rico and Barbados, Brad cruises from yacht harbor to yacht harbor, finding new and willing "first mates" along the way. "You'd be amazed how people lose their inhibitions when they leave the country, have a few tropical rum drinks, and go sailing on a moonlight cruise on a yacht in the Caribbean," he says.

Every night, as he stretches out on a deck chair on his little ship, while the girlfriend du jour is asleep below in the cabin, Brad smiles and hopes his former wife is thinking of him, and stewing in her own juices. More likely, however, she has found a new husband by now (Brad was number three), and is eyeing new divorce court judges in search of retirement plan number four.

But it's no skin off Brad's back. He's cruising along in Paradise, financially sound and personally secure, a true citizen of the world. The last word I heard was that he was planning to sail the Mediterranean, but that may have been just a rumor, planted to send his ex on a wild goose chase.

Fortunately, not all of us have suffered woes on par with our friend Brad, but even so, we've all experienced the hunger to just get away and never come back. Perhaps that hunger is awakened by the flight of a flock of geese on a cool autumn night . . . or the whistle of an outbound train . . . or the roar of a plane passing overhead. As the routine pressures of our daily lives grow more complex, as more and more of us face vengeful ex-spouses, aggressive creditors, greedy lawyers, and that most insidious of entities—the Infernal Revenue Service—that hunger grows and grows. And for some of us, fantasy begins to take real form. More and more people find themselves wanting to just get away, and not come back, ever.

How about you? Wouldn't you sometimes like to disappear without a trace and leave behind all your personal or business problems and worries? Are you sick of the same old spouse, the same old job, the nagging in-laws, or the host of debt collectors or creditors that seem to call every morning at 7:00 A.M. or just as you are settling in for the night? You can make all of them fade away and disappear by doing just that: making *yourself* disappear.

There are many places in the world that would welcome you with open arms, especially if you have some money, skill or talent, or can help them do something new and better, employing some of their indigenous people. In many of these places, you can live in luxury or something very much like it, for a fraction of what you'd pay in the U.S, without the stress, hassle and grief that you have to deal with in your current situation in your current home life.

But what if you don't want to leave the security and benefits and comforts of the United States? Well, the comfort factor is hard to argue with, but personally, I think our rights and benefits are eroding far too rapidly and are going downhill fast. So the choice is up to you. Do you want a good living or a good life? One of my friends says, "Live fast, die young and go out with a bang!" Personally, I like the story my daddy told me of the two bulls on the hilltop, overlooking a heard of fine looking heifers. The young bull snorted and said, "Let's run down there and screw a few of those heifers." The old bull looked them over and told the young stud, "Save your strength, *walk* down and screw them all!"

Many folks would point to the IRS as the beast that has taken the most rapacious bite out of those rights and benefits. This agency, spawned by the devil—oops, I mean by a constitutional amendment—in 1913, is literally a law unto itself. The IRS has become synonymous with harassment, tyranny, and police-state tactics, stemming from the agency's assumption that all taxpayers are guilty until proven innocent. Very few people have ever fought the IRS and won. Here's the story of one man who did win—well, sort of.

Daniel Neal Heller, a high-profile Miami trial lawyer, says his troubles began because he represented the now-defunct *Miami News* in the mid-1970s. The newspaper had broken a sensational story about a rogue

IRS project known as Operation Leprechaun, an overzealous intelligence operation that targeted Miami politicians, lawyers, and judges. The newspaper story was the beginning of . . . well, let's just say a public relations nightmare for an agency that was already P.R.–challenged.

In accordance with responsible journalism standards (remember those?), the *Miami News* refused to divulge where it got its information for the story. I.R.S. agents, suspecting a leak within the agency, marched into Heller's office one day demanding to know the paper's source. "No can do," said Heller; his sources were privileged. He says he threw the agents out of his office, but not before he had a "heated exchange" with agent Thomas A. Lopez, who had been identified by the *News* as the head of the investigation.

Lo and behold, Mr. Lopez turned up four years later among the agents investigating Heller's taxes. Coincidence? I don't think so. Heller claimed that the IRS's actions against him were pure retaliation, but despite his claims he was indicted and convicted of tax evasion. The key to the government's victory was that Heller's own accountant testified against him after being visited by a trio of special agents who made him "an offer he shouldn't refuse."

Heller was sentenced to three years in prison, and in 1987 he began serving his sentence. Fortunately he was released after four months, when the 11th U.S. Circuit Court of Appeals overturned his conviction. The appeals court based its decision on arguments prepared mostly by Heller himself. It determined that Heller's accountant had testified falsely; the court blamed IRS intimidation. Heller later settled a lawsuit against his accountant for $5 million, which was the insurance limit.

He filed a separate $30 million lawsuit against the three agents who had investigated him, including Lopez. The defendants continually denied wrongdoing and maintained that Heller had indeed cheated on his taxes. But as the trial date neared, the two sides agreed on a $500,000 settlement, which was paid by the IRS. Though neither the agents nor the IRS admitted any liability, Heller declared the settlement his long-overdue "apology" from the agency. For him it wasn't the money that mattered; it was the feeling of vindication and the return of his good name. He let his wife give the settlement money to charities.[1]

---

1 "IRS Pays Lawyer $500,000," *ABA Journal*, May 1994, page 28.

Although Daniel Heller's story was described by the *ABA Journal* as a man-bites-IRS story, his case is the exception that proves the rule. Being a lawyer and, by his friends' descriptions, "incredibly aggressive," he was uniquely suited to fight back. Even so, the settlement was paltry compared to the $30 million he sought, and, when you consider all the hell he was put through—a 12-year battle and a stint in a federal prison—$500,000 seems a pittance.

Heller's case, and many other of the IRS's worst abuses are documented in a book written by my good friend, David Burnham, called *A Law Unto Itself; the IRS and the Abuse of Power*. Read it sometime if you really want a good scare, and a reason to hide your assets and disappear.

Unfortunately, few us have Heller's skill and stubborn aggressiveness to aid us when the tax-man focuses his wrath on us. Therefore we have one of two choices: pay up or bug out. In other words, we can hide our assets and disappear from the good old U.S.A. altogether or stay and face the music. It's really not that bad being a man without a country. You would be amazed at how many of Uncle Sam's tax refugees are roaming the world, outside of the reaches of Uncle Sam.

Skippy and Mary fled the U.S. over a little personal tax dispute of about a million dollars, give or take a few thousand. They moved to Manzanillo, Mexico, and rented a beautiful garden apartment overlooking the harbor on the bay. (Americans can't own land on or near the coast, but you can rent or lease it for a lifetime.) Their total living expenses, including rent, a full-time live-in maid, food, and liquor (a big expense for them), is under $1,200 a month—and that's less than half of what they were paying on their mortgage in their stateside home.

For many years this couple has lived in quiet luxury off the interest income from their disputed tax money. They have given up very little in the way of their personal lifestyle and probably live healthier lives than they did at home. They're still close enough to their friends to visit them occasionally, and their habits remain very much the same, except for minor adjustments such as shopping. There are no megamalls where Skippy and Mary live, but the local market has everything they could possibly need, and all the food is fresh and preservative-free.

Best of all, they have eliminated all of the heartache and grief of their old life. They no longer fret over the social problems that seem to have taken over many U.S. neighborhoods and communities. In Manzanillo there are no teenage gangs and no drive-by shootings. The worst offenders are pickpockets, beachside prostitutes, and the occasional rowdy drunk on holidays and weekends. And there's no urban blight; the view outside Skippy and Mary's window is that of a sparkling bay and pristine beach under a pure blue sky. (One night, after drinking too many margaritas, we were entranced by a beautiful fireworks display in the harbor, only to find out when we sobered up the next morning that the beautiful display the evening before was actually a ship that had burned to the waterline.)

If, for whatever reason, you still want to stay close to home, there *are* ways to hide within the United States, ways that ensure no one can find you. We'll go into those in Chapter 1.

Your mission, whether you choose to stay in the U.S. or sail to distant shores, is to make a fresh start, with a new identity and a new personal outlook. To do so, you must give up those ties to your old life—*all* of them.

This may be more difficult than you think. When I say you have to cut the ties, that's just what I mean. You can't check in on your parents on holidays, nor can you maintain any of your social, business, or credit connections with your old life, because these can be traced right back to your new world. Oh, and don't even *think* of calling your ex-spouse and declaring your undying love for her when you get drunk now and then—because if you do, "They" *will* find you. Count on it.

You don't think so? As you will see, it is the little things that give you away every time. Use this story as an example of how anyone can be tracked through those simple and seemingly inconsequential things we all hold near and dear to our heart.

Bob's Gold Card Strikes Gold—For His Creditors

A man we will call Bob Jacobson flew everywhere on business, traveling coast to coast on a near-weekly basis, on sales calls for his company. In doing this, he collected hundreds of thousands of frequent flyer points. He was awarded a frequent flyer gold card for his faithfulness to Continental Airlines, who lavishes all kinds of benefits on their frequent flying one pass members.

When Bob decided to bug out and disappear, he changed his name, got a new identity through the graveyard gambit (see Chapter 4), and walked away from all of his friends, neighbors, and family. It was no great loss to him; he was fed up with them and needed a change anyway.

What Bob didn't give up, though, were his frequent flyer points and gold card. He loved to travel, and he especially liked the automatic first class upgrade—which gave him free drinks, better food, classier flight attendants, and personal attention from the airline staff. (You *do* know that there is a world of difference in the service between first class and coach, don't you?) So, whenever Bob traveled, he used his airline gold card and his real name to get his frequent flyer miles on his gold card.

Unfortunately, he didn't realize this information put him in the database that told the world every city he traveled to and from, as well as his method of payment and his home address (which was the post office box where his frequent flyer statement went every month).

Guess what . . . Bob isn't hidden anymore! A creditor, to whom he owed a surprisingly small amount of money, found him and traced him to an address where he could be served with a lawsuit and brought to task for his folly. That legal action told everyone else in the world where he was and the rest was history. (So was Bob.)

The latest poster boy for brainless bozo of the month is Marty Frankel, the computer geek who scammed somewhere between $300 million and a billion from a bunch of bloodsucker burial insurance companies looking to make a killing in the market.

Our boy Marty, a stockbroker dropout (his license was pulled in 1992), used a dozen bogus companies and phony names to create a paper financial empire wrapped around a hocus-pocus charity to amass millions that he invested in his personal pleasures rather than such dull investments as stocks and bonds.

As a moth comes to the flames, Marty Frankel flew to the high life, buying houses for $3.5 million and $1.6 million, a brace of sports Mercedes, and a ton of toys for the women whom Marty wooed on the Internet, with the help of his newfound wealth. Not only did Marty get brave, he turned seriously kinky, playing bondage games with his harem until one of them turned up dead.

As a balloon fills with air until it bursts, his kingdom exploded as his investors asked hard financial questions. Seeing this end of the rope, Marty torched his records and flew the coop. Along the way he bought, $10 million in diamonds for the girlfriends that he brought along for the ride.

To make a long story short, Marty and his friends wandered around Italy, France, and Germany for a number of weeks and were finally bagged through a tip by an informant trying to cash in on the $100,000 reward offered by the FBI. Money talks, don't it?

As I said, it's the little things that catch you every time: the magazine subscriptions, the charge cards, the hunting and fishing catalogues, the calls back home, the frequent flyer clubs, and the sports associations that you just can't seem to give up because they define who and what you really are.

It is my hope that after reading this book, you will be prepared, both logistically and psychologically, to successfully make the transition to your new self in your new world. You will have the best information available on how to go, where to go, how to live, and even who to become once you get there.

So settle in, take notes if you need to, and get ready for the ride of your life. You are about to create a whole new living, breathing personality. If you do it right, this new person will be someone with whom you can enjoy spending the rest of your life. And very soon, you just may be cruising along in your own Paradise with a new life, a new attitude, and a hell of a lot less baggage.

Happy trails!

FOREWORD

Forget About Asset Protection!
It doesn't work if:

Your creditors claim and prove fraud.

Your problems don't pre-date your asset protection.

You are involved in drugs (even if you didn't inhale).

You have facilitated organized crime or money laundering.

The government really wants you *bad*.

Your spouse (or partner) slept with the judge.

Forget fancy legal maneuvers and asset protection planning, they don't work! If your spouse, enemies, creditors or their smart attorneys, or the government alleges fraud against you, they can freeze any of your assets and cut through any trust, estate, or annuity, just like a hot knife through butter. If they can show that you have had the intent to hinder, delay, defraud, or deceive, or have committed acts of fraud, your most carefully laid plans can go to hell and fall apart. You can be charged with triple the actual damages by a judge who deems that you have schemed and planned to keep your assets from the jurisdiction of his or her court. And, if you are just planning to do it now, and you already have knowledge of a potential or existing personal or business problem in the future, forget it. Why? Because it's far too late for you to start taking the steps necessary to shelter your assets if you already are in the soup.

You don't believe it? Just ask F. Lee Bailey, one of the nation's finest legal minds and attorneys who specialized in representing clients against the government. In 1997, Lee Bailey represented Claude Duboc, a client charged by Uncle Sam in a drug-dealing scheme of titanic proportions. When Duboc was ultimately convicted, the government went after his assets, which included a 74-foot yacht and 400,000 shares of publicly traded stock worth close to $16 million.

To protect his client's assets, Bailey, who once represented O. J. Simpson, claimed that the assets were now his payment for legal fees in his representation of Mr. Duboc. Bailey claimed that he was entitled to his fees and refused to obey the order of the court. The judge, U.S. District Judge Maurice Paul and the prosecutor felt that Bailey was protecting the stock and the yacht for his client. Lee Bailey was placed in jail for contempt in refusing to turn over the assets ordered by the court.

After spending 44 days in the Tallahassee County Jail, not the semi-luxurious Club Fed in Pensacola, Florida, Bailey decided that disgression was the better part of valor and ponied up the stock so that he could get out of jail. The judge firmly admonished Bailey and told him that he could go back to jail if he didn't pay an additional $700,000 within one year.

If F. Lee Bailey couldn't talk his way out of this kind of deal, do you think you could? Neither you nor I could afford that caliber of legal defense, and he still lost!

If you really want to protect what's yours, then you really do need to hide it all and disappear by becoming invisible and taking your assets with you (by becoming a man or woman of the world, away from the law and a lawyer that wants to get his hands on you).

Can Asset Protection Planning Ever Work?

Is asset protection planning a legitimate strategy, and can it save your assets from your spouse, creditors, and the IRS? The answer is, well, maybe sometimes. If you have a million dollars or more to protect and shelter from Uncle Sam, then you can afford to hire the attorneys and accountants to *delay* the inevitable tax process, hopefully till you are old and gray.

You see, asset protection planning requires (actually demands) a great deal of affirmative action to create legitimate roadblocks between your assets and your creditors, while still allowing an acceptable level of direction and enjoyment in your hands (or the hands of your designee). Once put in place, these roadblocks are designed to either prevent the seizure of your assets by creditors or, at the very least, slow them down by making the collection process so difficult and expensive that the bloodsuckers will view settlement at a substantially reduced amount a better deal than throwing the dice for the whole enchilada. After all, who wants to throw good money after bad!

A well used strategy, used by many savvy self-employed entrepreneurs, has been the filing of a bankruptcy, usually a Chapter 11, with no intention of ever going through with it. One of our illustrious U.S. Senators has done this at least three times (that I know of) without blinking an eye. Every third year, he files a business bankruptcy just outside his own jurisdiction, and claims that he is flat broke. He sends his new bankruptcy petition to all of his creditors and ducks behind the bankruptcy shield for a year or two, or at least until the judge orders him to produce schedules of income and assets, and then he tells his creditors that they can get 20 cents on the dollar, if they settle with him right now. (If not, well then, you have to take your chances, because I'm going to have to convert to a Chapter 7, and nobody will get anything, except the lawyers). Faced with the chance of getting nothing, and still having to pay high-priced lawyers to have lunch with the bankruptcy trustee, most of them settled for the 20 cents on the dollar and went home to lick their wounds.

Did he do anything illegal? Did he violate any laws? Nope, he didn't even get judged to be bankrupt, so he can do it again any time he wants to. And, he beat his creditors out of 80 percent of his debt. If you read the newspaper, you can see that the banks and "big businesses" are trying to close this loophole through bankruptcy reform. The proposed new laws and government guidelines currently in effect allow "smooth operators" to tap dance all around the law by filing bankruptcies, in remote jurisdictions, with no intention of following through, but those days are numbered, my friend. For most of us, asset protection is too expensive and complex. Besides, if the creditors or government can get an expert to testify as to your intent to commit fraud, or you have just a little criminality in your heart (like Jimmy Carter has lust there), then all bets are off as far as asset protection is concerned. Asset protection relies on statutory authority in the U.S.'s and the foreign country's laws and treaties used to encumber assets located in the U.S. If you act outside that authority, then your goose is cooked.

For asset protection to even have a chance to work, timing is critical. The closer in time action is taken to the knowledge of a financial obligation or judgment, the less effective the power of the protection. To be successful, the asset protection must be "old and cold," predating the forseeability of the obligations, debts, judgments, and criminal acts of the defendant. The vehicles used by the plaintiffs and their attorneys to pursue their claims are made under the Fraudulent Conveyance Acts of many states and the U.S. Government and the Statute of Elizabeth in the British Commonwealth.

Basically the creditor tries to take apart or unwind the asset protection strategies by convincing the judge that the plan was set up to defraud the creditor and create roadblocks from letting the creditors get to their due. The test used by the court and by the experts retained by the plaintiffs is the intent of the debtor, and his or her state of mind, at the time the trusts and plans were set up and the assets removed from their jurisdiction. If the creditor can convince the judge or jury that the asset protection was enacted specifically to defraud, then the best-laid plans go to hell. If, however, the defendant can persuade the court that there was a legitimate purpose for the creation and continued existence of the strategy, and that it pre-dated the financial problems that the plan just happened to protect, then you have a shot at saving your bacon!

If you want to consider asset protection as a temporary measure or want to try to gut it out in the U.S.A., then you need a plan. First, lets make a review of your current financial statement (the real one that you gave the bank last year, when you had to borrow money). This document, and others like it, defines your assets, their value, and the sources of income, which become the target of your post judgment creditors and Uncle Sam. Once you lay out your full financial picture, you then need to maximize state and federal law exemptions in your favor. Some of the most important things you should consider are the following:

Personal Residence
Personal Property (like vehicles, boats, aircraft, artwork, etc.)
Life Insurance and Annuities (with equity)
Wages
Spousal Separate Property
Trust Assets and Property
Partnership Property
Business and Corporate Assets and Property
Corporate Stock
Inheritance

By putting all possible property in a category that is exempt, you thereby avoid the issues and claims of fraudulent conveyance and create a barrier between the asset and the creditor. Once you use up all of the possible exemptions, then it's time to begin the asset protection process by using a combination of domestic and offshore strategies to further protect yourself and your hard-earned wealth.

At the top of the list of assets to be protected are the negotiable liquid assets such as cash, savings accounts, and brokerage accounts. If you have the guts, take it offshore, using one of the many methods we have discussed in this book. If moving your assets is not to your liking, then you can try the expensive process of purchasing a foreign annuity or life insurance contract in a friendly foreign country. If we can assume that you pick a favorable and stable country as the host for your policy and contract, then you will be exempt from attachment by U.S. judgment creditors. Next, you must legally make a one time filing of IRS form 720 and the payment of a 1% excise tax on the amount expatriated. The only additional cost is the cost of the annuity, which may vary from 1% to 5% as an upfront fee plus a small annual maintenance charge.

In most cases, premiums paid to insurance companies are limited by U.S. tax law, where contributions to annuities are unlimited. Each of these products offers the inducement of tax-deferred growth and offers an additional benefit in life insurance and non-taxable policy loans to the owners of the policy. Combine these features with the benefit of self-direction of the investment portion of the product and you can see why this is the vehicle of choice for the well-heeled tax and debt avoider. (Note: The big difference between tax avoidance and tax evasion is that avoidance is legal. We all have a legal right, and I think a legal obligation, to minimize our taxes by taking advantage of every word of the tax code.)

Once you have divested yourself of your liquid assets and cash, the next order of business is to shelter the more tangible assets, such as real estate, vehicles, boats, aircraft, and the like. The best way to protect assets of this type is to load them up with debt.

Fred Bogart's pride and joy, the apple of his eye, was his 85 foot sailing yacht, anchored in St. Barts, in the Netherland Antilles. This yacht, worth more that $2 million, was bought in trade for company stock that headed south in a heartbeat in the oil and gas stock market debacle of the 1980s. This devaluation of his paper millions raised immediate claims from the former owner of the yacht that he was swindled in a fraudulent conveyance of stock that was known by the company president to be worth far less than its trade value.

To protect his new toy from litigation and seizure by U.S. courts, Fred created an IBC that loaned $1.5 million to Fred, with the yacht as collateral for the loan. With this encumbrance in place, even if the previous owner won in court, he would have to pay off the note before taking possession of the boat. (Oh yes, Fred took the deduction for the interest on the loan against his taxes, but forgot to declare the interest gained by the IBC, which just happened to be issued as bearer shares, thus maintaining the privacy of the ownership of the lender and saving him a bundle through the deduction on his taxable income in the U.S.A.)

To take maximum advantage of asset protection (you are paying for it, so you might as well) you should change the title to the property and encumber the asset with debt, just like this:

1. **Personal Residence:** The only two states that offer unlimited homestead exemptions at this time are Texas and Florida. (Ask Bowie Kuhn, the commissioner of baseball, how he bought a $3 million home and then declared bankruptcy, with his new home as his only asset.) All other states protect homesteaded property up to a specific dollar amount over mortgaged debt, *if* the home is homesteaded. Nevada's limit is $125,000, Colorado is $40,000 and California is $100,000 to name a few examples. (There is currently legislation pending to limit the homestead exemption *everywhere*!)

2. **Real Estate:** In most cases, investments in real estate are held either in the name of the debtor or in a limited partnership with other investors. To protect this asset, the prudent asset protection specialist will usually recommend the transfer of the asset from an individual debtor's individual estate to a Family Limited Partnership (FLP), which offers protection from a personal judgement.

3. **Corporate Stock** held in a C corporation, not held in an S Corporation, can also be transferred out of the name of the debtor to a Family Limited Partnership (FLP) or encumbered by loans wherein the stock becomes collateral for personal or business loans of the stock's owner.

4. **Pension plans, IRAs, and Keoghs** are protected by state law in most instances and further covered by federal law. The two states that

offer 100 percent protection on retirement funds are (you guessed it) Texas and Florida. Without the protection of his NFL retirement, our famous football friend O. J. Simpson (as well as many other professional sports figures), might well be bussing tables instead of playing golf and contemplating retirement in Florida, where his assets cannot be touched by the multi-million-dollar judgment awarded against him to the Goldman family.

5. **Wages and Income** are two of the most difficult assets to protect from creditors. One of the only ways to protect this kind of asset is to have it paid or made in a state that does not recognize wage garnishment (you guessed it, Florida!). Other income, such as inheritance, can be placed in an irrevocable trust for your or your family's benefit and partnership income can be protected by transferring the interest in the partnership to an FLP, which makes the interest also exempt.

Last, but not least, once the asset protection strategy is in place, it must be managed, directed, or controlled (at least on paper) by an independent entity. This means someone who is not connected by birth, family, or control by you. All of your best-laid plans can be sabotaged if the opposition can prove that you "really" direct the strategy, either by showing "alter ego" (meaning that the asset protection strategy is really a ruse directed and controlled by you) by your nominee or by the use of the vehicle to buy goods, transact business, or pay obviously personal expenses such as a swimming pool for your house, a new set of wheels for your honey, or vacations for you and Ms. Fifi Latour. *Warning! Warning!* A woman scorned can be very, very dangerous. If you dump a sweetheart or trade in your very personal secretary (particularly if you trade her in on a new model, one with bigger bumpers and shinier hubcaps) then you may have created the vehicle for your own destruction.

Bill Golden owned a prosperous pornography business, actually the biggest X-rated bookstore in town, until he was done in by his former "squeeze," compliments of the IRS.

Every week, Billy counted his cash proceeds from his thriving business and doled out his money as follows: "One for the government, one for the bank, one for me. One for the government, to hell with the bank, two for me. To hell with the government, to hell with the bank, three for me." (You get the picture, right?) Bill then took "his" money and placed it in a Federal Express envelope and mailed it to his sister in Canada. She then placed the money in a new Federal Express envelope and mailed the cash to a well-known Canadian bank in the Cayman Islands.

Over a period of three years, Bill deposited over $500,000 through his little scheme. He would have gotten away with it except for a clerical error in the bank. It seems that the account (made up in the name of Bill's retired mother-in-law) experienced some "technical difficulties" wherein a clerk improperly credited Bill's account for $100,000, which brought the matter to the attention of bank officials.

When the bank couldn't locate its account holder, who had been in a nursing home for the last five years, they contacted your friendly neighborhood investigator to locate the woman so that they could recover their monies.

A quick search of public records revealed that the account holder was 87 years old and a resident of Sleepy Glen, so a search was then conducted of her family members to find the real account holder. A quick scan of marriage records disclosed that a woman with the last name of the account holder was married to Mr. Pornography. *Bingo*! Billy was caught!

Billy was confronted by the bank's investigator and offered the opportunity to return the $100,000 to the bank or face the consequences. Billy stupidly decided to keep the money, thinking that the Cayman Banking Secrecy Act would prevent the bank from disclosing his ill-gotten gains to Uncle Sam. (A lot of good that lawyer's advice did!)

Two weeks later, the investigator, who is not under the jurisdiction of the Cayman law, delivered a present of the bank statements to the IRS Criminal Investigative Division, who already had an investigation of Bill on their books. The IRS agents took the bank statements and combined it with the anonymous "tips" provided by Bill's former "squeeze" and presented Bill with an invitation to "Club Fed."

By using asset protection planning properly, you will save money not only for yourself, but your next generation as well. Remember "keeping it is the best reward" or as one of my best friends said, "he who dies with the most toys wins!" Asset protection and planning can't stop you from getting into lawsuits and legal or financial trouble, but it can cover your backside from everything but criminal acts, in most cases, if you plan ahead!

1

So You Want Out ... What Are You Going to Do and Where Do You Want to Do It?

If you have come to the big decision that you want out of your old life and into a new one, you now have many more decisions ahead of you. Perhaps the most basic one is this: Do you want to stay in the United States or do you want to flee to another country? You don't have to answer that one just yet. In fact, you may want to read this entire book before you decide, one way or the other, which decision is best for you.

My own biases in this matter will perhaps become apparent as you read on. For many reasons, I think a person stands a better chance of success at creating a new life by moving out of the country altogether. Much of this book is geared towards doing just that. Even so, I realize that many people, for many reasons, may want to stay in the U.S. So we'll discuss this option first—including its perils and pitfalls—and then we'll talk a little bit about the alternative: expatriation.

The Long Arm of the Credit Bureaus

Within the boundaries of the United States, it's very easy to move anywhere without setting off any alarms and whistles in the government itself. While government agencies maintain vast databases of information, they are not particularly well-equipped (or motivated) to track the majority of the information contained in these databases.

When they do, they usually move very slowly. The IRS charts you by your tax return, which is filed yearly, and the Social Security Administration by your employer payroll, filed quarterly and the police by your driver's license, renewed whenever the state gets around to it.

The only way they narrow in on you is if you get a speeding ticket, a DWI, or are arrested for ringing someone's bell. Now, if they have good reason to target you, it's a different story. Uncle Sam has his way to track your foreign travel, your financial transactions (over $3000) and your public record filings around the country. Oh, so you never heard of FinCen? FinCen is the Financial Crime Enforcement Network, a semi-secret division of the U.S. Treasury.

Unfortunately, this is not true of the massive credit bureaus and collection agencies. They track every single transaction you make: your credit card purchases, loans, payments on insurance policies, mortgages, car loans, credit applications, voter registration, bank accounts, and driving records. They even keep track of your new car purchases and leases, so they know when you are ready for a new car. (You've gotten those discount coupons for a new car, haven't you? They arrive right on schedule, exactly two years after your last new auto purchase.)

The credit bureaus buy tons of information from Uncle Sam that the government won't sell to you and me. We can no longer go to the post office and obtain someone's change of address information for a dollar, as we could several years ago. This information *is,* however, sold daily to the major credit bureaus like TRW (now Experian), TransUnion, and Equifax, and merged into skip tracing and locator databases called *Missing Links, Discover, People Finder, Sleuth, Tracker,* and *Wizard.* Where does it go after that? It is resold to marketing agencies, government and private investigators, collection agencies, and skip tracers that want to "reach out and touch someone" like you or me.

Let's face it: In this country it's far more difficult to hide from the credit bureaus, private investigators, information brokers, and collection agencies than it is from the city, county, state, and federal governments. The federal government recognizes this, and is now outsourcing and subcontracting many of its locator, background investigation, and asset searching functions to the investigative arms of the huge credit bureaus, and also to private investigators specializing in such work. For example, the IRS has now hired collection agencies to find and collect the millions of dollars in unpaid taxes and student school loans, which it has been heretofore ineffective at collecting.

In later chapters, we'll discuss some of the different agencies and the ways they can and do use information against you. (In particular, see Chapter 7, "How the Pros Will Look for You.")

For now, suffice to say: *You can run, but it's getting harder and harder to hide, especially in the computerized society in the USA.*

Slipping Through the Cracks

Despite the intrusiveness of the credit agencies, it is still possible to "slip through the cracks." But it may take some major re-shuffling of your spending habits and lifestyle. If you intend to hide within the United States, here are three basic rules to remember:

1. Cut up all of your plastic. Pay cash for all of your daily, weekly, and monthly purchases. If you have to have these for identification (you can't rent a car or check into a hotel without one) get a debit card—in another name!

2. Close your bank account. (C'mon, you don't really need a checking account.) The infamous Meyer Lansky, financial wizard of organized crime, did have a checking account—but he only wrote one check a year off of the account, and that was to the Infernal Revenue Service, for his tax return. (I should know. I'm the guy who collected it from him.) Your bank account, especially if it is of the interest-bearing kind, is a government snitch. Every year, your bank faithfully reports your interest, by social security number, to Uncle Sam. The IRS and a few other nosy agencies calculate the amount of money needed to make that interest and compares it against your last tax return that would indicate any major increase in your net worth. If new accounts suddenly appear or the amount of interest rises substantially, your chances of becoming a target rise substantially.

3. Keep your real name out of the public records. This includes driver's license, auto registration, marriage license bureaus, property ownership, voter registration records, business filings such as corporate officers, UCC borrowing documents and other local and national registrations. (See Chapter 4 for information on how to create a new identity.)

Don't forget the agencies that issue hunting and fishing licenses. One Montana man, who decided that disappearing was cheaper than a divorce, was found five years later when he applied for an elk hunting permit in the neighboring state of Wyoming. Only a few such permits are issued each year, and they are verified through a driver's license. Our hapless hunter thought he was long gone and forgotten, but he forgot that old adage: "Hell hath no fury like a woman scorned."

Knowing his greatest loves were hunting and fishing, the "wife from hell" religiously called every state fish and game department within a thousand miles every year, looking for her husband to make that one fatal mistake, which he ultimately did. Armed with his private post office address, the wife hired a private investigator, who in turn bribed the minimum-wage, equal-opportunity employee at the storefront mailbox company to sound the alarm when the errant spouse came to pick up his mail. He then became the hunted instead of the hunter.

This brings us to another point you really need to remember: *Many people will rat on you for money*. In fact, one of the best ploys in an investigator's bag of tricks is to pull out a twenty-dollar bill and cut it in half in front of the new source of information. The investigator then hands one half to the snitch, lets him hold it and feel it in his greasy little palms, and tells him that he'll get the other half when the proper information is provided. Take it from a pro: It works every time.

The government also knows the value of paying for information. Why do you think that the FBI, DEA, and IRS offer substantial rewards to informants who provide them with original information on criminal violations? The IRS currently pays a 10 percent reward for monies recovered in investigations, if you provide original information that results in a recovery of funds, or an arrest of someone they really want.

City Mouse or Country Mouse?

If you want to stay within the United States, should you live in a big city or move out to the country? There's a lot to be said for urban living. The city's denser population offers greater anonymity and a lower expectation of community involvement on the part of its residents. As we see all the time on the boob tube, most city residents look neither left nor right, know nothing about their neighbors, and have no interest in anything even resembling community spirit. With a million stories in the naked city, the chances are nobody will be too interested in yours.

What if country living appeals to you? You should be aware that rural communities often bring their members together out of a sense of isolation due to distance between each other. They try to support each other because of their common need for companionship.

This, of course, can work against you. Citizens of rural communities are much more aware of new members in their midst, and are far more curious about the new members' activities, simply because they have fewer people to observe than they would in a city. Besides, they are always looking for a new subject of gossip or a way to marry off the local spinster. As a result, each individual receives a greater share of their attention. A new resident may remain an outsider for years, a source of speculation at coffee klatches and storefront gatherings—especially if he or she doesn't work in the vicinity, doesn't have a visible source of income, or doesn't join in activities with the new neighbors.

If you're going to move out to the country, you should *really* move out to the country, away from the small towns and outside of the rural communities. The Unabomber was able to elude authorities for more than 23 years because he made his home, quite literally, out in the sticks, but who wants to live like that? Not me! I gotta have satellite TV. (Oops! They can track you through your billing on that, too.)

Stranger in a Strange Land

By far, the easiest and most foolproof way to disappear is to leave the country and start anew as a stranger in a strange land. There are, of course, some potential drawbacks, such as language and cultural barriers, but it's often easy to find a thriving American community within certain countries. Such a community caters to the power of the American buck, affording you the best of all possible worlds:

- Anonymity
- Legal protection
- An inherently disorganized and decentralized foreign record-keeping system
- Amenities compatible with your previous lifestyle
- Lower cost for comparable living
- Drinking and fishing buddies
- Lonely hearts looking for love, especially if it can improve their lowly lifestyle

We will discuss, in detail, the various places that meet these criteria in Chapter 3. But first, let's talk a little more about the subject of expatriation—what it is, and why so many people are choosing to do it every day.

"Give Me Your Tired, Your Rich, Your Huddled Masses Yearning To Live Tax-Free": The New Refugees

If America ever was the land of milk and honey, the milk has curdled, the honey has gone sour and the bees sting us in the ass—we can lay much of the blame for this transformation on the U.S. government. As Uncle Sam becomes ever more willing to pry into every aspect of our lives (and as we, unfortunately, become ever more willing to let him do so), cherished principles such as privacy and freedom are rapidly losing their meaning.

From recent newspaper articles and the hearings held about IRS abuses in the Senate and House, it is clear that the public feels confused and abused. Congress has recently enacted new legislation to create a "kinder, gentler IRS," one where the burden of proof is no longer on the taxpayer (but rather on the IRS in making claims of additional tax due or criminal charges). Tax court is the only court in the land where you are guilty until proven innocent.

But it's not just the principles, it's the money. Consider, for example, our $5 trillion national debt, which amounts to about $20,000 for every man, woman, and child in America. Consider the U.S. tax system, which is becoming more complex and more oppressive by the year, just the opposite of what they claim.

We're not just talking about income tax, either. Case in point: our federal estate taxes really do soak the rich, or even the moderately affluent. While a very wealthy Bahamian citizen, for example, pays zero estate tax, a rich American—defined as anyone with an estate worth $3 million or more—pays 55 percent. A fairly stiff marginal rate of 37 percent kicks in for Americans leaving as little as $600,000 to their children (it will go up to $1,000,000 by the year 2006), and from there it can range up to 60 percent if you don't have a smooth legal beagle probate lawyer.

Indeed, the United States is virtually the only country in the world that imposes significant income *and* death taxes on the worldwide income and assets of every citizen—even if the citizen is domiciled elsewhere. Even semi-socialist Canada did away with estate taxes years ago. The United States even wants to tax you if you move to another country and renounce your U.S. citizenship.

Well, according to an article in *Forbes* magazine,[1] quite a few wealthy Americans get mad as hell, and they aren't going to take it anymore. They took their assets offshore!

Okay, so maybe you don't have a $3 million estate. But you don't have to be wealthy to fear and loathe the taxman; we all feel the effects of increasing tax burdens, and in many ways the middle class is hit hardest of all.

Many people, fed up with outrageous taxes and other threats to their quality of life, are simply leaving the United States. Roger Gallo, author of *Escape From America* (Manhattan Loft Publishing, 1996), writes that Americans are leaving the country in record numbers. Most of those who are leaving are not telling anyone and they are not surrendering their passports, either. You see, though there are records of those who enter America, there are no requirements whatsoever for anyone to register that they are leaving. That's why there are no hard figures on the exact number of American expats worldwide. Under its current system, the government has no idea of what is really going on in the outside world.

However, there's considerable evidence that the number is large and growing. The U.S. State Department claims that there are 2.5 million Americans living abroad, but they are basing those figures on expatriate Americans who are paying taxes. Gallo believes that if you take into account the vast numbers who may have chosen to quietly slip out of the U.S. tax system altogether, the head count of expat Americans could easily be three times the State Department's official estimate.

And for every doer there are countless dreamers. Statistics gathered by *Money* magazine show that one in five Americans has considered leaving America, and that three million Americans would do so right this moment if they only knew how. (So here's your chance!) Another endless wealth of information to expat living is *International*

---

1 "The New Refugees" by Robert Lenzner and Philippe Mao, *Forbes*, Nov. 21, 1994, pp. 131–135.

Living,[2] a newsletter devoted to detailing the most desirable places and best investments ripe for the picking in the newly formed third world.

Though many people are interested in leaving the country for tax reasons, a lot of them lose interest when they find out that to accomplish much of a tax saving they have to renounce their U.S. citizenship.[3]

"Gee, that sounds pretty drastic," you might be saying. "Why do I have to give up my citizenship?" Well, the U.S., unlike virtually every other country, levies income and estate taxes on its citizens living abroad. So unless you plan to cheat on your taxes, just moving abroad won't accomplish much at all unless you don't have that much money to report to Uncle Sam.

Moreover, former citizens can be subject to income tax on U.S. income, including capital gains from real estate situated here and from stocks in U.S. corporations. If the IRS suspects you are renouncing your citizenship to avoid taxes, it will try to tax your holdings for another ten years, no matter where you live. All the IRS needs to establish is that it is *"reasonable"* to believe you gave up citizenship to avoid taxes. Then, the burden of proving the move was *not* for tax reasons falls on you. And when a citizen, or former citizen, gets toe-to-toe with the IRS, you know who usually wins. That's why I strongly recommend you hire an ace attorney *before* you make any big financial decisions.

Still, in spite of the drawbacks, many nations put out the welcome mat for tax-rebellious Americans. Some of the big boys who have taken the plunge in recent years include:[4]

- Michael Dingman, chairman of Abex, and a Ford Motor director. Dingman is now a citizen of the Bahamas and lives there in abject splendor.
- Billionaire John (Ippy) Dorrance III, an heir to the Campbell Soup fortune. Dorrance is now a citizen of Ireland and lives there as well as in the Bahamas and Devil's Tower, Wyoming. (Guess which country he claims for tax purposes!)

---

2 To subscribe to *International Living* (published by Agora Press), mail your request to: International Living, 105 W. Monument St., PO Box 17473, Baltimore, MD 21298 or call: 800-851-7100, 410-223-2611, fax: 410-223-2696.

3 "Flight Capital" by Brigid McMenamin, *Forbes*, Feb. 28, 1994 pp. 55–57.

4 "The New Refugees" by Robert Lenzner and Philippe Mao, *Forbes*, Nov. 21, 1994, pp. 131–135.

- J. Mark Mobius, one of the most successful emerging market investment managers. Born a U.S. citizen, Mobius has chosen to accept the German citizenship of his ancestors and lives in Hong Kong and Singapore.
- Kenneth Dart, an heir to Dart Container and his family's $1 billion fortune. He is a citizen of Belize and works in the Cayman Islands (if you consider sunning and fishing work).

Are these moves worth it? Well, consider, for example, that the heirs of John (Ippy) Dorrance III, the Campbell Soup heir, won't have to pay Uncle Sam the maximum bite of 55 percent on the 26.7 million shares of Campbell Soup that make up most of his $1-billion-plus fortune. His new homeland, Ireland, assesses a 2 percent estate, or probate, tax. Not that Dorrance has escaped the full federal income taxes; there's a U.S. withholding tax of 30 percent on the $30 million he gets in dividends every year from Campbell. Even so, it's pretty obvious that he is saving a bundle and it is well worth the ride, as well as the journey.

Despite the clear financial advantages of expatriation, many people agonize over the decision. "I have serious reservations about expatriation for patriotic and practical reasons," says William Zabel, senior partner of Schulte Roth & Zabel, one of the nation's foremost authorities on trusts and estates. "It is extraordinarily difficult for Americans to get back their citizenship once it is given up. To get it back you have to start like any other nonresident alien, with a green card, and go through the naturalization process.

"Before expatriating, I make my clients consider all the limitations on loss of citizenship—like giving up the ability to travel to the U.S. more than 120 days a year." Even so, losing that American passport isn't as dangerous for the pocketbook as it once was. Recklessly wasteful government policies are steadily eating away at the value of the U.S. dollar, making overseas investments increasingly preferable for the wealthy. Investments in emerging markets are looking more attractive all the time. And the end of the cold war has made it much safer for Americans to live in developing nations safely. In addition, cheap jet travel and global communication make an offshore lifestyle easy. With computers and cable or satellite TV and access to the World Wide Web, you can be as well informed, and as quickly in touch with the world markets living in a remote Caribbean paradise as in downtown New York City.

In Chapter 4, we'll go into the details about changing your citizenship and acquiring second (or third) passports.

Some folks who are not yet ready to give up their U.S. citizenship have taken the less radical measure of only moving their assets abroad. This group includes former congressmen, entrepreneurs who created entire new industries, rock stars, physicians, and wealthy investors.[5] Again, unless you want to lie on your IRS 1040, merely moving your money into a Swiss or Cayman bank won't save you from the woes of U.S. income taxes as a U.S. citizen. You are taxed on your income worldwide as a U.S. citizen and don't you forget it! In fact, some of these partial exiles are motivated less by aversion to taxes than by fear of future restrictions on capital movements.

Expatriation of assets has a long and venerable history.[6] Rich Europeans have expatriated their money to safety ever since the French Revolution, when they began hiding it in Switzerland. In recent years many wealthy Kuwaitis have established offshore trusts in the Channel Islands and the Isle of Man to protect their fortunes from Saddam Hussein. Offshore investing in countries like Liechtenstein and Switzerland are S.O.P. for the filthy rich in Latin America, Southeast Asia and the Middle East—areas notorious for unstable, corrupt, or tyrannical governments and presidents who flee to fight, live, and spend another day. (My childhood TV hero, Maverick, once said, "A coward dies a thousand deaths, a hero dies but once! At the odds of 1000 to 1, I will take the coward every time.")

Now, many Americans, Australians, and New Zelanders are beginning to feel the same sort of insecurity about their worldly possessions. They see our courts eroding their property rights. They read about bureaucrats who talk about "tax expenditures" when referring to that part of your earnings that they permit you to keep. We live in a society that changes the tax rules so frequently that long-term planning is almost impossible. You can hardly blame us for casting more than a wistful eye to offshore investment opportunities. In Chapter 5, we'll talk more about moving assets offshore safely, and managing it once it's been moved.

---

5 "Flight Capital" by Brigid McMenamin, *Forbes*, Feb. 28, 1994, pp. 55–57.
6 "The New Refugees" by Robert Lenzner and Philippe Mao, *Forbes*, Nov. 21, 1994, pp. 131–135.

I guess you can see that if you decide to expatriate, you're in good company. Take stock of your situation, and you may very well decide to join the flood of "new refugees" who are *leaving* the hallowed shores of America in search of a better life.

Before you pack your bags and hop aboard the first flight to some Caribbean paradise, however, some cautionary notes are in order. (That's what Chapter 2 is all about.) And then, of course, you have to decide if the Caribbean is really where you want to go; perhaps Greece or Tonga would better suit your temperament and your financial status, or you might want to visit your relatives in Ireland. That's what we'll cover in Chapter 3.

In fact, after further reading you may decide you want to stay in the good ol' U.S.A. after all. Even if you feel that's what you want, you will still need the information herein—e.g., establishing a new identity and getting new I.D. (Chapter 4), keeping your financial affairs hidden (Chapter 6), avoiding those who may be looking for you (Chapter 7), and so on. So hold off on the packing for awhile, and read on, my friend.

Hide It All–In the U.S.A.

2

No matter what the problems and dangers, I am sure that some of you are going to try to gut it out and hide your assets at home. Maybe you don't want to leave the life that you have strived so hard to build for the past twenty years, or maybe you just don't see yourself living like a stranger in a strange land without all the comforts and support that you are used to at home.

Whatever the reason, you can certainly try to protect your assets by hiding them in plain sight in the U.S.A., but if you are caught and your assets located, then you can just kiss your safe and secure life good-bye. One of the reasons that it is so hard to successfully hide in the United States, is that so many people have tried it before you. Everyone from peons to presidents have sought to hide or disguise their net worth, creating a body of knowledge that both government and private investigators draw on every day, to check up on your personal, business, and financial activities. (If you don't believe me, go to the nearest mega bookstore and read some of the fine literature published on sneaking and peeking into the public record. Then read some of the government's own publications written by the IRS, such as "Financial Investigations: A Financial Approach to Detecting and Resolving Crimes" at your friendly neighborhood U.S. government bookstore.)

The second problem is that the United States is the most computerized country in the world, and the computers are merging data at an all-encompassing way that cross-references every personal business and financial transaction made by each man, woman, and child. From our social security number (not required at birth) to the death insurance policy that electronically closes our lives, the mega-credit bureaus document every move we make.

They wheedle our work history out of employers, pry our spending habits out from our lenders, and suck out personal transactions such as voting and marriage and property transactions from the public records.

Every move you make in the United States is reported, analyzed, massaged, and sold to anyone and everyone who will pay the price.

Your best hope, if you want to hide your assets at home, is that whoever tries to find your stash does not have the brainpower or financial resources to look into all of the places you can hide. Asset searching costs money, and the harder you make it to search, the more expensive the process becomes. Many creditors don't want to throw good money after bad and limit their searchers to a finite budget or ask their attorneys, collectors, and private investigators to work on a contingent fee, where the searcher gets a percentage of what is recovered. If the initial investigation doesn't disclose a pot of gold, or at least the potential for one, then a lot of the foxes will drop out of the hunt. (The exception to this is most often a person who abandons reason and is after you for revenge, like your ex.)

Johnny Darden was a brilliant businessman, but a lousy husband. Like many of us, his idea of holding up a marriage was for him to pay the bills; the house payments, the car notes, the grocery bills, the shopping bills, the million other bills that his wife and children dumped on him each month, all in the name of love. After ten years of this, Johnny and Sally rolled up their sleeves and duked it out one night over the high cost of living and her spending habits. Johnny, seeing no way out of this mess, decided to get a divorce and take his money and run. Being familiar with international business, Johnny had one of his clients open an account in Liechtenstein, a country that offers one of the highest degrees of financial secrecy, where he proceeded to funnel over $1 million dollars from his brokerage account, into a new account in only his name.

Being smarter than the average bear, Johnny didn't rush into a divorce. He played the part, made it look like business had turned bad for him, and told his wife that they were losing it, they would have to sell the house and she would have to find a job.

Johnny might have gotten away with it. He didn't count on his wife having the determination of Hannibal and his elephants, and the good luck to find the man that wrote the book on asset searching. Given a little direction and a few pointers on searching the house for clues, Sally scoured the place clean and found Johnny's stash of private papers in the attic.

They say a picture is worth a thousand words, but I will bet that the picture of Johnny grinning from ear to ear, in front of the foreign bank, cost him at least a million. The revealing photo, plus the bank statements that Johnny had to produce to the judge (who had no sympathy for someone who lied to him when asked if he had hidden any money), cleaned Johnny out for keeps.

If you insist on hiding your hoard at home, then here are a few ideas that you should keep in mind. You can move your assets into a variety of places that can be difficult to find, but remember the chance you take if you get caught. Your creditors don't have to be smart if they hire a pro who is!

Transfers to Family Members or Friends

The easiest way to move money out of your name, but still keep control of it, is to put in the name of someone whose name and identity you can use. Your mother or your spouse has a maiden name, in addition to their married one, and they probably still have an I.D. from an old driver's license that they can show when needed to open a bank or brokerage account in that name.

If you don't trust your mother or your spouse, then you might place your trust in a business partner, attorney or personal friend. A caveat: If you take these steps with the intent to defraud, both you and your nominee may be breaking the law and be subject to a criminal charge. You don't want to put other people in the position of going to jail for you.

When you put assets in the name of someone else, you run several risks. They may feel that they could spend the money better than you could, they could rat out on you for a reward from the other side, or they might cave in under the bright light of a court or government inquiry.

Another problem is that this is the first place that good investigators look when they see that the assets of their target disappear. Experience shows that nine out of ten people that hide money hide it in the maiden name of their mother or their spouse. When money is found to have disappeared from your account, these are the first people and records to be subpoenaed. So, if you are going to even think about trying to keep the money in an account at home, then you need to think about putting it in the name of someone that investigators aren't going to be able to quickly identify, such as an old, but trusted, friend (who does not show up on your home or cellular telephone records) or a new identity that you have created through the graveyard gambit or some other means that does not involve breaking the law.

Corporate Cloaking

One of the most common means of diversifying assets is to play the corporate shell game, by creating a number of business entities that hold your assets and spend your money, in their own name. Many states now offer a degree of anonymity from prying eyes (Delaware and Nevada come quickly to mind) by requiring very little recorded information about the officers, directors, and stockholders of their client corporations. All they require is the name of one corporate officer, namely the registered agent, who is usually your lawyer.

In recent years, the wonderful world of computerization has made it easy for investigators to conduct a national search of corporate records to locate companies and their officers and directors in a heartbeat. Not only will they search your name, but the name of your spouse (yes, in her married and maiden name), your lawyer, your accountant and any other business associate that shows up in any corporation you have been registered with in the past.

With a clean corporation, one that has no ties to you in any way, you can open bank accounts and get credit cards that allow you to do business in the name of the corporation, which is just as good, if not better, than having a new personal ID. You can spend money and transact business in the corporate name with a good deal of anonymity. Just don't let anyone in your old life know or find out about this new entity. (Remember, three can keep a secret, if two of them are dead.) Don't keep the new corporate credit card in your wallet for your spouse to find and don't keep the receipts of this newborn baby in your briefcase. Burn them all before they lead right back to you.

Trusts, Trustees, and Estates

One of the most touted ways to protect your personal assets is through the setting up of various legal entities such as trusts, living estates and family partnerships that purport to own and protect your assets from creditors and collectors. This type of asset protection involves a complicated legal process (and thereby expensive) of transfers and sales of your worldly goods to an entity that theoretically you no longer control.

In this program, you give or sell your assets to your family and children as a means of estate planning, ostensibly to avoid future inheritance taxes and probate. To make this type of plan work, you have to be able to show that you did not have an intent to defraud creditors through the transfer of assets to a third party. The test for intent is whether or not you had a liability, debt, lawsuit, or knowledge of a potential liability that could or might encumber the assets that you are seeking to protect.

In a matter close to my own heart, there exists a court case where I sued a former business associate for fraud and won a big time judgment against him and his business. During the trial, he was the epitome of confidence, but when the jury came back with a verdict against him, he deflated like a two-bit balloon. The next day, he sold all of his business equipment at auction, skipped out on his office lease, and transferred his business telephone lines to his home.

Since he had a goodly amount of personal assets, and was found personally liable for the judgment, Johnnie cut a deal with his wife and gave her *all* of his personal assets in a friendly divorce agreement. I mean everything: the house, the lake property, the cars, the money in the banks, and all of his stocks and bonds. He claimed that he had to give her everything because she had evidence on him that would have cleaned him out in court.

Three months after the supposed divorce was final, our little love-birds got back together again and purchased a new home together, as husband and wife. No, they didn't get married, but they might as well have, because Texas is a Common Law marriage state (if it walks like a duck and talks like a duck, then by God it is a duck). They clearly showed their intent to co-mingle their assets again by signing the note and deed for their new house as Mr. and Mrs. (*Gotcha!*)

If you are going to try to protect your assets through a trust or estate, then be sure that you do it before you get into deep yogurt financially. Do it now, don't procrastinate and hope to get away with transferring your assets once you step in the doo! If you don't believe me, then read your state UCC (business code) and see what they say about fraudulent transfers and sales of assets for less than fair value. That's what you will have to face in court.

Bankruptcy Blues

A few years ago, it was very fashionable to be in bankruptcy; everyone did it, from shoe salesmen to senators, crooks to congressmen. Some liked it so much that they did it three or four times, filing for bankruptcy, dropping their claims before they had to disclose their assets, and filing again just to drag out the legal process.

Today, many judges have gotten sick of such antics and have begun to take legal action against people who abuse the bankruptcy process. Some have gone so far as to put blatant violators in jail for fraud. Congress is trying to enact new rules and guidelines for bankruptcy but the business lobby, particularly the credit card companies who help us create all of our debt, is dead set against anyone making it easier to get out of the trap.

Many people have used the bankruptcy courts to stall their creditors or to make creditors settle for 25 cents on the dollar, rather than hire an attorney to pursue their claims in bankruptcy court. Everyone knows that the first money paid back in a bankruptcy is to the trustee and the lawyers, and that there is usually very little left for creditors, so most creditors would rather get paid something rather then nothing, and settle out of court.

Many people trying to hide it all will put all of their money in a new home purchase and buy everything they need for the next year or so, then file a bankruptcy in a user friendly state like Texas or Florida. The home becomes protected under the state's homestead law, exempt from the bankruptcy, and protected until the bankruptcy is settled or completed. Then, once the debts have been discharged, the house can be sold and the proceeds pocketed free and clear.

The real problem with any of these methods is that your friend or spouse is going to blow the money you entrusted to them or that the creditors are going to get together and pool their knowledge, information, and money to pursue you either in state or bankruptcy court. If they all get together, and compare the financial statements given to them by you and can show that you gave different information to different lenders, or claimed different assets in different financial statements, then they have a good chance of convincing a judge and jury that you have committed *fraud*.

Once the court finds that you have acted with the intent to delay, deceive or defraud your creditors, it can strip you of all of your legal defenses, freeze any assets in your name or the names of the parties you transferred them to, and force you to repatriate those assets or go to jail, à la F. Lee Bailey. Then you are in real trouble!

3 Cautionary Notes: What You Should Know Before You Go

Okay, so you think you might be ready to bug out and start a whole new life. Before you do anything, there are a few points you need to seriously consider in order to hide and remain happily hidden. That's what we're going to talk about in this chapter.

Are You Skipping Out on the Law—or Just on Your Life?

Depending on your reasons for skipping out, life can be simple or life can be complicated. If you are running from the law and you have decided you want to leave the United States, you need to make sure that:

1. Your new home has not signed the MLAT (Mutual Legal Assistance Treaty) or does not have an extradition treaty with the United States.
2. The crime you committed is so minor that the law enforcement establishment is not going to bother spending the time or expense to return you to the United States once you are located in your new home. (If the crime you committed is a felony, and the government wants to make an example of you through prosecutorial body count, then you need to consider an alternative course of action.) This will entail a little more planning and a whole lot more consideration, because you are making a conscious decision to break the law and you should learn all of the ramifications before even thinking of it.

Here's a viable "Plan B." You leave the United States and create a new identity in another country—an identity that you can afford to have "discovered." What they (the people looking for you) won't know is that you will have used that country as a "cut out." Meanwhile, you'll have moved to a third country, where you will create a third identity by opening an appropriate bank account and applying for a passport and citizenship in a name separate from the first two. Your detractors will chase these other two identities for years to come, and never get close to you (unless, of course, you make a major blunder). In Chapter 4, you'll find more about creating a new identity via a second (or third) passport.

Three Can Keep a Secret—If Two of Them Are Dead

If you remember nothing else from this book, remember this one simple truth. It is so important it's almost worthy of a book in itself. Believe me, I have more than a whole book's worth of stories about people who forgot the number-one rule, the Prime Directive for those with something to hide:

THREE CAN KEEP A SECRET IF TWO OF THEM ARE DEAD.

The surest way to get caught is through your own mouth. Most people are their own worst enemy when it comes to keeping a secret. It seems to be a quirk of human nature: very few people can pull off a crime, do a dirty deed, or get away with something spectacular—and be able to keep their mouth shut about it. They always have to tell someone, to show off how clever they are, and that is their ultimate downfall.

If you really want to disappear however, you can't tell *anyone* of your dreams and plans. Your spouse, your friends, your in-laws, your ex-laws, your old relations, your new relations, your bird (if it's a talking bird), or your dog (if there's any chance the dog is wired, the room is bugged, or there's another soul listening in on your confessions).

All it takes is one p.o.'d sweetheart or one big-mouthed "friend," and your carefully crafted plans have gone to hell in a hand basket. Everything you worked for and built on can be shattered instantly through one stupid slip of the tongue.

Don't tell your lawyer, your doctor or your shrink of your intentions; don't even tell your priest or minister or rabbi. The law is getting less and less respectful of client or parishioner confidentiality.

And for God's sake, don't write about your plans in a diary or journal. Don't send an outline of your battle plan by e-mail, snail-mail, or carrier pigeon to your pen pal in India. Don't even use a cellular phone in making calls to people or places that you want to go to. The written word has a way of rising up and biting you in the behind when you least expect it. (Now, why did I even write this book? Hmmmmm.)

Of course, you don't want to pull the old Tricky Dicky disaster and make tapes of your innermost secrets either. Use your head, or "they" may end up *having* it on a platter.

You Can't Go Home Again—Or Phone Home, Either

The one thing you *must* remember is that once you leave, if you really want your new life to work, *you can't go back*. This means you can't call your relatives in the United States, you can't go across the border to meet them on holidays, and you can't send back to the good old U.S.A. for your medical, dental, or prescription records. *You have to take these records with you when you go.* (More on that in a moment.)

In the Introduction to this book, we touched on this need to sever your old ties, so forgive me if I belabor the point—but it is very important. It's so easy to slip up and screw up even the best-laid plans.

Having been indicted for bank fraud and embezzlement in the failure of his financial institution, a prominent banker decided it was smarter (and cheaper) to leave the country than to spend his money on lawyers, who would eventually give him over to the clutches of the law anyway. Our banker made his plan, bought all the books he could find on disappearing, and converted all his assets to cash, which he took with him to his new home somewhere in Central America.

Everything went well for months, so the banker, feeling brave, bullet-proof, and invisible, contacted his wife from a pay phone and arranged to meet her in Tijuana during the Christmas holidays. The wife, who was unable to whistle and chew gum at the same time, asked her husband to meet her at the border because she didn't know how to speak Spanish, convert dollars to pesos, or arrange for the auto insurance required for driving in Mexico. Our bright little boy, forgetting all his best-laid plans, went to pick up his wife at the border-town hotel one block from freedom.

I bet you know the rest of the story. The FBI collected the spouse's phone bills, saw the call details showing the long-distance call from

Central America, and looked up the next major holiday on their trusty calendar. With a little deduction, they figured out that a Christmas visit was a distinct possibility, and so they followed Mrs. Banker to the little border town and the local no-tell motel. When our hero showed up at the hotel, his goose was not only cooked but also served on a platter to a Federal Judge with an appetite for "justice." He is now serving 25 years in Club Fed wishing that he had not made that one mistake.

Remember what happens to the best-laid plans of mice and men. Don't ever take anything for granted; don't count on the stupidity of the government, the naiveté of your ex-spouse, or the incompetence of an eager-beaver investigator. You can beat them one hundred times in a row, dance like a butterfly, sting like a bee—and then get caught forever through one foolish mistake. They don't have to win the game or the war, just one battle, and then, despite all your minor victories, you go directly to jail (or, perhaps worse, back to the spouse and creditors you were running from in the first place).

Out with the Old Past, in with the New: A Final Word on Secrecy

Picasso once said, "Every act of creation is first an act of destruction." Those are wise words indeed. By now you've surely gotten the message that before you can begin a new life, you must first get rid of your old one. Once you have done that, once you've rid yourself of all the old baggage, old ways, and old troubles, *then you have to walk away and really let the past die*. In a sense, you've got to "kill" your old self.

But the good news is now you get to be creative by inventing a brand new "past." The idea is to fabricate a history that is different from your real life, but not so much at odds that you will have a problem with credibility. Most importantly, you want to create a past that doesn't provide enough information for someone to find your old hometown and identity. (You will find details on the logistics of creating a "new you" in Chapter 4.)

Once you have created your new identity, you must then guard it as if your life depended upon it. In a way it does. If you tell any of your old friends—and especially if you have them come visit you when you are lonely or in need of emotional repair—you had better realize you are digging your new identity a grave. Before your friends are back in town three days, they will be telling two more friends, who will each tell three friends, who will each tell four friends, and so on, and so on.

And every time someone tells your story, it will just keep getting bigger and bigger. Before it's over, you will be a multi-million-dollar drug lord with an army of mercenaries and a harem of exotic women answering to your every beck and call. There's no way you can live down a story like that, or keep it from spreading like wildfire. This and more could happen to you, if you don't remember the number-one rule (all together now, boys and girls):

THREE CAN KEEP A SECRET IF TWO OF THEM ARE DEAD.

The moral of the story is: Make new friends, but *don't* keep the old ones.

Don't Leave a Trail

There are other ways you can give yourself away without even opening your mouth. You can sabotage your plans completely before you've even left the country, simply through carelessness. Take a few sensible precautions now, and you won't leave a trail for those who may be looking for you later.

Meds and Feds

Before you bug out, be sure that you—and all of your family members who are coming with you—have obtained copies, or, preferably originals, of all medical, dental, and prescription records from your local health care practitioners. These include medical doctors (G.P.'s and specialists), psychotherapists, dentists, optometrist, and pharmacists. Also consider any "alternative" practitioners you may have seen, such as herbalists and acupuncturists. Once you've arrived in your new country, you certainly don't want to send a message concerning your medical needs back to your hometown. That would make it only too easy to trace your whereabouts.

Ask your medical providers to give you all of your records. This, of course, may be easier said than done. Be aware that some doctors are reluctant to give records directly to patients because their policy is to send them directly to the patient's new physician. (Note that if you have medical insurance through your employer, and said employer is self-insured—as many large companies are these days—the employer technically owns the records relating to any health claims.) In any case, *stand up for yourself.* Legally, your rights to your medical records vary from state to state, but with persistence, you should be able to get your records. It might help to explain that you will be on the road for an extended period of time, that you don't have a new physician lined up as of yet, don't have any idea of when you will have one, but want to have your records with you in case of an emergency.

By the way, medical record privacy is a hot-button issue among privacy advocates. (Also see the section in Chapter 5 on air travel privacy.) While computerized medical records are beneficial in many ways, the truth is that technology is seriously jeopardizing confidentiality. Once records have been digitized, they can be transmitted without a trace all over the globe. Your entire medical and insurance history is now complied online by an insurance industry database service called the American Index Bureau.

For privacy advocates, the trends are truly alarming. *Consumer Reports* magazine says, "Medical information has become a commodity that can be traded." A couple of years ago Equifax, the giant credit reporting company, announced an alliance with AT&T to push aggressively into the medical records business.[1] Agencies such as the Medical Information Bureau (MIB), the Property Insurance Loss Register (PILR), and the National Insurance Crime Bureau (NICB) collect your medical claims and insurance policy records, and can use them to follow your medical history all over the map.

Insurance company lobbyists, information conglomerates, and the computer industry are fighting for legislation, under the pretext of medical privacy, that will legitimize the establishment of an electronic medical register. This is nothing more than an attempt to legalize their intrusion into the previously sacred doctor-patient relationship—without any say-so from either doctors or patients. (In fact, the state of Maryland has passed a law *requiring* centralized compilation of patient-identified data, including private psychotherapy.[2])

In the unlikely event that your doctor's records aren't all computerized, it may be a bit easier to protect your own privacy and cover

---

1 "Medical Privacy," article by Denise Nagel, *Newsday*, Oct. 27, 1995 (available on EPIC (Electronic Privacy Information Center) website at epic.org.
2 *Ibid.*

your trail. Do insist on getting the original records, and, if you can manage it, don't let the practitioners keep copies.

Of course, if the government is really, really *after* you, all bets are off. The feds can confiscate any existing record on you—paper or electronic—from virtually anybody. If that happens, there's not much you can do about it, though in some states you may have the right to ask the court to either disallow the opening of your file, or to allow only a specific portion of your medical record to be seen. In that case, a judge will decide what parts, if any, of your medical record should be considered private and who can have access to them.

For the person who is trying to disappear, the important point is that even though the records may reveal intimate information you'd rather keep to yourself, you're not too bad off as long as they don't also contain any clues about where you've disappeared *to*.

A couple more points before we leave this topic. First, I would suggest that you and your family get a good thorough physical check-up before you depart, so you'll know about any new or potential problems before you take off. If you need to take care of small problems, surgeries, or therapies, do it before you go, if you can. Get as much as you can over and done with before you have to establish new medical relationships. That way, you can start over with a clean slate in your new home.

Second, if you're going to move outside the United States, particularly to a tropical climate, check the immunization requirements or recommendations for your new destination. The Centers for Disease Control (CDC) in Atlanta can provide you with all you need to know about this information. Their number is (404) 639-1938. Or check out their Web site at www.cdc.gov.

I cannot over stress the importance of getting your immunizations. Here in the United States we tend to focus our concern on AIDS, a relatively "new" disease, while we remain quite complacent about many of the nasty diseases that have plagued humankind for millennia. This complacency is bad enough within the borders of our country (particularly when you consider, for example, the steady increase in tuberculosis here) but to venture unprotected into less-developed areas is downright stupid. Tropical and sub-tropical regions are home to all manner of insects from Hell, and some of these areas have less than sterling sanitation systems as well, making them a Paradise for nasty bacteria. There's nothing like a diagnosis of malaria, yellow fever or diphtheria—or tetanus, for that matter—to spoil your stay in Paradise.

You don't believe it can happen to you? Well, a friend of mine, who recently moved to Central America, poo-pooed the idea of immunizations—and just last month came down with a minor case of malaria. And once you've got malaria, you've got it for good.

So don't neglect this very important step. (By the way, be sure you stay current on your tetanus shots.) In most places shots are not expensive; for example, in Honduras, as of this writing, you can get virtually all the inoculations you need for under three dollars each at the local medical clinic.

Clean your house. I don't just mean this metaphorically; I mean it literally, too. And when I say "clean your house," I mean be sure you take all your photos, bills, mementos, business and personal correspondence, invoices, computer printouts and disks, and travel brochures when you leave. Oh, and if you're not taking your computer with you, wipe its hard drive clean, for crying out loud.

If you don't want to keep all your letters, bills, magazines, and other items, don't just throw them in the garage or dumpster, and don't leave them in a pile for the landlord or Realtor to clean up after you're gone. You must be absolutely certain that you don't leave any identifying information in your old home that will tell about your social activities, your business, or, most importantly, your future plans. Just look at what these Florida goofballs did.

A gang of Miami jewel thieves, connected with the infamous Murf the Surf, found out that they could case their future victims' residences by buying copies of the local *House Beautiful*-type magazines. These publications featured the architecture, décor and furnishings of South Florida's most expensive homes, as well as the jewels and collectibles of the homes' inhabitants. The only trouble was that these clowns tore the pages out of the magazines containing their chosen targets, and then threw the torn-up publications in the trash.

Federal agents and local police investigating the thieves found several of these magazines in their trash and naturally wondered why certain pages were missing. So they bought copies of the magazines and looked at the pages in question, and pretty soon, with a little deduction, they figured out why these pages were missing from the thieves' copies. (They were the places the crooks picked to rob.) It didn't take a rocket scientist to decide to set up surveillance at these homes, wait for the jewel thieves to do their dirty deed and bag them in the act. Oh yes!

A search of their apartments also disclosed travel brochures with hotels in the Bahamas circled in red. Guess what the judge thought about their chances for bond when this evidence was put in his hands.

Not that you are or might consider being a jewel thief of course, but, a similar scenario could happen to you if you leave behind any travel brochures, phone bills, or other identifying information that:

1. Gives clues to your future plans or destinations
2. Reveals the names of friends or relatives who might know where you went
3. Lists your favorite magazine or mail order subscriptions

Destroy all such items that you are not taking with you. Cancel your subscriptions. Whatever you do, don't just send in a change-of-address notice; *cancel* all of those subscriptions to the *Robb Report, International Living, The Coconut Telegraph Belize Weekly News*, etc., and all of those specialty catalogs, too. Once you're settled in your new home, re-start them in your new name. Sending an address change notification in your real name is just like laying bait for a subpoena by the evil empire.

Have a Contingency Plan (In Other Words, Cover Your Assets)

Now that we've pretty thoroughly gone over the need for keeping your mouth shut and severing your old ties, there's one more factor to consider. Whether you are running from the law or are just running out on a spouse or creditors, you must make plans for all possible eventualities. One of your contingency plans has to include the means to funnel assets to you in case of need or through inheritance. You need a clean means of maintaining access not only to the money you have now, but to assets that may become yours in the future—for example, through inheritance from a family member.

If the possibility exists that you are going to inherit from your parents or another family member, then you must plan for this eventuality and see that your creditors cannot attach these assets before they are transferred to you. You should also make sure there is no trail from the probate of the inheritance estate to you in your new home. (This is where a well-chosen lawyer comes in.)

One way to do this is to get a worldly legal beagle to create an irrevocable "family trust" to own and shelter the assets and thereby head any creditors off at the pass, so to speak.

In addition, it would be wise to make arrangements for the distribution of your assets in the event of your demise. Not a very pleasant thought, I grant you, but a little advance preparation could mean the difference between your assets being bequeathed to someone you care about and being used to stuff the pockets of some lower-level bureaucrat in your new home.

The most common means of ensuring that your chosen beneficiaries receive what you intended are by the establishment of a Living Will or a Trust. It is well beyond the scope of this or any other book to advise you on all the details, which must be attended to, as each country's laws are unique. Also, due to the dynamic nature of the developing nations' legal systems, the laws within a given country are subject to change very quickly. Therefore, I cannot stress strongly enough the importance of consulting a tax attorney who is an expert both in the United States and in the specific country you have chosen—an expert who knows their laws and idiosyncrasies, and is capable of helping you plot your course through these unfamiliar waters.

You will note that I advise consulting with a tax attorney, as opposed to an accountant or consultant. The reason for this is simple and straightforward: In a court of law, an attorney has a limited privilege from testifying against you, should Uncle Sam, your creditors, or an angry ex-spouse decide to nail you to a wall. An accountant or consultant, on the other hand, is not afforded this exemption, and I've seen too many of them squeal like pigs when the pressure to testify against their clients got too great.

Unfortunately, these are issues that most people never consider until it is too late—usually after some creditor, an ex with an attitude, or the IRS has slapped a lien on the assets, thus preventing their sale. Remember: An ounce of prevention is worth a fifth of cure.

Later, we'll go into more detail on finances: specifically, on moving your money and keeping it hidden. But for now, since we've gotten most of the caveats out of the way, let's concentrate on deciding just exactly where you want to go. In the next chapter we'll take a look at some choice expatriate dens all over the globe.

Where Are the Best Places to "Hide It All and Disappear"?

4

Now that you've decided you want to pack up and go, and you're on your way to being mentally and logistically prepared for doing so, the crucial question is, where? Deciding this can be a challenge. The world is changing so fast these days that historians, economists, and political analysts—not to mention map-makers—are having a hard time keeping up with it all. Nevertheless, the information in this chapter should give you a pretty good idea of the global outlook, from an expatriate's perspective, for now and the near future.

First This Disclaimer: My Criteria

I don't present my choice of locations as being a complete, definitive list of all viable places to start your new life. I base my recommendations on certain criteria, which in some cases stem from my own biases—to wit.

Proximity To The United States

Obviously not all of the areas discussed are going to meet this criterion—Vietnam, Malaysia, and Turkey come to mind immediately—but you will notice that I place a favorable emphasis on areas closer to home, such as Central America and the Caribbean, because I travel back and forth on business, and that gets expensive. Rumor has it that a new airline "Honduras Air" is bringing in a route direct to Roatan Island from Houston for $359. The companion fare is said to be half the price of the $359 round trip fare. This is what is known as a good deal. See your travel agent for current information, *but* don't book your ticket through them.

Weather

This is one place where my own personal bias definitely comes in. I happen to prefer a balmy, tropical paradise; I shy away from lands that offer eternal winter. If you want to hide it all in Antarctica, Iceland, or Greenland, more power to you, but you won't find a five-star rating for your new home (or even a discussion of it) in *this* book. W. C. Fields and I both agree that ice belongs only in drinks!

Available Amenities

I've considered not only necessities for the body, such as health care, but necessities for the soul, such as good restaurants, cheap liquor, and other delightful diversions which make a place truly a Paradise.

Administrative Details

No expat guide would be complete without consideration of investment opportunities, banking, and privacy laws, and, of course, the existence or lack there of, of extradition agreements with the United States.

Infrastructure

Without good roads, reliable power, and clear telecommunications, a paradise can quickly turn into a purgatory. If you intend to hide your assets and disappear, it only makes sense to do so in a place where you can live with a minimum of frustrations and a maximum of suitable amenities. Do a little homework on your new home and be sure that you can be happy there and can live with any local problems or without any missing services that are not available in your new host country.

Value

In many of the places I've mentioned, real estate is still an incredible bargain, and the cost of living is a fraction of what you'd pay in the United States Not all of the countries listed, however, are such bargains; in some cases, you get what you pay for (not much); in other cases, paradise has been "discovered" and the prices reflect this. (Real estate in Costa Rica rose 500 percent in the last five years, Honduras doubled in two.) As the song says, "you better shop around."

As a matter of fact, you will notice that I've listed a few places I don't particularly recommend. I have various reasons for including them, depending upon the country in question. Perhaps they're located close to some of the areas I *do* endorse. Or perhaps they once were suitable ex-pat locales, and have the potential to be so again. Or they may just be countries I've frequently been asked about, so I have included them for your benefit.

Conversely, there are several viable expat destinations that I've not covered in this chapter, such as Canada, Ireland, Israel, Russia, and the countries of Eastern Europe. Granted, one of these countries may very well be the ideal place for you. For example, Canada, our good neighbor (or is that neighbour?) to the north, welcomes entrepreneurs, investors, and retirees after three years of residency—but as I said, I'm a tropical species, and, baby, it's *c-c-c-c-cold* up there! In Ireland and Israel, it's possible that you could be entitled to citizenship within a few months of arrival, based upon your ancestry. There's no denying Ireland is beautiful and romantic, and it is also developing into quite the expatriate's haven, but again, the climate is a bit too cold, damp, and gloomy for my tastes. As for Israel—now, there's a land rife with history; unfortunately, there's still entirely too *much* history being made in this tiny country, if you ask me. More to the point, it's an interesting place to visit, but let's face it, not just anybody can disappear there. As for Russia and Eastern Europe, see Canada, above.

Notwithstanding my disclaimer of incompleteness, I believe I have presented a rich variety of locations for you to consider. And I've certainly not ruled out including other countries in future editions of this book, or perhaps in my newsletter or on my Web site (I've got two of them, www.hideyourassets.com and www.pankau.com.) I'll be relying on your feedback to help me decide which countries to include in the future. Meanwhile, you can find information in periodicals and on the Internet about the countries not covered in this book—e.g., Ireland, Israel, and . . . oh, yeah, Argentina (where, I hear, you can get ranch land cheap).

Before we go any further, I want to recommend again that you read the current edition of a terrific monthly newsletter called *International Living*. They publish analyses by some of the world's foremost legal authorities and economists, and, being a periodical, are not inhibited by the requirement of maintaining information that is accurate over the long term. They report conditions as they *presently* exist, with educated projections as to future trends. As the Chinese philosopher once said, "The only thing that is permanent is change."

The editors of *International Living* keep up to date on all of the latest expatriate hot spots and often give names of people in those cities and countries that can give you up to the minute information on their locale and the ins and outs of living or doing business there. If you need a man on the ground to point you in the right direction, then *International Living* is the source for you! See the Resource List at the back of the book for more information on *International Living* and on other valuable sources of data.

So Enough About Me Already . . . What Are *Your* Criteria?

For me, Paradise is a place where I can run around in shorts, a tacky Hawaiian shirt, and a sombrero all year round if I want, and where the United States is just a short plane trip away. The presence of a Free Trade Zone is pretty darned attractive to me too. But maybe you'd rather be further away from the United States, and maybe you don't care what the weather is like because you spend most of your time indoors anyway. Perhaps you have particular legal or business needs that would make my Paradise your Hell.

Before you can make a truly rational choice about where you want to go, you need to sit down and think about your situation. That's why I've included this little check list for you to determine what *you* want and need in a home country. Once you've determined this, the charts and information on the individual countries I've provided will have more meaning.

What I want you to do right now is take the time to fill out this little table, placing a mark in the box which most closely matches your own personal priorities (see Table 4.01). Then, as you look over the countries described later in the chapter, you'll have a rule of thumb by which to judge how well a country "fits" you, just by comparing your answer table with the ratings table for each country. You may be living in your new home for a long time, so you had best be very clear and honest with yourself in your choices. This isn't a pop test, but if you move to a new home with eyes that aren't completely open, you may very possibly fail.

TABLE 4.01

Personal Checklist
How Important?

Factor	Less 1	2	3	4	More 5
Location	☐	☐	☐	☐	☐
Weather	☐	☐	☐	☐	☐
Legal System	☐	☐	☐	☐	☐
Banking	☐	☐	☐	☐	☐
Extradition	☐	☐	☐	☐	☐
Infrastructure	☐	☐	☐	☐	☐
Value	☐	☐	☐	☐	☐

Before you assign an importance level to each category, I'm going to give you a few questions you need to ask yourself. Don't hurry . . . think about each question very carefully. Remember: We're playing for *all* the marbles here, and we're playing for *keeps*. This is the rest of your life we're talking about.

Location

When answering the questions below, keep in mind the caveat from previous chapters: If you really want to disappear completely, *you can't go home again*—at least not as your "old" self (see the next chapter on how to create a "new" self). Keeping this in mind, ask yourself the following:

- How important is it to remain close to the United States?
- Do you have affairs that require your physical attendance in the United States?
- Are there people you want or need to visit frequently? (Remember that caveat, though!)
- Will proximity to the United States put you in danger of extradition?
- Is it a "security" thing that keeps you close to home? (But also ask yourself: What price "security"?)

Weather

When you're looking at the ratings charts below for the individual countries, you'll need to keep in mind the subjectivity of this category.

Remember that I like my countries warm and balmy. So if you're a life-long member of the Polar Bear Club, you won't necessarily agree with my five-star rating for the weather in some Central American Eden.

- Do you hate cold winters?
- In your opinion, is Paradise a place that is always warm, or a living icebox?
- Do you believe that ice is something that only belongs in drinks?
- Do you enjoy outdoor activities? Or do you enjoy your indoor sports?
- Do you feel that sweat is sexy, or is it repulsive?

Legal System

Most countries don't want dangerous felons, but they do cater to folks with big-time tax miseries, domestic disputes, and other financial entanglements in which the courts are used to try to confiscate assets. Often cash-poor and with little in the way of natural resources or internal income, these nations throw out their arms in welcome to people seeking financial freedom.

On the other hand, some of these countries suffer from hopelessly disorganized or corrupt governments, some are strangled by bureaucracy, and some operate under tyrannical laws that are arbitrarily enforced. Think about your needs and do a little bit of research on the country you're considering; don't jump out of the frying pan into the fire.

- Is privacy a primary motivator in your move?
- Are you fleeing a civil judgment, creditors, or something potentially criminal?
- Will your business affairs suffer in a less-than-orderly legal environment?
- How important to you are the day-to-day functions of the government in your new home? (Or do you even give a damn?)

The worst thing you could do is to isolate yourself in a self-made prison. Ted Kaczynski did it in Montana, but he definitely has a screw or two loose. You can have your cake and eat it too, if you spend a little time planning out your self-imposed exile in the most enjoyable means.

Banking

Many countries have specific laws against providing financial information on their customers and citizens unless it is through very specific, very targeted agreements and treaties, such as the various "bank secrecy" acts (see Chapters 5 and 6 for more on said treaties and bank secrecy acts). You'll notice that several of the questions in this section are repeats of those in the previous section, "legal." That's because you need to consider them in the context of your financial as well as your legal matters.

- Do you want, or require, privacy in your business dealings?
- Are you fleeing a civil judgment or creditors?
- Do you plan to manage the majority of your assets from your new home, or elsewhere?
- Do you have passive income that you want to shelter?
- How important is it to be able to fully trust the banks in your new home?

Extradition

Many countries offer immunity from extradition back to the United States, as long as your crimes are not drug-related or are not major felonies such as crimes of violence or organized crime.

- Are you fleeing criminal prosecution or even imprisonment?
- How serious is the crime you fear prosecution for?
- How significant are your liabilities to creditors?
- How much does your ex-spouse hate you?

Infrastructure

If you absolutely must have your MTV, your CNN, your ESPN, or, for that matter, your ISP (Internet Service Provider), *and* you've gotta have 'em 24 hours a day, you might be somewhat disgruntled in a place where they turn off the power at 8:00 P.M. A relatively sound infrastructure is one of those things we take for granted here in the United States, but, as the song on the jukebox says, "We don't know what we've got till it's gone." So consider . . .

- Do you require absolute reliability in your electric and telephone service?
- Are smooth, comfortable rides in the country important to you?
- Do you experience a high degree of anxiety when driving?

Value

One of the most common reasons for starting a new life is to improve your quality of life without spending any more to do it. To determine whether this is a prime factor for you, consider . . .

- Does the idea of living like a king for less than you spend now appeal to you?
- Are you going to be living on a fixed income, with no outside money sources?
- Are you an habitual coupon-clipper, who will drive five miles out of your way to save fifty cents on a six-pack of beer?
- Is the beer an off-brand or generic in the first place?
- Do your friends tease you, accusing you of drinking bear whiz if you can get it at a discount?
- Did you steal this book from the public library?
- Are you one of those cheap bastards that sees fit to haggle with the cashier over every item you purchase?
- Did you wait for it to go on sale before you bought it? Where do you live? (Hey . . . it's my money you're messing with on these last two!)

Take as long as you need to complete this personal checklist. Once you're done, mix yourself a margarita or a smoothie, settle back in your armchair or lawn chair, and let's get the show on the road.

The World Next Door (And We Don't Mean Canada)

Of all the places you can go, for all the reasons that you can think of, it's hard to beat Latin America—specifically Central and South America, and parts of Mexico. Latin America is an opportunist's dream. Both Central and South America are in the early stages of a once-in-a-lifetime real estate and financial boom, the likes of which we may not see ever again.

Justin Ford, managing editor of *Latin American Index*, says that a tremendous shift in wealth, similar to the one in Asia over the last twenty years, is in the process of beginning in our own backyard. (We will go into more detail about that in a little while.)

For the person seeking a place which offers the best of everything—comfort and secure living; the potential for realizing substantial gains on real estate and business investments; and the lure of living in luxury for far less than you spend at home—the Latin American countries beat the rest of the world hands down.

But what about crime . . . ?

While we're on the subject of secure living, we might as well address a concern which, even if unstated, is very present in the mind of anyone considering relocating to a Latin American country: *crime*.

It seems that every day, we are treated to the image of some new act of violence occurring in one or another Latin American country. It would be all too easy to come to the general conclusion that life in Latin America is inherently more violent than life here in the United States Such a conclusion would, in fact, be grossly inaccurate. While varying degrees of political and social unrest do exist in a number of the countries of the region, the actual instances of violent criminal acts are, if anything, less frequent than what we have grown uncomfortably used to right here in the good old U.S.A. As a matter of fact, the United States has the world's highest rates of murder, assault, and robbery.

I think the frequency of incidents south of our borders appears so high to us partly because of our tendency to generalize "Latin America" as a region, rather than looking at individual locales as being independent of each other. Were we removed from the United States, for example, we would be appalled by the frequency of violent crimes which occur in virtually every American city. Such incidents have become so commonplace here in this country that only the most outlandish and grisly crimes are even reported in the media (just watch the news on the boob tube). It all comes down to a matter of perspective as much as fact.

Naturally, there exists a criminal element in every corner of the world, including Latin America—an element which seeks to prey upon the careless, unwitting, or poorly defended victim. As such, the traveler would be advised to use common sense in his or her travels, regardless of the destination.

For example, you wouldn't think of walking alone in one of the more economically disadvantaged sections of an American city, flaunting "wealth" by wearing expensive clothes and jewelry and waving large sums of cash around. Nor would you venture at night into a neighborhood which had been the scene of recent unrest. Yet, you would be amazed to learn how many foolish travelers will do just that while vacationing in a foreign country. Even more amazing is the fact that they are shocked when, in so doing, they fall victim to criminals.

Perhaps they are infected with that grotesque symptom of "Ugly American-itis": the arrogance to honestly believe that just because they are Americans,[1] they are immune to danger. Perhaps they are simply not too bright. Either way, they tend to inflate the crime statistics, even as they improve the average intelligence of the gene pool by the simple act of getting themselves killed.

One must acknowledge the higher probability of being mugged in many Latin American countries, particularly when venturing out alone or at night. You should realize that in Latin America, the division between the wealthy, privileged class and the poverty-stricken masses is not buffered by a "middle-class" citizenry to which we pay such great lip-service in the United States Once you wander from the confines of the wealthy, you step almost immediately into a world much like our American ghettos, only worse. If you venture into these areas alone, or at night, you are placing yourself at very real risk, just as you would be by walking through an American ghetto looking like a potential victim. If you want to explore the nightlife, don't get into the first cab you see downtown. Get the hotel to take care of that problem because they know the score and will see to it that you don't disappear or become a victim of the local Robin Hood.

In short, if you are considering traveling to even the most highly publicized "crime centers" of Latin America, say Colombia, then go right ahead, and count on having a wonderful time in this beautiful country. If, however, you feel compelled to satisfy your curiosity about what a coca field looks like, or feel you simply *must* absorb some "local color" at a bar, far removed from the main centers, or that perhaps you must sunbathe at the end of some remote airstrip there . . . well, I'd appreciate being named as beneficiary in your life insurance policy! Simple common sense is about all it will take to keep you healthy.

---

1 Or, specifically, United States citizens. If you want to get nit-picky, people in Mexico (which is part of North America) consider themselves "Americans" too, and so do many folks in Central and South America.

There are, of course, a few precautionary measures you should consider taking when traveling in Latin America.

- Don't carry a lot of cash, or any obvious signs of what will be perceived as wealth. Leave the diamonds, Rolexes, Nikons, and Hasselblads at home or in the safe deposit box at your hotel. Same goes for the Armani suit; leave it in the closet. While these items make a wonderful statement about you in your professional life, they mark you as a target on the street.
- Carry a "sacrificial wallet," stuffed with small bills, scraps of paper, and perhaps an expired credit card or two. Typically, a mugger will run like hell as soon as he thinks he's gotten your valuables. By the time he realizes that he didn't get very much from you, you will be long gone. Of course, if he pushes the issue, hand over everything you've got without resisting. Nothing in your wallet is worth losing your life over.
- Be sure to get about $50 US converted to local currency before leaving the airport. In Cali, for example, they won't let you back into the terminal once you've left, and a taxi stand outside an airport is no place to be attempting to get currency exchanged.

What Can You Offer Your New Homeland?

Many of the developing countries in Latin America have tremendous natural resources: mineral wealth, fertile land, teeming fisheries, and pristine real estate. The things they lack, and need, are investment capital and the entrepreneurial know-how for which the citizens of the U.S.A. are famous. These countries need almost every kind of twentieth-century amenity, the capital to get them started, and the ability to fix them when they break down.

While I can't say this is a bad thing, most of these countries *don't* have fast food restaurants (outside their capitals), video stores, coin laundries, or "critical" amenities such as repair/maintenance shops for televisions, radios, and small electronic appliances. Anyone who can "fix" anything from automobiles to VCRs—and has access to the parts through a United States supplier—has a sure-fire business opportunity in any Latin American country that you can name. It's definitely a business owner's dream, for in Latin America you can start on a shoe-string and take your firm as far as you desire.

In addition, the very progress that these countries are experiencing leaves them with a real need for all types of semi-technical and administrative expertise. For example, sales of personal computers in Latin America have skyrocketed in the last few years as more companies and individuals come to rely upon these machines' incredible capacity to store and process information. The number of skilled software technicians and trainers, as well as the quantity and quality of written documentation, have by no means kept pace with this growth. As reliance upon computers continues to grow at an ever-increasing rate, the lack of essential support elements will become even more critical. The people with the knowledge to solve support-related problems will virtually be able to write their own ticket in these emerging countries. And they will have far better job security than their United States counterparts who are laying off people left and right.

Although most of us don't want to get back on the treadmill and work at a full time job, many of these ventures could be undertaken part-time from home, or by making house calls, a service long since lost in the United States. Because of the lack of qualified repair persons in most areas, many people use their cars and other machines until they break, and then they just throw them out. This creates an opportunistic gold mine for a handyman who, recognizing the necessity for used parts, creates a "second-hand-rose" repair and reclamation business or deals in used merchandise that can be resold to a ready market.

Investing in the Future

If your tastes run to the big time, and you have money to invest, the *Latin American Index* indicates that it is, indeed, an exciting time to be involved in Latin America. Current success stories are just the tip of the iceberg. A few samples of the financial activity going on in these countries include the following developments:[2]

- Credit card markets are booming here. Visa's Latin American sales have quadrupled since 1989 to over twenty billion dollars.
- British Petroleum is investing heavily in a joint venture in Colombia, to the tune of seven billion dollars.
- Intel has opened a computer assembly factory in Costa Rica that is truly world class.

---

2 *Latin American Index;* Winter 1996.

- Coca-Cola says it will invest 1.5 billion dollars in Mexico, and six hundred million dollars in Argentina in the next several years. Coca-Cola of Mexico stock has been one of the hottest items in the country for many months.
- General Motors is investing two billion dollars in Brazil in the next three years. Mercedes is planning to spend four hundred fifty million on new car development.
- Investments in the Peruvian stock exchange grew almost 80 percent in 1994 alone.

When many of the smaller nations join NAFTA, it's possible that their exports to the United States will double within the first three years. A great change is under way in Latin America, and if these countries hook up with North America to form an Americas trading bloc, there will be an economic potential larger than either the European or Pacific Rim groups. The North American bloc alone will exceed the European Community by 35 million people and 34 percent percent in gross national product.

If a country such as Chile, which will probably join NAFTA, opens up its borders to international trade, both their market size and their stock market could go ballistic.

Many of the Latin American countries have significantly lowered or stopped inflation in the last few years and have little or no debt. This scenario leaves them poised for an unprecedented period of financial growth, now that political turmoil has diminished significantly. Add to this the stringent banking privacy laws in most Latin American countries,[3] and you have an environment which fairly begs the adventurous entrepreneur to get involved.

And get involved they have. In some Latin American countries, the number of investment corporations and banks exceeds the total population of the country—a distinction once reserved for Liechtenstein, long considered the banking Mecca of the privacy oriented world.

---

3 The prospective investor should remember, however, that the United States government, ever the tireless pursuer of funds it believes (rightly or not) it is owed, is actively seeking a means to circumvent foreign countries' banking privacy laws. As a result, a given country's status as a tax haven can change quickly. To protect yourself and your money from greedily clutching hands, you may someday soon need to convert all your assets into another currency before investing it offshore. As I often stress, enlist the services of an expert in setting up investments in your area of choice—one who is up to date on international treaties as well as offshore financial procedures. This is no place for the do-it-yourselfer!

Russia is out of the picture as the most effective proponent of international socialism nowadays. With the elimination of Russia's political and financial support to Cuba, Europeans and Asians are now flocking to Cuba, the Caribbean, and Latin America to avoid high taxes in their own countries, and to beat Americans to the punch in the rush for profits in the New World. The Swiss, Germans, and many other Europeans now threaten to engulf much of Cuba, as well as Costa Rica and its neighboring Belize and Honduras, which will cause real estate prices to rise dramatically in the next decade. The Chinese and Koreans have already begun developing their own cities in Honduras, with more planned.

I won't attempt, in the confines of this book, to advise you on the detailed procedures for setting up your business and investment portfolio in your new country. You will find, however, an appendix at the back which lists a number of valuable sources of information, as well as specialists whose expertise can smooth the transition and make your life as an expat infinitely more rewarding and enjoyable. I owe a great debt of gratitude to some of the people listed there, for providing specific information pertinent to this book, as well as for their advice and counsel over many years.

That said, let's take a look now at some of the individual jewels in the crown of Latin America.

North America

Mexico

For over a century, saying the word "expatriate" immediately brought to mind images of Mexico, with its quaint villages tucked

TABLE 4.02

Mexico
Livability Rating

Location	****
Weather	***
Legal System	**
Banking	**
Extradition	***
Infrastructure	**
Value	***

away in the mountains or nestled on some sleepy shore. While newer, more trendy locations have emerged to overshadow our neighbor to the south, Mexico remains one of the true bargains in the world, and offers great location to boot. You just have to know where to go.

Certainly, the economic woes that have ravaged Mexico have had some unwanted side effects for the traveler who wants to come here to disappear. As the Mexican government grows increasingly dependent upon United States foreign aid and trade agreements, they are growing ever more cooperative in exchanging information about the activities of Americans living there. Where once, the meanest, most notorious outlaw could start a new life just by crossing the border and paying off a few *federales*, the modern felon is forced to sneak deeper into the country and pay off a *lot* of people who aren't satisfied with the pittance bribes once paid.

For the expat who isn't fleeing the government and creditors, however, life in Mexico is still much more economical than in the States. And, if you want to stick to more familiar environs, you can find huge communities of American and European expats in the area around the thoroughly modern city of Guadalajara.

Some thirty miles away, the village of Ajijic (pronounced A-HEE-heek) boasts a large expat community which, while maintaining their former countries' culture, have thoroughly integrated into the placid Mexican society. Residents report a significant improvement in the overall quality of their lives, and a noticeable reduction in stress. Medical facilities are readily available here, and Guadalajara boasts facilities on a par with (and, according to some reports, better than) those found in the United States for a fraction of the price.

There are, of course, some areas you will want to avoid, such as the more destitute sectors of border towns, and, far to the south, along the borders with neighboring countries. Or Mexico City, if you are fond of breathing . . . it has, perhaps, the world's worst air pollution, spectacular earthquakes, and some impressively daunting crime statistics.

In short, if you use good sense, good planning, and good information, your dreamed-of Paradise may well be closer than you think.

TABLE 4.03

Belize
Livability Rating

Location	****
Weather	****
Legal System	*****
Banking	****
Extradition	****
Infrastructure	**
Value	****

Central America

Belize

Belize, which has been an independent nation only since 1981, today fulfills the fantasy picture that was Costa Rica ten or twenty years ago. Where Costa Rica has been heir to two decades of unchecked growth and development, Belize is just now getting its feet wet as a haven for expatriates and the international business they bring with them. It truly epitomizes the picture of a "tropical paradise," with miles of unspoiled beaches, lush rainforests, and waters so blue they deserve to be named with a color all their own.

Here, you can still find real estate at bargain-basement prices, and the procedure for a foreigner to purchase land is not so fraught with obstacles and pitfalls as is the case in many Latin American countries. Further, the Belize government is offering free leases on land to people who come in and buy adjacent property and develop it for the purpose of creating jobs for their countrymen. A dentist I met last year bought 80 acres of property on the Belize River and cleared the land for development as an RV park and camp site for American tourists. Once he cleared the original property, the government granted him an additional 60 acres and gave him a tax-free development status for five years as an inducement to employ local villagers. He now tells me that he is going to build palm-thatched bungalows called *palàpas*, and start tours to the Mayan ruins that were recently found in the nearby jungle.

The economy in Belize is booming, helped along by the relative political stability of the country, as well as the government's inclination to encourage foreign investment. For example, it is quite simple to form your own corporation here, in the form of a Belizean International Business Corporation, or IBC. For an annual fee of $175 to $750 (as of this printing), paid to the Belizean government, you may establish your own IBC, and be in business.

Privacy is ensured by the fact that the assets of most IBCs are held in bearer shares—which brings up another important point: Whether you're considering playing the stock market or forming your own IBC, you should know that stock shares are usually issued as bearer certificates. This means they're good to anyone who holds the paper—just like currency, in fact—and transferable (invisibly) at your whim.

Since Belize currently has no information exchange agreement with the United States—or with any other country, for that matter—nobody can know the details of your business dealings unless you want them to. Belize, bless its soul, has steadfastly refused to sign a Mutual Legal Assistance Treaty (MLAT) with the United States We'll talk some more about MLATs in Chapter Five; for now, I'll just say these agreements have provisions that require bankers to fill out reports on your financial transactions if there's even a hint of suspicion that you might possibly in some way be involved in the drug trade. The word is that Belize is not going to participate in any sort of MLAT unless the reporting requirements are removed in all cases except those that are definitely drug-related or involve other serious crimes such as terrorism. Obviously, Belize knows where its bread is buttered, and where its future lies.

Belize is very jealous of its independent status and will not "bend over" for other nosy governments and their agents. Two IRS CID (Criminal Intelligence Division) agents were recently caught snooping around in Belize City, trying to allegedly bribe or intimidate Barclays Bank employees into divulging clients' financial information. The agents soon found themselves run out of the county on a rail, wearing the local equivalent of tar and feathers. Since then, no others have come back (what a shame).

Furthermore, since the country has now established Free Trade Zones, no taxes are levied upon goods you import and export, nor upon any income you may realize from them. Now, I don't know about you, but this is really beginning to sound like Paradise to me. Excuse me while I phone my travel agent.

Well, things aren't quite perfect yet. As Belize is a newly developing country, it should come as no surprise that the Belizean infrastructure is less than ideal. Roadways remain primitive outside the urban areas, and service facilities are few and far between. While communication networks continue to improve, there remains significant room for improvement. At least in the near future, don't count on a clear voice connection on your telephone line—much less a reliable data connection—if you're located in one of the more pristine areas. You might want to look into the purchase of a satellite telephone before you go. (In another year or two, the technology of wireless communication will be such that you will be able to easily afford a portable cellular telephone that has international calling capability.)

Although the crime rate in Belize is still fairly low, there have been instances of pickpockets, minor thefts, and even armed robberies in the more crowded tourist centers. Again, the use of simple common sense will ensure that you, and your possessions, are at no greater risk in this beautiful country than in any location in the United States.

Costa Rica

Advertised as the "Switzerland of the Americas" as much for its economic stability as its breathtaking countryside, Costa Rica has experienced an unprecedented rise in land values in recent years—a 500 percent increase in a five-year period. The very real potential now exists for these prices to go through the roof. The new entrepreneurs, having already seized the tremendous opportunity in Costa Rica, are now venturing out to Honduras, Guatemala, and Belize, which are developmentally five to ten years behind their southern neighbor. Many are even starting to sniff out Nicaragua. They are finding truly bargain-basement prices on *ranchos* and *haciendas* in these newly developing countries.

Like most other Latin American countries, Costa Rica has an

TABLE 4.04

Costa Rica

Livability Rating

Location	*****
Weather	*****
Legal System	*****
Banking	*****
Extradition	*****
Infrastructure	****
Value	****

infrastructure which could be called "nostalgic" by American standards (in other words, if you long for the slower pace of the '50s and early '60s, this is the place for you!). Road conditions are generally fairly good, especially in proximity to the major urban areas, but some rural roadways require high-clearance, off-road type vehicles to be success-fully traversed. Telephone and other utility services can be sporadic, especially in rural—and even many suburban—areas.

These services are improving in the urban centers, however, as they become critical to continued development and increased commerce. This improvement is due in large part to the wonders of the modern satellite communications technology, (which is being rapidly imple-mented even as I write this) to replace the previous antiquated systems.

Costa Rica's health care system is considered one of the finest and least expensive in the world, thanks to a constitutional mandate to provide universal health care to all citizens. Naturally, more facilities are available in the capital city of San Jose, but medical care is still accessible—albeit on a smaller scale—throughout the country. And it's cheap. It is no accident, therefore, that life expectancy in this beautiful country ranks third in the world, bested only by Japan and France, and ahead of the United States.[4]

The Costa Rican health care system, under the auspices of the *Caja Costarricense de Seguro Social* (CCSS), is available not only to citi-zens, but to foreign residents and visitors. They may join the CCSS for a small monthly fee, or may alternately purchase low-cost health care insurance from the state-run *Instituto de Seguro Naccional* (INS). While the state-run system, like other aspects of the infrastructure, is highly overburdened, more timely health care may be obtained by vis-iting the physicians in their private practices, to which they typically devote their afternoons. Although care at these private facilities is more expensive than the same care, by the same physicians, at state-run facil-ities, it still costs a small fraction of its North American equivalent.

Considering the excellence of the available facilities, the wealth of internationally trained physicians and support personnel, and the remarkably low (by United States standards) cost, it is no wonder that nearly 15 percent of all tourists who come to Costa Rica come with the primary goal of having some medical procedure performed. Costa Rica

---

4 *The World Health Report, 1995*; World Health Organization.

has definitely become the new Mecca for the "health tourist." This definitely includes cosmetic surgery clients. Chances are that those beautiful breasts which the young sun-worshippers so proudly display are a product not of good genes, but of local commerce.

The traveler should be warned, however, that American health care insurance is not generally valid outside the United States, and that most providers expect immediate cash payment for services. While an ever-increasing number will accept payment by credit card, one would be wise to carry, or have ready access to, sufficient cash to make payment. Or consider purchasing the aforementioned CCSS membership or INS insurance. For additional information, check out the Health Tourism Corporation of Costa Rica's Web page at www.cocori.com/ healthtourcr. They are so upbeat and enthusiastic that you may find yourself wanting to head for Costa Rica just to see the doctor!

Overall, life in Costa Rica is on a level above other areas of Latin America. And with its impressive 96 percent literacy rate, this small nation has much to be proud of.

Honduras

Honduras is considered by some experts to be the best buy in all of Latin America, with its lush mountains, pristine beaches, and one of the lowest costs of living in the Western Hemisphere.

Those who prefer a simple life, enjoy the beauty of the outdoors, and are looking for the opportunity to have a comfortable *casa* with no questions asked, would be well-advised to consider the island of *Roatân,* just off Honduras' Caribbean coast. Roatân has all of the advantages of being in a foreign county, one not necessarily enamored

TABLE 4.05

Honduras
Livability Rating

Location	*****
Weather	****
Legal System	***
Banking	****
Extradition	*****
Infrastructure	****
Value	*****

of the U.S.A., while at the same time possessing all of the benefits of being an American community, because of the many expats there (including yours truly), who have already made Roatân their home.

In fact, virtually all of my neighbors are former Americans who have fled the United States because of financial, legal or domestic pressures that they chose to avoid or evade. On the island, these people live much like you and I are used to living in the United States; they simply don't choose to go back to the States to face the music (dum-dee-dum-dum).

Another place to consider is the coastal port city of *Trujillo*. This pearl of the Caribbean boasts several excellent European-style hotels at rock bottom prices. Adding to the intrigue: a fort built by Columbus, and the irresistible lure of gold. This fort was the staging area for the Spanish treasure ships that looted the Americas and carried the plundered wealth back to Spain. Hundreds of these ships, piled high with booty, never made it back to Spain, and now lie broken and scattered throughout the Caribbean. Many are believed to be off the Honduran coast, upon whose beaches gold is found after every heavy storm, washed ashore from the watery grave of the Spanish conquistadors.

Who knows? An individual on an extended scuba vacation . . . a retiree . . . or—why not?—an expatriate . . . could make one of those "finds of the century" that enriches its owner beyond his wildest dreams.

Years ago, I was plying my trade in the Bahamas when four divers came into the bar, hooting and hollering about the treasure-laden ship they had just found in 20 feet of water, right in the middle of the bay. Within hours, every able-bodied diver was churning up the bay trying to grab their piece of the rock, or at least a few gold doubloons, before the government got in on the action. They found a huge treasure trove of over $25 million, right in the harbor, but soon began fighting over it, pouring blood in the water to draw sharks to other divers—and themselves.

I bet you can guess what ultimately happened: the government stepped in and took the lion's share of the loot and kicked all of the prospectors out. This incident shows the importance of remembering our cardinal rule (you didn't think you'd get by with not hearing this again, did you?):

THREE CAN KEEP A SECRET IF TWO OF THEM ARE DEAD.

Rumor has it that the smart money is already nosing around Roatán, and that several exclusive "but still inexpensive" international communities are being planned on the hillsides and beaches of its beautiful bay. These country-club enclaves will offer a full range of private financial services and will come complete with medical, communication, and shopping facilities, all within the confines of the communities themselves. Perhaps best of all, it is rumored that Roatán is in the process of setting up a Free Trade Zone.

If your ultimate goal is to *hide your assets and disappear* in comfort, follow the trail of promise to Roatán, moving ever Southward through the United States, through Mexico to Guatemala and on into Honduras, snaking your way down country roads past the capital to that sleepy little country—where you will hear whispers of a community of like-minded Americans and Europeans who ask no questions and tell no lies (at least not *too* many).

It's truly amazing how comfortable, relaxed, and free you can feel when you move to a place where there are few lawyers practicing their trade, and no tax collectors or collection agents. A place that costs less than twenty-five cents on the dollar compared to what you are used to in our highly taxed society. It's remarkable how quickly you can fall in love with a land where life moves at a much more leisurely pace, where the sun always shines and the water is always blue, where beer and margaritas are cheaper than Coke, and "*Mañana* is the only girl for me."

Panama

Panama used to be a wonderful place for smart investors and people who wanted to disappear. At least it was until Manuel Noriega went overboard with his avarice and greed. He was so blatant in his association with the drug trade that the United States finally got fed up with him (no pun intended), broke the door down, and plucked him from his well-feathered nest. As a result, Washington decided to keep its finger on the pulse of financial operations there.

Why? Because Panama was the money-laundering center for the drug lords of Bolivia and Colombia. Noriega was reputed to have personally received 1 percent of all drug proceeds cleared through the Banco de Panama—a princely sum indeed.

Today, you would have about as much chance of avoiding Uncle Sam's scrutiny there as you would in the storage chambers at Fort

TABLE 4.06

Panama
Livability Rating

Location	***
Weather	****
Legal System	***
Banking	***
Extradition	****
Infrastructure	***
Value	***

Knox. Add the element of anti-American sympathies, and the abject poverty left in the ruins of Noriega demise, and Panama becomes one place to scratch off your list—at least for awhile, until things cool off.

On the flip side, they have inexpensive real estate, gorgeous beaches, and some of the finest salt water fishing in the world. Their Pacific coast has been immortalized by Hemingway, Zane Grey, and many other world class fishermen who live to fish. (One of my ex-wives thought fishing was a jerk at one end of the line waiting for a jerk at the other end of the line.)

Roger Gallo tells me that the time to buy is now. There is a sleepy little fishing village that is one of the best-kept secrets of Latin America, but it won't be for long if too many of you find it first.

Guatemala

Guatemala is a stunningly beautiful but perennially troubled country. In recent years, it has been virtually impossible to read an article in

TABLE 4.07

Guatemala
Livability Rating

Location	****
Weather	****
Legal System	**
Banking	***
Extradition	***
Infrastructure	***
Value	***

the world press which mentions Guatemala and isn't followed almost immediately with the word "rebels" or "human rights violations." The instability of the country's political climate has kept virtually all foreign investors away, and Guatemala has suffered greatly because of it.

On December 29, 1996, a "final" peace accord was signed between the Government of Guatemala and the Guatemalan National Revolutionary Unit, marking the potential beginning of a new era for all Guatemalan society. Naturally, putting pen to paper does not ensure stability, or even an end to the conflict that has so disrupted Guatemala's emergence into the Latin American bloc. It does, however, indicate an awareness on both sides that the overall well-being of the Guatemalan people can best be served in an environment of peaceful coexistence, and real progress is being made toward that end.

Guatemala benefits from its proximity to established trading centers, being a 90-minute flight from Miami or Mexico City. It also enjoys a climate highly conducive to year-round cultivation of crops, as well as tourism. Despite political upheavals, the country has maintained a relatively low rate of taxation and inflation, necessary requisites for consideration as a viable investment milieu.

One step the government has taken which may provide lucrative investment returns is the decision to privatize the majority of state-owned enterprises. For the adventurous investor with very deep pockets, the purchase, lease, or concession management of such major facilities as railroads, ports, airports, telecommunications, and electrical service utilities may well prove to be a virtual windfall. I must, however, stress the significance of the word "adventurous" in describing prospective investors. For my money, I think "foolhardy" may be a better term, especially considering all the opportunities available in more stable environments in the region.

Also worthy of note is that the United States Government's Overseas Private Investment Corporation (OPIC) has already expressed interest in financing some privatization projects in Guatemala. If good old Uncle Sam spends billions of dollars to shore up the Guatemalan system,[5] how inclined do you think the Guatemalan government is going to be to keep your piddling (by com-

---

[5] As it turns out, Uncle Sam and Guatemala have a mutual history that goes back decades. For example, do the words, "1954," "CIA," and "United Fruit" ring a bell?

TABLE 4.08

Nicaragua
Livability Rating

Location	***
Weather	****
Legal System	**
Banking	*
Extradition	****
Infrastructure	**
Value	***

parison) affairs hidden from him? In short, I feel there are much better places to hide it all and disappear. Like maybe Cleveland.

Nicaragua

After the Sandinista revolution of 1979, Nicaragua was literally a country in ruins. Staggering national debt, a legacy of 50,000-plus dead as a result of the war, and a virtually decimated infrastructure all contributed to a bleak near-term picture for the country.

Although there has been some improvement in the nearly twenty years since the revolution, Nicaragua remains one of the poorest countries in the Western Hemisphere. Though bolstered by foreign aid and some private-sector investment, Nicaragua's growth remains impeded by a predominantly unskilled workforce, lack of continuity in a legal system rife with corruption, and a mountainous backlog of still-unresolved asset-redistribution cases left over from the toppling of the old Somoza regime.

Settlement of property claims continues to be dominated by an inherently corrupt, despotic system, leaving investors unsure as to their future ability to repatriate assets. Granted, Uncle Sam has offered his "benevolent" hand in the form of Overseas Private Investment Corporation (OPIC) financing and insurance, but, by accessing this system, the investor is literally handing his information over to the United States government. Call me paranoid if you like, but this book is about *avoiding* this kind of visibility! To have any reasonably secure investment in Nicaragua, you would need to make yourself about as invisible as you would be signing the visitor's register at CIA headquarters. Need I say more?

The final factor which should be considered by the prospective expat is the lingering, if occasionally subliminal, dispute which continues to fester between the Sandinista regime and the Contra rebels. The political and social problems so long prevalent in this country are by no means resolved, and are, if anything, exacerbated by the United States government's overt and covert intervention efforts.

Having said all that, however, I just can't entirely dismiss Nicaragua as a future possibility. In the last year or so, several tour groups, led by publishers of the expat newsletter *International Living* (see Resource List at the back of this book), have ventured into Nicaragua to get a birds-eye view of the situation. I've joined some of these tour groups and am among those who came back—well, let's say, *interested*. While Nicaragua is still a far cry from Costa Rica, or even Honduras, we did see a great deal of potential in this country, and are definitely keeping an eye or two on its future prospects.

With a little outside investment, a few years to recover from the war, and laws friendly to expatriates, this little piece of Central America could bloom and develop into a real gem.

South America

Colombia

Probably no country in recent history has received as much negative publicity as Colombia. Forget all those commercials about Juan Valdez and his coffee beans; you and I and the rest of the world know that coffee is not the big cash crop here. Hardly a day goes by that we aren't assailed with a new story of corruption and violence. Think

TABLE 4.09

Colombia

Livability Rating

Location	***
Weather	****
Legal System	**
Banking	***
Extradition	****
Infrastructure	**
Value	**

about it . . . when was the last time that you heard or read the word "Colombia" when it wasn't in close proximity to other familiar words such as *cocaine, cartel, kingpin,* or *drug-lord?* Naturally, the State Department regularly issues dire warnings against travel to this beautiful country. If you took all of the State Department's warnings to heart, however, you'd never leave your living room.

I know people who travel in and out of Colombia regularly, and they tell me that you would have to be either profoundly unlucky or profoundly stupid (or both) to get into trouble there. One man goes so far as to say that he feels less at risk in a restaurant in Cali, Columbia, than he does in a similar establishment in a stateside city. Naturally, you wouldn't want to go ambling through some farmer's coca fields, or exploring in some wholly unknown area, but you would be just as ill-advised to do so here.

That said, I still cannot recommend Colombia as a desirable location for starting your new life. For one thing, the banking privacy statutes which make so many other Latin American countries desirable simply aren't in place in Colombia. Secondly, the tax rate and cost of living is much higher there than in many other Latin countries. Thirdly, the infrastructure is years behind other countries you could choose; roads, communications, and medical facilities are sorely lacking in all but the more affluent urban areas.

Also worthy of mention—and this is just a gut feeling—is the amount of pressure the Colombian government feels from Washington regarding their drug trade. It's my belief that the Colombians would gladly serve up an American expatriate who was trying to hide, just to get in some sort of good graces with Washington. I may well be off-base on this, but it's a feeling I just can't kick.

The bottom line here, for whatever reasons you may choose, is that Colombia is not where you want to go, at least for the time being.

Venezuela

From the Orinoco, the third longest river in South America, and Salto Angel, the world's tallest waterfall, to the grand vistas of the Sierra Nevada de Merida at the northernmost tip of the Venezuelan Andes, Venezuela claims more than its share of breathtaking scenery, beckoning nature-enamoured tourists from every corner of the earth. Speaking of breathtaking scenery, I have observed that there are about five women to every man in Venezuela.

TABLE 4.10

Venezuela
Livability Rating

Location	****
Weather	****
Legal System	***
Banking	****
Extradition	***
Infrastructure	***
Value	*****

While such things as meals and housing can be had cheaply in Venezuela, they have an economy that goes up and down more frequently than the space shuttle, and the country just isn't stable enough to consider as a place to hide and disappear. As with so many other countries, my advice on Venezuela is to visit, see what there is to see, then move on. Maybe someday things will change, but for now, you can do much better in some of her more friendly nearby neighbors that cater to the expatriates of the world.

The Islands of the Caribbean

Not too long ago, some of the best places to consider were those that the Beach Boys sing about—you know, island paradises such as Bermuda, Bahamas ("c'mon pretty mama"). Many of the tropical islands in the Caribbean offered not only perfect weather and gorgeous scenery, but also financial privacy, immunity from extradition, and a very high standard of living for the dollar, compared to what we are used to in the United States. In these countries, you could live in elevated style for a fraction of what you would pay in the States.

Things began to change somewhat as these areas got "discovered." Developers rushed in and real estate prices soared. Even worse, Uncle Sam woke up to the fact that folks were hiding their assets and/or themselves in these Caribbean havens. (I'm shocked!) Now many of these once-ideal places are, as a screenwriter or novelist might say, "too obvious."

I'm not suggesting you rule out these beautiful islands entirely, but be aware that recent changes—e.g., astronomical real estate prices, changes in bank privacy laws, and the like—may have transformed some areas into a less-than-perfect Paradise for you.

For up-to-the-minute information on the many countries in the Caribbean and the present status of their economies and their legal and banking systems, I again recommend you take a look at the newsletter I mentioned earlier, *International Living*. Whereas I can give you some good generalities here, the folks who publish *International Living* make it their job to keep current on the details you'll need to make a truly informed choice. Meanwhile, let's sail away on a brief tour of some of the islands of this region, so you can get a head start on deciding whether or not the Caribbean would indeed be Paradise for you.

The Bahamas

For years the Bahamas have been known as a desirable location for people who wish to escape taxation. There has been no taxation here since it was founded in 1717. It's almost as if the region were established with expatriates in mind, as virtually the entire legal system is geared favorably towards foreign investment.

The major drawback to this well-established system is that you will be far from the first to get there. While the infrastructure is well developed, and the economy is quite stable, the Bahamians have grown accustomed to a preponderance of dollars—and prices for everything from meals to accommodations to real estate reflect it. With its beautiful beaches and first-class amenities, the Bahamas are truly a paradise, but if you intend to live there, you'd better have deep pockets, stuffed with cash. And if you have a mind to start an IBC here, be prepared to

TABLE 4.11

The Bahamas
Livability Rating

Location	****
Weather	****
Legal System	***
Banking	****
Extradition	***
Infrastructure	***
Value	***

invest a minimum of $1 million to even have your charter considered.

One other thought, since, after all, we're talking about disappearing and hiding. Everyone knows about the Bahamas. If you truly want to hide and disappear, you don't want to go to such an obvious hiding place. It may be "better in the Bahamas" if you're a tourist, but the serious expat should take the path less traveled and find a country with a lower profile (and lower prices to boot).

For the ecology-conscious traveler, it is worthy of an aside note that the group EarthWatch has regularly scheduled research trips in the region to study marine mammals. For the hardy, adventurous traveler, serving as a volunteer on these research studies affords a unique opportunity to study not only marine mammals, but the region itself. For more information, see EarthWatch's website, which is listed in the Appendix.

The Turks and Caicos Islands

One area of the Bahamas that is an exception to the overdevelopment of this area is the Turks and Caicos islands, in the far southern quadrant of the Bahamas chain. These little gems are enjoying both a building boom (for their size) and a flurry of financial activity.

The banks and accounting firms headquarted in the Turks have become the latest "in" place to set up IBC's and offshore trusts. These financial services firms offer disgression and a level of service comparable to the Cayman Islands, and have the advantage of being not so well known and targeted for examination by the minions of the government as the Caymans have become.

They also have first-class condominiums for sale, rent, or timeshare that make this a very hospitable and enjoyable place to contemplate your immediate financial future.

Barbados

All I can say about Barbados is, "See Bahamas, only more so." While Barbados offers good banking and tax structures and wonderful amenities, and enjoys close proximity to the United States, it is geared very much toward the extremely wealthy investor. My advice is to come down to this beautiful isle, located just 100 miles east of the Netherlands Antilles, enjoy the beautiful setting, wonderful restaurants, and pristine beaches. Take lots of pictures, buy the T-shirt, then go somewhere else to live. If you do choose to stay, bring lots of money, because believe me, you'll need it.

TABLE 4.12

Barbados
Livability Rating

Location	***
Weather	****
Legal System	***
Banking	*****
Extradition	*****
Infrastructure	***
Value	**

Now, if you do have money to play with, one of the best things about Barbados is the excellent banking system. Barbados' banks do still adhere to strict financial privacy laws. (See no evil, hear no evil, speak no evil!) These institutions offer a full range of trust and management services, allowing their customers to do business worldwide, on all recognized (and some unrecognized) stock exchanges and investment vehicles. (You may want to live in a more economical country and maintain your banking here, both for stability and investment purposes.)

The beaches are beautiful, views spectacular, but the prices, for daily living, cut wide and deep into your pocketbook. Also there are too many English speaking expats there. If you like company and need good conversation on a regular basis, you may have a problem here.

Cayman Islands

One very valuable rule of thumb which I use in deciding whether a country would be a good place to hide it all and disappear is this: *Have I seen the country being promoted on television often enough that I can recall its musical theme or slogan?* If the answer is yes, it's probably too late to get in on any bargain-basement real estate.

The Cayman Islands are a perfect example of a country that meets the above criterion. Now don't get me wrong: The place is incredibly beautiful, and has all the amenities you could ever ask for in Paradise. You can enjoy some of the world's most beautiful reefs, just begging you to don snorkel and fins. You can thrill to some of the best game fishing there is. If you're more interested in catching dinner than a trophy, all you have to do is walk a few yards from the dazzling sugar-white beaches into the crystal blue waters, squirt a little Cheez-Whiz

TABLE 4.13

Cayman Islands
Livability Rating

Location	****
Weather	****
Legal System	***
Banking	****
Extradition	***
Infrastructure	***
Value	*

into the water, and wait a few moments. Before you know it, the yellowtail and mutton snapper will rush up to get their snack. You, armed with only a dip net or spear, can scoop up the entrée of your choice. It ain't sport, but it's sure fine eating!

The Caymans are also a well-known international banking center. According to the legendary tale of the "Wreck of the Ten Sails," the Caymans won their independence from England for heroically saving the crew and passengers of a fleet of ten of the Crown's ships that crashed on their shores in November of 1788. If one chooses to believe this long-debated legend, the most probable assumption is that these indigenous "good Samaritans" were actually rushing out to loot the ship, and that the saving of lives was merely a secondary concern.

The story goes that, because they saved the lives of his sovereign citizens, King George III gave them independence and exemption from British taxation and conscription. Thus were they given the means to become a self-directed, duty-free port—again, according to unsupported legend. I guess it doesn't really matter *how* it happened; what matters is that the Caymans took advantage of their autonomy and created a financial sanctuary that brought almost all of the world's banks to their doors. Through the years they have also attracted countless expatriates from the world over, who came with a desire to maintain bank accounts without sharing their wealth or financial information with their home government.

So the place is beautiful, and a money haven to boot. What's not to like? One big problem with the Caymans (and a few places like it) is that it is geared totally toward the tourist dollar. Land prices are through the roof, and the rental properties that are available are either pure squalor, expensive as hell, or taken. There's no diversified culture;

virtually all the residents are natives and salaried employees of one aspect of the tourist industry or the other.

Nor is there any expat community to speak of on the islands (except for a significant European community, and I won't even go into the "pleasures" of hanging with *those* homeboys). The expats have avoided this area, perhaps because they inevitably get last pick on job offerings—with first pick being the locals, followed by their English compatriots. As a result, an American expat would stand out like a sore thumb: not a desirable attribute for someone who wants to disappear. Besides that, let's face it: you could very well go stir crazy after the first rush of island living wears off. The big island, Grand Cayman, is only twenty miles long and six miles wide at most points.

There also may be trouble in banking paradise. The Caymans are one of a growing number of countries and regions that have entered into a Mutual Legal Assistance Treaty, or MLAT, with Uncle Sam. The effect on banking privacy may ultimately be quite chilling, even in this traditional haven of the offshore entrepreneur.

In short, savor this place for a little while, then leave. The Cayman Islands remains one of the most enjoyable vacation spots you'll ever find. But don't buy into the illusion that this is the Paradise where you want to live. After a few weeks or months, the reality would set in, and it would truly be a Paradise Lost.

Warning! Warning! Last year the IRS busted a Camanian "money manager" and squeezed him until he rolled over on his more than 500 clients who were holding accounts in the Caymans.

The IRS says that the information provided by a financier has given them valuable insight into the Cayman banking establishment and may

TABLE 4.14

Cuba
Livability Rating

Location	****
Weather	*****
Legal System	*
Banking	*
Extradition	****
Infrastructure	**
Value	****

well close this door to offshore investments seeking to protect their assets there.

For now, pick a new place to stash your cash, as the IRS has their eagle eye on this third-world money haven.

Cuba

In the early '60s thousands of American soldiers stood poised in Florida to invade Cuba through the Bay of Pigs. Today, thousands are still poised to take over Cuba, but this time purely for economic purposes. You see, with its beautiful beaches and clear water, and its location only nintey miles from Miami, every real estate huckster and dreamer is ready to charge into Cuba the day that Castro dies or rolls over on his cherished Communism.

Remember the movie *The Godfather*? There was a character, based on the real-life Meyer Lansky, who developed Havana into the gambling and vice capital of the Western Hemisphere with his Mafia-made millions. Before Castro, the tourist business made Havana a literal gold mine, where "anything goes" was the motto. Because it was outside of United States laws and jurisdiction, this was "The Place."

Today, Europeans are flocking to Cuba with francs, marks, lira, and kroners, buying up every piece of beachfront for literally dirt cheap prices. Right now, unfortunately, we can't, because of United States law, but the moment that the laws (and the State Department policy) change, we will have a land rush on that you wouldn't believe.

My advice? Forget Havana and head out to the Isle of Pines in the southwestern part of Cuba; it's the most beautiful piece of beachfront you ever saw. My father sold outboard motors to all of the fishing resorts in the Isle of Pines during the Batista regime, and he swore it was the most exquisite place on earth. My best bet is that the United States government is going to posture its way out of having any say in how this Caribbean gem develops. This will make it high on our list of suitable places for entrepreneurial expats who wants to have their cake (a home outside the United States) and eat it too (not *too* far outside—it is just ninety miles from Miami).

It will take a while to restore the infrastructure that Castro let fall apart during his soiree with socialism. You might consider sailing there on a boat and living on it until the systems get re-built to a decent standard, but this is definitely a place that will be worth visiting or possibly living when the time comes.

TABLE 4.15

Netherlands Antilles
Livability Rating

Location	****
Weather	*****
Legal System	*****
Banking	*****
Extradition	****
Infrastructure	****
Value	***

Netherlands Antilles

The Antilles, which include Aruba, have arisen as some of the prime destinations for American expatriates and their money. This is due to several factors, including the broad range of available facilities, proximity to the continental United States, and the highly favorable Dutch banking and privacy laws in effect.

Naturally, these auspicious conditions have inspired the U. S. government to pry as best it could into the details of business in this little island chain. In 1987, the United States Treasury Department convinced President Reagan to end a long-standing tax treaty with Netherlands Antilles, effectively forcing the little country to open its books to Washington's gaze. As you would expect, much hell was raised in response to Reagan's announcement.

What was surprising was the *source* of the maelstrom. The "objections" came not from the government of a sleepy little island chain, nor from its European affiliates, but from a roster of complainants that looked like America's own Fortune 500. Realizing where its political bread was buttered (and, for that matter, who bought and made the butter), Washington tucked its tail between its legs and announced that it had "reconsidered" its decision. The treaty was left unchanged.

Where the Antilles offer the same lush tropical environment as other locales, they also offer a degree of "civilization" that is a cut above many other Latin American countries. The infrastructure of this chain of islands is quite advanced in comparison to other countries in the region, with roads being in generally better condition and more easily traversed. Other critical utilities, such as water, electric, and telephone service, are available in all but the most remote areas, and are quite reliable.

These amenities, however, do come at a price. Being as developed as it is, this country does not offer the "bargain basement" real estate that some others do, and is geared more toward the well-heeled "major players." If you wish to disappear into a land with all the comforts of the life you've left, the Netherlands Antilles may well be just what you're looking for. But be sure to bring lots of money!

It is also quite a beautiful sailing area. If you plan to visit before you move (which I highly recommend), take a day or two out on a sailing yacht, dive up your own lobster, and eat it as you stand watching the sunset over a bottle of Chablis. It's hard to beat!

Oh, one other thing: The French tend toward nudity, especially on their beaches. Be sure that your heart can stand the sight of nubile young things sunning and rubbing lotion *all* over their bodies on the beach (or on the boat next to yours)! Believe me, it *is* an experience.

Europe

When one thinks about financial privacy, or, for that matter, banks, the first name that springs to mind is Switzerland. After all, the Swiss have been handling Europe and the world's banking for centuries. They are the ones who originated the concept of Offshore Banks. On a slightly smaller scale (but with a higher ratio of banks per capita) is Liechtenstein. There are more "corporations" than citizens in this tiny country, most of them "letterboxes," or receiving and registry points for foreign investors.

In recent years, however, these countries have fallen under the influence of both the American dollar, and, more to the point, the American government. The privacy of records in their banks is not nearly so absolute as it was in years past, and, as a result, they are no longer recommended as desirable places to "hide and disappear." Just for starters, there are those devious little agreements we've already talked about, known as Mutual Legal Assistance Treaties, or MLATs. Furthermore, the sharing of information brought about by the institution of the Common Market will compromise the level of your privacy, to say the least.

When you compound this with the fact that the Swiss Franc continues to hold very strongly against the dollar, and that everything in these little countries is significantly more expensive than in America, it becomes a wonderful place to visit, to say you've visited, buy the

T-shirt, and then leave. And, by the way, Swiss banks pay little or no interest, viewing themselves as service organizations as opposed to investment organizations. If you want your money to make money— as opposed to just sitting there—don't invest in Switzerland. Also, I believe that only the Swiss can own land in Switzerland.

However, this doesn't mean Europe is a dry hole for the expatriate on a budget. Ireland, as I mentioned earlier, could definitely be worth your consideration, and you'll find information about the Emerald Isle in Roger Gallo's book, *Escape From America*. But as you know, my tastes are for spots where the sun is always shining and the sky is always blue—places such as those the Beach Boys sing about.

The New Europe
One food for thought, and a very real possibility for future consideration, is the countries of the new Europe, the ones created in recent years by the breakup of the Soviet Union.

Moldova and Estonia, two of the new independent countries situated above Turkey, on the Black Sea, are extremely pleasant and appear to be financially friendly to PT's and investors who like the weather and atmosphere of Switzerland, without the price. Moldova has the potential to be one of the real sleepers of the hide and disappear society, with many of the benefits of the Caymans, the weather of the Mediterranean and the prices of Mother Russia (which have gone to hell in a hand basket recently). If the opportunity presents itself to visit these little gems, take it and see for yourself. I may even see you there!

TABLE 4.16
Greece
Livability Rating

Location	**
Weather	****
Legal System	***
Banking	***
Extradition	****
Infrastructure	****
Value	*****

Greece

Few images inspire the lust for travel to exotic lands as completely as do pictures of the breathtaking beauty that is Mykonos. Ruins that proclaim a grandeur of time beyond comprehension and beaches with sand that is blinding in its whiteness and touched by waters so perfect that no mortal color may describe it—these are testaments to a land of past greatness that will never die. It is no wonder, then, that the mythical gods chose Greece as their "contact point" with mortals.

At one time, living in Greece was dirt-cheap. Though this isn't the case anymore (especially in the tourist Meccas such as Mykonos, Paros, Santorini, and the like), it is still possible to enjoy a visit to Greece in relative comfort for under $50 US a day—relatively cheap by American standards. With judicious shopping around, an expatriate can live quite well in many areas, especially on a boat.

The serenity of this pastoral land is interrupted at times by the liveliness of the club scene in Athens and some of the other more popular tourist attractions, and is belied by the rumblings of a centuries-old conflict with neighboring Turkey. Both are avoidable to the savvy traveler, however.

The woman traveler, especially the fair-skinned European or American traveling alone, should be aware that attitudes toward women in this alternately placid and boisterous country are not necessarily consistent with those in the United States and Europe. *Machismo* is not a derogatory label in Greece; it is an accepted fact. Many locals assume that a foreign woman traveling alone is seeking romance, a perspective from which they are not easily dissuaded. There is rarely any malicious intent on the part of these gregarious, friendly people; it is merely a deeply ingrained part of their culture.

By all means, the prospective expat should visit this enchanting land, and drink deep from its centuries-old culture, its age-old natural beauty, and its cutting-edge night life. Taste its glorious repast, and laugh with some of the friendliest people you will ever meet. As a place to settle into a new life, you could do far worse.

The Middle East

When most people think of the Middle East, the images that come to mind are often conflicting, and, just as often, not very pretty. On the one hand, we have the quaint, trendy refuge so brilliantly portrayed in the movie classic, *Casablanca*. On the other hand, we have, burned into our consciousness, the images of buildings destroyed by centuries-old wars and modern terrorists. But, as we pointed out earlier, if we relied solely upon the information offered by our own State Department and intelligence services, we would never venture past our own front door.

So what is the true image of this tumultuous region? Well, it's somewhere between the extremes noted above. Yes, there are trendy enclaves of terribly chic expats, and, yes, there are fanatics who destroy, allegedly for the glory of their Creator. But there are also simple folk who yearn to live their lives, undisturbed by the events of the world, and who offer a hand in friendship to all who come to cherish their homelands. The tricky part, for the expat, is finding the one, while avoiding the other. It can, indeed, be done, but it requires knowledge, planning, and a special type of personality which allows others to live as they will, no matter how different they may appear.

It is this unique type of individual who, having done their homework, has the greatest chance of living peacefully and happily in the Middle East. To those unsure as to their qualifications in these areas, I advise seeking Paradise elsewhere. But if you're one of the few who truly posses the necessary qualities, this region, so steeped in history and passion, may well be your own personal Shangri La—particularly if you love camels and hate mowing a lawn.

Your only worry should be that your new home could become the next atomic bomb testing site in the neighborhood. War is always a distinct possibility here; just read the Bible for its history.

TABLE 4.17

Turkey
Livability Rating

Location	**
Weather	***
Legal System	**
Banking	***
Extradition	****
Infrastructure	**
Value	*****

Turkey

I have heard reports of late that Turkey is the least expensive country in the world to live in, and, frankly, I'm not surprised. When you venture onto the streets of Istanbul or Ankara, you are literally stepping back hundreds of years, even as you are surrounded by the sounds of a modern city. The area fairly screams of a picture-book image of the Middle East, with a rural ambiance being felt, even in the large cities.

Driving in Turkey can best be described as acting out a death wish in the midst of apparently suicidal hordes. If there are traffic laws, they exist only on paper in some bureaucrat's office, certainly not out on the streets. And riding along the streets themselves is certain to test the condition of any vehicle's suspension, not to mention the integrity of the traveler's dental work. The experience certainly comes under the heading of "the ride of your life." Maybe even the *last* ride!

Much has been said of the dangers of traveling in Turkey, especially in the Eastern region, and most especially at night. It's all true. I have heard, however, that the separatists who cause so much trouble in the East are now making their presence known in the resort and commercial centers in western Turkey. Ah, commercial enterprise! Even the terrorists are flocking to where the real money is. The Western coast is, by any measure, beautiful, westernized, and expensive. Other areas are reminiscent of Greece twenty years ago: a great bargain.

My advice: Visit Turkey, soak up its charm, and do some sightseeing and shopping. But steer clear of antiquities and drug sellers. . . . The movie *Midnight Express* was, if anything, a sentimental look at Turkish prisons, which are much easier to get into than out of. Oh, and don't wear an "I love Greece" T-shirt.

If you enjoy the hybrid East-West atmosphere of Western Turkey, and find the cost of accommodations within your budget, then settle into your new home and enjoy it. But, if you're like me, you will soon long for more Western shores, and when you've fully tasted the age-old delights of this fascinating country, you'll leave, and go someplace where the culture shock will be of a lower voltage.

The Pacific

Palm trees swaying in rhythm with soft island breezes . . . tangy, exotic dishes, as colorful as they are delicious . . . beautiful young women, clad only in grass skirts, gyrating to the pounding beat of native drums. . . . Well, two out of three ain't bad! The scenery is really just like it's described, and the Polynesian dishes are frequently delicious beyond description. However, you're much more likely to see the swaying breasts attached to a vacationing coed from New Jersey than a bronze-skinned island girl.

The Pacific Islands have grown up when we weren't looking. The "natives" all live in brick houses and apartments, drive Chevys, and raise hell about low wages, just like the rest of us. They may be a little more laid back about it, but the once-idyllic islands of the Pacific have come full-steam into the '90s. They will, indeed, provide the visitor (or expat) with a taste of paradise, but they now accept American Express instead of mirrors and trinkets.

One of these island groups, the Cook Islands, excels in offering financial privacy and intricate corporate legal structures for the interested expatriate. They have recently become the Switzerland or Cayman connection of the Pacific to those in the know of such things.

All this means is, you may well find the life you are searching for here in the Pacific, but if you come expecting the innocence which Captain Cook encountered, you will be very disappointed. There are still a number of remote and pristine islands in the Pacific that offer incredible value and beauty. Their drawbacks, and to some their allure, is that they are truly remote, many accessible only by the infrequent trading ship or private yacht.

If you really want to get away, never to be found, this is the part of the world to disappear in. Some of the island groups to consider and visit if you *really* want to disappear include the Marshall Islands, southwest of Okinawa (for great offshore fishing if you don't mind glowing

TABLE 4.18
Australia
Livability Rating

Location	**
Weather	**
Legal System	****
Banking	***
Extradition	**
Infrastructure	****
Value	**

in the dark), the Solomons (for super snorkeling and diving, if you can outswim the sharks), and the Caroline Islands, east of the Philippines.

Australia

Once a penal colony for the outcasts of the British Empire, Australia is now a thriving, bustling, raucous country that still carries a touch of the wild west. If you have heard all of the stories of the lonely women there, take heart, because some of them are true. (I still get letters and photos from one Sheila who wants to, uh, warm my buns down under.)

The only problem with Australia is that it has become *too* successful and prosperous, and therefore too conservative for the ambitious expat. In years past, the Australian government provided lots of enticing incentives to anyone who wanted to emigrate there, such as free land, start-up financing for a business, and even subsidies on passage to the country. So many people took them up on their generosity that they began restricting the benefits to married couples. These days they only want working families, with job skills and a significantly British background to allow them to instantly assimilate into the culture before being given the blessing of Aussie citizenship. This should serve as a lesson to anybody who is considering starting a new life in a promising new country; if *you* wait too long, the opportunity *won't*. Somebody else will claim your little corner of Paradise.

Personally, I wouldn't pick Australia, anyway. It is too far away from the United States for my taste, it has real winters (which, as you can guess, I hate), and it also has the greatest abundance of poisonous snakes on earth. If I were a religious man, I'd say that the last item alone would qualify as a message, telling me to "Stay Away." I'm not a devoutly reli-

TABLE 4.19

New Zealand

Livability Rating

Location	****
Weather	*****
Legal System	*****
Banking	****
Extradition	****
Infrastructure	*****
Value	****

gious man, but the message still comes across pretty clear. I'll take my island a little smaller, a lot warmer, and without all the snakes, thank you! (But go there for the Olympics, it should be a trip of a lifetime.)

New Zealand

When one fantasizes about an ideal Paradise in which to start a new life, New Zealand doesn't usually leap to mind. And yet when you study the factors that qualify a place for such a title, it's difficult to come up with a better example than these Pacific Islands.

Granted, they're a long way from home, but consider these points. New Zealand is:

- A proponent of British Common Law, as Hong Kong has been for so many years. Privacy and fiscal freedom aren't just policies here; they're a state of mind.
- Free of significant political strife from within, or turmoil from without.
- Rich in natural resources, minerals, and livestock.
- Emerging from a socialist history, and possessed of a passion for capital ventures (particularly from foreign investors).
- Blessed with a well-developed infrastructure, thanks to long-standing British involvement.
- Strikingly beautiful, with some of the most dramatic landscapes in the world.
- Host to some of the world's best trout fishing, and the prettiest sheep you ever saw.

So if you don't mind being a long way from the United States (and for many, that may be a real plus), you might want to consider this wonderful spot. It has been reported that a single visit to the awe-inspiring Milford Sound, on the South Island, will inspire even the most sedentary homebody to sell the house and update the passport. (I almost did it myself years ago.)

New Zealand enjoys the pastoral life most of us only dream about. The pace of life there is similar to that of the United States in the 1950s, steady, sure and safe. Here you will find excellent schools for your children, the safest environment on the planet and a standard of living that is the envy of much of the rest of the world.

The only problem, shared with Australia, is a government that is

TABLE 4.20
Asia
Livability Rating

Location	**
Weather	**
Legal System	*
Banking	*
Extradition	***
Infrastructure	*
Value	**

overwhelming its residents with outrageous taxes and a duty on everything from the outside world.

Asia

Living successfully and happily in Asia, like in so many emerging expat destinations in the world, is as dependent upon realistic expectations as upon proper preparation. If you are going there (or anywhere else) expecting a land filled with gullible, subservient citizens who live only to serve you for a few coins, you will inevitably have a miserable time of it.

Much of the average American's image of the Asian people is based upon Hollywood's depiction's of a citizenry decimated by wars and the ensuing famine and pestilence. The average Asian of today may well be poor by our standards, but they have seen "the promised land," and are highly motivated to acquire their piece of it. For the expat who settles in their home, accepts the value of their customs, and honors their social structure, Asia may well prove to be a fount of wealth and happiness. For the expat who ignores the sensibilities of this culture that predates our own by a millennium, the dream of Paradise may never materialize.

Malaysia

The islands of Malaysia are, perhaps more than other Asian countries, a true paradox. Politically, they are very much Chinese, with all the rigidity that implies. Yet the economy is purely Malay: market-driven and hungry. The visitor there can wander through, and get quite lost in, impenetrable jungles, untouched by man—yet the city of

Kuala Lumpur boasts the Twin Tower, which is the tallest skyscraper in the world.

For the expat whose interests run to more rigorous activities, there are breathtaking (literally!) mountains to climb, lush and beautiful jungles to hike through, and world-class snorkeling at Besar.

The factors that make Malaysia such a paradox serve to make it an interesting, if tenuous, place to live. There are plenty of laws to run afoul of, and not just in Singapore, which has received the heaviest press in these matters. Enforcement of these laws is seemingly quite arbitrary. Though the official attitude of the government is to encourage and welcome investment, actual practice is rife with the stereotypical Chinese cynicism toward outsiders. One should always remember that even a law on the books is only as reliable as the body charged with implementing and enforcing it. In many Asian countries, that enforcement is still driven by paranoia and a fear that their traditional way of life is endangered by the very people they are trying to attract.

Do I endorse Malaysia as a place to hide and disappear? Frankly,

TABLE 4.21

Malaysia
Livability Rating

Location	**
Weather	***
Legal System	***
Banking	***
Extradition	***
Infrastructure	***
Value	****

I'd have to advise you to give it a few years before packing your bags. A paradox is interesting to observe, but grows quite uncomfortable if you have to live in it. But, many of my most knowledgeable friends swear by this region of the world and consider it the best value on the globe for the life you can lead there. I guess that it just takes some time on the ground there to bring out the best in the place?

One other note: Whether you're going to Malaysia as a tourist or as a prelude to moving there, you won't want to go during the rainy season between November and March. If you do, you will learn first-hand the true meaning of the word *monsoon*. It is so intense that the nicer beaches are completely dredged up and the sand packed safely in bags to prevent it from being washed away. (Think Seattle, hot and with an *attitude*.)

Philippines

The Philippines is unique among locations we have studied, in that it has developed beyond its rustic origins primarily due to a long-standing American military presence. Also unique is the absence of anti-American sentiments displayed by so many other locations which have "benefited" from that same presence.

Said presence may have been what started this island nation's "progress," but its continued growth is due more to non-United States investment. In the Subic Bay Export Processing (Free) Zone, for example, there are presently 107 companies in operation, most of which are owned by Japanese and Taiwanese investors. Another $65 million in future projects is already committed.

I wouldn't be too quick to rule out United States involvement,

TABLE 4.22

Philippines

Livability Rating

Location	***
Weather	***
Legal System	***
Banking	**
Extradition	**
Infrastructure	****
Value	***

however, as the United States government still perceives a need to maintain a strategic presence in the area. If they can't do it directly, with military bases, they will at least be certain to maintain a significant economic toehold. It is for this reason that, even though the Philippines offers significant investment opportunities, it does not really meet my criteria as an ideal place to disappear.

I have heard, however, that it's a great place to be if you're an avid shoe collector. I'm not certain about laws directly affecting such an activity, but the Filipino government has alternately been very supportive or highly suspicious of aficionados of this pastime.

Oh yeah . . . one other thing: The biggest commodity being exported by the Philippines seems of late to be mail-order brides.

Vietnam

Few countries inspire as emotionally charged reactions in the American mind as does Vietnam. The wounds of a long, costly, and highly controversial war are slow to heal. For Americans, however, nothing promotes "healing" as quickly as the potential for economic gain.

And in the eyes of Vietnam, as a country struggling to emerge from widespread squalor into a fully developed player in the modern

world, the American dollar is viewed as an even greater panacea. Add to this the continuing movement of the communist bloc towards capitalism, and the stage is set for Vietnam to become another haven for foreign capital investment.

Unfortunately, the country still struggles beneath the burden of its own inherently corrupt bureaucracy, and it is bound together by an infrastructure that, even by the kindest description, is terrible. I look for some improvement in the latter, but see no dramatic changes in the foreseeable future where the bureaucracy is concerned.

To the foreigner, the country puts on a friendly, welcoming face, but upon closer inspection, one can see the sharpness of the teeth. For example, a traveler in Vietnam who is brave (stupid?) enough to drive may expect frequent stops by police, each time to be assessed a small "fine" for some nondescript, or nonexistent, infraction. This is a minor irritation, but it is indicative of an attitude which reaches all levels of the government, and could potentially pose much more grievous difficulties.

Some months back, the *Wall Street Journal* wrote a glowing travelogue on the wonders of Vietnam and the ability to live there on five dollars per day. However, unless you relish the idea of living in an armed camp—one that still looks upon Americans as the foreign Satan—I think I would pass on this one if I were you. (*But*, then again,

TABLE 4.23

Vietnam
Livability Rating

Location	**
Weather	***
Legal System	*
Banking	**
Extradition	*****
Infrastructure	**
Value	***
Land Mines	******
Ghosts	******

one of my friends just came back from Ho Chi Minh City, and told me that Vietnam has improved a zillion percent in the last few years, and that he found it to be one of the best values of the Far East.) I guess that I am just pissed that we never got to buy that beachfront property in Hanoi in the early 1960s, when they promised that it would develop into the eastern Riviera!

I'd take the much-touted investment opportunities with a grain of salt too. Even though the Vietnamese government has been actively encouraging foreign investment by establishing favorable banking and capital repatriation policies, implementation of government policies has historically been quite arbitrary—in short, not conducive to a favorable and secure investment climate.

Having experienced the country in darker times, I admit to some degree of distrust where the integrity and motivation of the Vietnamese government is concerned. This distrust is not assuaged in any way by the more recent reports coming back from Vietnam.

In summary, I cannot recommend Vietnam as a favorable place to hide it all and disappear. Too many have disappeared there already and may have been hidden against their own wishes, and no accounting seems forthcoming for me to add this country to our list.

The Whole World

Maybe you haven't found that ideal spot that matches your description of Paradise. If you've lived your whole life in one place, you might

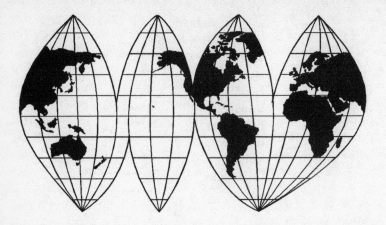

even hunger for a continually changing environment. Understand that we're not talking about becoming a hobo. The modern term is "P.T.", which, depending upon who's talking, can mean "Perpetual Traveler", "Permanent Tourist", or even "Previous Taxpayer". Some wags claim it also means "Parked Temporarily" or "Passing Through" . . . well, anyway, you get the drift. Though the concept dates back to the earliest nomadic tribes, the connotation was created by Harry Schultz, who wrote a number of popular investment books over the last three decades, such as *Financial Tactics and Terms for the Sophisticated International Investor; Bear Market Investment Strategies;* and *Panics and Crashes: How You Can Make Money From Them.*

You would be surprised at how many people just like you have picked a "haven" from which to base their financial dealings and are now simply spending the rest of their lives traveling around to whatever places tickle their fancy and their pocketbook.

You may be wondering why you should even have a "home base," in the form of residency or country of origin. Look at it this way: just as a ship on the high seas maintains a registry in a specific country, yet constantly roams the world, the P.T. needs someplace secure from which to operate and perform financial transactions. And, just like the ship, the P.T. needs to select a country of origin whose legal and financial structure is geared towards his or her privacy, mobility, and fiscal well-being. The good news is that by not declaring actual citizenship in any country, the P.T. is exempted from most of the scrutiny that the country's citizens must endure. So, at least until the dreaded and much-predicted "World Government" comes into power, the "P.T." option seems pretty attractive.

Well, then, how does one become a Perpetual Traveler? The process is really quite simple: after researching different countries and selecting the one that best suits your needs, you establish either a trust or an International Business Corporation (IBC) in that country, and funnel all your financial transactions through it. As you need money for your living expenses, you simply draw upon your trust or IBC account that is tied to a credit card issued by an International Bank. This process allows you to keep your money in a safe, secure Internationally recognized bank, but gives you access to your money anywhere in the world through the magic of Visa or MasterCard.

Oh yes, by using an account of this type, you leave no paper trail except at the point of sale, and in the country maintaining the records of your bank/credit account. A country that excels in protecting the financial records and independence of its clients and customers.

Where do you find one of these International Visa and/or Master-Card accounts? Just look in your international airline travel magazines for their ads, or ask your friendly neighborhood International Banker; he just may happen to have an application handy.

As an IBC, your company's privacy is protected from scrutiny, and, since you aren't a citizen of any country, you are exempted from any country's requirements, such as military service and income tax. Furthermore, if you do it right, you can make yourself invulnerable to liability in many civil proceedings. Even while living a high-profile life, you can remain, for all practical purposes, invisible to governments and creditors. And if you want to really disappear, you can do so quite easily, leaving a trail so convoluted that it will confuse even the most astute public, private or creditor's investigator.

If the P.T. idea intrigues you as much as it does me, you might want to do some investigating on your own. You'll find some useful information on the Internet.

A Few Points to Consider No Matter Where You're Going

Now that we've taken our quick armchair tour around the globe, I want to point out a few general factors you need to consider in making your decision about where to live.

When contemplating your ultimate destination, you must keep in mind that you are not going there as a tourist (unless, of course, you choose the P.T. option and become a "person without a country"). If you're seriously considering settling down in one place, you need to remember that this isn't a vacation; it's your life. Give more than a passing thought to these questions:

Do you speak the language? It's very important to consider whether or not the local language will cause problems for you and your family. Can you fluently speak the language of the indigenous peoples, or is English a predominant second language? While many South and Central American and Caribbean countries use some dialect of Spanish as their primary language (and in Brazil the predominant language is Portuguese), many of them have become increasingly fluent in English out of necessity, due to the massive influx of American tourism and business activities. Many of these countries also have substantial expatriate communities, who build themselves a little Mayberry, U.S.A., right in the middle of their host country.

For the expat who wants to fit in, however, there's no substitute for being fluent in the local tongue. Since you'll be able to speak with the locals, it will be much easier for you to find the information you will need to live well—such as the location of less expensive housing and supplies, and even the local gossip about who the scammers are. (If you don't want to take the time to learn the language, get a housekeeper, girlfriend, or boyfriend who does.)

Do you have special medical needs? Does the country in which you plan to make your new home have adequate medical facilities to deal with your present and future medical needs? What does this treatment cost? We covered these issues briefly in some of the country descriptions above, and we discussed them in a general way in Chapter 2, but you should probably do a little research on your own to find out if you would really be adequately served in your chosen destination.

Will you really be able to "disappear" in your new home (if that's what you want to do)? At this point, it would be wise to inject a little advice about fitting in. In a later chapter we'll go into more detail on maintaining your lifestyle, but here are some factors you should consider before you go.

First off, even though the idea of a homey little American community right in the middle of a foreign country might sound appealing, you should remember that this is the first place any investigator worth his or her salt would begin to search for you. (See Chapter 7, "How the Pros Will Look for You.") If you really want to disappear, you must be as unobtrusive among the locals as possible, and not affiliate too publicly or openly with the American expat community, especially until you get to know a little more about your new home.

On the other hand, if you aren't actually trying to hide from anyone and are in the new country simply to lighten your tax burden, the Internal Revenue Service will look very closely at your activities and affiliations in your new home to determine whether you are, indeed, a permanent resident and entitled to the ensuing tax exemptions, or if you are merely a temporary visitor. In the IRS's eyes, a true resident of a new country would become as involved in their community as they did in their community back in the United States. If you still own a house in the United States, and don't involve yourself in your new community, they will assuredly try to determine that you are merely visiting, and will expect you to pay all your appropriate United States taxes.

In the event that you're not thinking of disappearing entirely from the eagle eye of Uncle Sam, but simply don't want his hand so deeply in your pocket, there is an attractive loophole known as the foreign-earned-income-exclusion, or the "$70,000 exclusion." We'll discuss that further in Chapter 6, when we talk about how to move your money to your new home, and manage it (or hide it) once it's there. Should you consider this option as an alternative to taxation?

It's a judgment call *or* a crapshoot, depending how you look at it. Only your friendly neighborhood tax attorney[6] can tell you the best way to go for you.

Wherever you decide to go, it would behoove you to get as much information about your new home before you make any serious commitments of effort, time and money. The best way to do this is by making a trial run, in your prospective new homeland (if you have the time to make such a run).

Some people like to venture out on their own, find their own little

---

6 Again, I stress engaging a tax *attorney* here for very good reason: If subpoenaed to testify about your actions and whereabouts, a tax consultant or CPA does not enjoy the same protections under the law regarding client confidentiality. Information shared with your attorney, however, is privileged. Maybe *two* can keep a secret—if one of them is the other's lawyer!

secret sources and quietly fade into the woodwork. Many others, especially those who do not have the same spirit of adventure, would rather not go where no (unknowing) man has gone before, and opt for a guided tour that exposes them to both the lifestyle and potential business attributes of their future getaway, and also offers introductions to bankers, lawyers and real estate brokers that have all of the local connections at their fingertips.

If this is your cup of tea, it's hard to beat the tours put together by *International Living*, both for content and for quality. As they frequently write about some of the world's most interesting and (not so more) anonymous hideaways, *International Living* has begun to promote package tours to the most promising and newly developing nations that offer privacy and a pleasurable lifestyle, for a price that might even surprise you.

In the last year or two, this Perpetual Traveler's tour company has made several trips to interesting havens such as Ireland, as well as the more convenient countries in our own backyard, such as Costa Rica, Guatemala, Honduras, and Nicaragua. Everyone who has gone on these trips has gotten their money's worth many times over and quite a few never came home.

One of my best friends took *International Living's* tour of Central America, looked at the amenities of Costa Rica, the unbelievably cheap prices in Nicaragua (he seriously considered a 50-acre estate with a villa prices at $40,000 US) and finally settled on buying a small hotel in Honduras, close to the newly discovered and developing Mayan ruins in Zewantapecke. With tourism doubling every year there, and real estate prices jumping over 200 percent just in the last year, I hear that he is a very happy camper in his new home. (Oh, yes, his new nineteen-year-old native wife is glad that he moved there, too!)

Wherever you go, kick back, enjoy the ride, and don't sweat the small stuff. Just think of the good times to come, and let your old life just fade away, just like the troubles you left behind!

I hope you've enjoyed our little journey across the globe, and that I've gotten your imaginative juices flowing. Now that you have chosen, or are on your way to choosing, your new home—whether it's one country or the whole wide world—let's take a look at how you can become a brand new "you."

How to Create That New Identity

5

If you really want to disappear, you have to create a new identity —one that will bear close scrutiny. To have a new identity, of course, you need new identification, with documents "proving" that you are who you say you are. These documents will give you the ability to travel and conduct financial transactions under your new name. Most important of all, they'll throw others off your trail.

There are multitudes of ways to get new identities, some legal and some not so legal. In the past there have been numerous books— mostly published by Paladin Press, Eden Press, and Loompanics Unlimited—that give instructions on obtaining someone else's identity. These procedures are tried and true, and they still work in many places. Some of the steady sellers are *Mail Order I.D.: A Consumer's Guide*, (Loompanics Unlimited, 1981).[1] For other helpful titles, see the Resource List at the back of this book.

Now let's review some of the ways to get a new identity. We'll go over a couple of the old ways first, and then discuss newer, legal methods.

---

1 You should keep in mind that the government has not been idle since this, and many other, source books have been published. Many loopholes have been closed, and others opened. *Always check to see whether information in these references is current.*

The Graveyard Gambit

One of the tried-and-true methods for assuming another identity is to go to the local cemetery and look for someone who was born around the time you were and is now peacefully reposing at Club Dead or the Hotel Forest Lawn. Pick somebody a) of the same sex, b) a little younger than you, if you look or feel youthful and think you can carry it off, and c) someone who died before they turned sixteen. Write down that person's date of birth, date of death, and their full legal name.

You should choose someone who died no later than their early teens, because a person of that age would not yet have acquired a driver's license or other identification that puts them in the system. More than likely, they also would not have obtained a social security number. Of course, the latter will probably not be true of future generations. (While most of today's adults didn't get social security numbers until they applied for their first job or joined the military, children these days are assigned numbers at birth, or within their first year of birth.) Shades of Orwell? Well, not quite (at least not yet), but parents can no longer deduct a child on their tax return unless the child has a social security number. That's a "Gotcha!" from Uncle Sam.

After you've found the person whose identity you want to assume, you can take the name and date of birth (of the deceased) and apply for a copy of their birth certificate with the state's Department of Vital Statistics. Even though the graveyard trick has been known and used for a long time, many states will still send you a birth certificate without trying to verify the identity of the person making the request. Some few will ask that you provide another form of identification, but this is the exception, not the rule. Use a private "store-front" post office, such as Mailboxes Etc., that will give you an address that looks and "acts" like a street address instead of merely a P.O. box number.

Once you have obtained a birth certificate, it is very easy to get a driver's license, a social security card, a passport, and any other identification in the new name, because all of them key back to a birth certificate as the ultimate source of identification. You may be asked why you don't have these other documents now. All you have to do is explain that you have been living out of the country and haven't needed a driver's license or social security number until now.

Now remember, obtaining government documents under false pre-

tense is a violation of the law; especially if they are used with the intent to defraud. Before considering this tactic, also consider that your next vacation may be at Club Fed.

An Old But Illegal Way—Don't Try This at Home

Another means by which individuals have obtained key identification is by buying stolen or forged passports. This has been a thriving industry for years. A mob attorney in New Orleans—a legal eagle who once represented Manuel Noriega—specialized in the sale of passports for a price. Noriega, as well, sold passports wholesale in Panama to the highest bidder. It is estimated that more than 10,000 Chinese obtained Panamanian passports, for $5,000 US each, through one of these sources, and then illegally entered the United States as citizens of Panama.

The lawyer in question had a pretty good thing going, at least until he got caught after one of his customers was stopped while entering the United States. It seems the customer's brand new store-bought identity was that of a wanted fugitive who was prominently highlighted in the TECS II and NCIC databases.[2] Oops!

Pretty Much Legal: The Phony Passport

If you want a "camouflage passport," you can buy one. For example, a company called Scope International, based in Hampshire, England, advertised as of this printing that they will sell you one for $550. In return you'll get a passport in whichever name, address, date of issuance, and profession you wish. Scope's suggestion for career choice, by the way, is "accountant"—an unobtrusive, plain-vanilla occupation. Other genuine-looking documents are generally provided to accompany the "passport," in order to help support your disguise.

The document(s) will bear the name of an imaginary country or a country that no longer exists. In fact, if you think about your geography lessons from high school, you'll realize that many of the countries from ten, twenty, or thirty years ago no longer exist today. They have either been renamed, absorbed by their neighbors, bombed into obliv-

---

2 TECS II is the Treasury Enforcement Communications System; NCIC is the National Crime Information Center. These are proprietary databases of Club Fed.

ion, or have gone through some other process that makes their old name obsolete. For example, Sri Lanka used to be Ceylon. Belize was British Honduras until 1981. Thailand was once known as Siam. Rhodesia has been reborn as Zimbabwe. And I can't even begin to keep the Belgian Congo/Zaire/Congo mess straight. As I've said before, the world is a busy place for mapmakers.

Of course you want to use some common sense here, and perhaps check a history text or reference book so that dates and names won't clash too noticeably. Don't get a British Honduras passport that says it was issued in 1996, for example. It's best not to count on the geographical/historical illiteracy of those who check your passport.

A camouflage passport is not an official government or legal document. It can be used to provide you with identity as a citizen of a country other than the United States. DO NOT use a camouflage passport on a customs inspector as a means to travel in or out of the United States or any other country. You may be in that country longer than you like—and not in a swank hacienda. The jury is still out on whether or not it's legal for United States citizens to purchase a bogus travel document, but the State Department probably isn't going to get upset by Americans using them to cross foreign borders. As a matter of fact, Scope says that among its biggest customers are United States government personnel. Given the volatile world situation, a phony passport could actually save your life someday by *not* identifying you as a United States citizen to some crazy terrorist intent on making an example of the "foreign Satan." The choice is yours alone to make, so let your conscience be your guide.

Mostly Legal but Sometimes Expensive: Adopt a Country

Money may not be able to buy happiness or love (though some would argue with that sentiment), but it *can* buy you a brand new identity. Yes, one relatively new and legal way to obtain that second identity is to get it the old fashioned way: simply purchase it. How do you do this? You buy yourself citizenship in another country.

Actually, this isn't such a new method, just one that's not widely known. Many countries have long offered citizenship to individuals who were willing to invest in these nations' futures and economies. The price varies, depending upon where you want to invest. Currently most

Central or South American countries require an investment ranging between $20,000 and $100,000; a good average is $50,000 (for example: Belize, Honduras, and Costa Rica) . . . Australia, New Zealand, Singapore, Canada, and Italy require $100,000 or more.

This money is deposited in an interest-bearing account that pays a tidy little sum of interest to the person seeking a new identity. (By the way, third-world banks pay far higher interest than their more solid United States and Swiss counterparts. As of this printing, for example, the interest rate paid on dollar savings accounts in Belize and Honduras is 8 percent to 10 percent—substantially higher than in the United States (Local currency accounts pay 25 percent or more, but carry a fair amount of risk through devaluation.)

To begin your quest for a new identity, and the new identification to go with it, you need to apply at the United States or foreign consulate of one of the countries offering passports for sale. A local attorney can expedite this process; I highly recommend you hire one. When applying, do so in your new name, of course. If you haven't already picked a new name, do so now. (I like Ernst Stavro Blofeld.) Immediately open a savings account in that country in your new name. This gives the host country hard dollars for investing and budget balancing—and in return, you get a new identity, a new country, and, of course, a new passport. Seems like a fair deal to me! What do you think?

In some cases, you may not even have to "buy" your citizenship. As I mentioned towards the end of Chapter 1, some countries offer instant citizenship if your ancestors were nationals, or if you are of a certain race or religion—for example, Thailand if you're a Buddhist, Israel if you're Jewish, or Lebanon if you are Muslim.

The truth is, many countries have well-established but little-known procedures for issuing passports under circumstances we might consider loopholes. But if you know these "exceptions," you can actually obtain multiple foreign passports. If you use them appropriately, you shouldn't run into trouble.

Oh, yes, there's one other advantage to legally adopting a new country (or countries): Even if you're not trying to "hide it all and disappear," the principle we pointed out in the section about phony passports applies here too. If you are unfortunate enough to get caught in a hostage situation where the terrorists have a grievance against Uncle Sam—and most terrorists do in fact share this grievance—that "alternative" passport could very well save your life by identifying you as a resident of some other country, with which they don't have a beef.

Again, no matter what your reasons for obtaining a second or third passport, I recommend you consult a competent attorney. Even before you retain legal assistance, however, you'd be wise to check out *The Passport Report* by W. G. Hill. This is probably one of the most comprehensive books on the market about this rather complex subject. Dr. Hill covers it all—the legal, logistical, and even psychological aspects of multiple passports, dual citizenship, and related topics. The book also examines the citizenship and residency laws and loopholes in more than one hundred-twenty countries throughout the world. The author has even included a contact list of immigration lawyers and consultants. *The Passport Report* is published by the aforementioned Scope International.

You may be interested in knowing that Scope International produces a variety of guidebooks for the potential expatriate or anybody wanting to legally avoid taxes and government interference. Though the books are rather pricey—about $100 each—they are quite comprehensive. Another Scope title you might find useful is *Tax Exile Report: Citizenship, Second Passports and Escaping Confiscatory Taxes*. The author is Marshall Langer, a London-based American lawyer who specializes in international taxes and often helps people expatriate. For more information on the complete catalogue, write to Scope International/Box 5725, Forestside House/Rowlands Castle, Hants./PO9 6EE, England, UK. Or contact *International Living* in Baltimore, MD.

Once you have your new passport, you can travel in and out of your new country as a legal citizen. In fact, you should be able to travel just about anywhere, if you take a few sensible precautions. Your passport should pass all but official government scrutiny (don't try it at the border if you're not feeling lucky, and don't carry more than one passport with you when traveling—bad news if you're caught). In Chapter 6, we'll discuss in more detail how to safely travel in, and out, of your new country, the United States, or anywhere else. But now it's time for another cautionary tale.

Embrace the "New You"

You cannot simply assume a new identity, you must *embrace* it. Know your physical description, your date of birth, your identification number(s), and your home address. Again, it's easy to slip up here. Your paperwork may say you are from Panama, but your accent and mannerisms may identify you as a citizen of the good old U.S.A. Consider what happened to Richard Minns.

Former Texan Richard Minns became an expatriate and an international fugitive after his live-in girlfriend was brutally shot in ambush in a parking lot while on her daily shopping tour. The shooters and their contact were quickly identified and caught, but Minns fled the country, and his go-between refused to identify Minns or anybody else as the party ordering the hit on our former beauty queen.

Minns flitted around the world, living first in the Bahamas, then in England, and later in Honduras. Unfortunately for him, his activities were reported back to his former girlfriend, and also to a writer who had taken up her cause. The writer, Suzanne Finstad, authored a book describing the Minns escapades: *Sleeping With the Devil*, now a made-for-TV movie. This book, as well as Finstad's considerable lobbying for Minns' arrest, brought his dark deeds to the attention of state and federal investigators.

Still, he continued to elude justice. Then one sunny day, for some unknown reason, he decided to travel to Canada on a plane that had a stopover in the United States He should have known better, for he was still wanted for questioning in the shooting case under investigation. I guess he simply thought his new identity made him invincible. At any rate, Minns waltzed right into the airport, found a Customs declaration line manned by a sweet little old lady in tennis shoes, and proceeded to clear United States Customs on the way to Canada.

With all of his knowledge about evading the police, Minns should have known that those little old ladies are the sharpest of the Customs inspectors. Experience has shown that women make the best investigators. I don't mean this in a sexist way, but women look at details that most men tend to shrug off in pursuit of supposedly bigger gain.

Well, this little old lady gave Minns the once-over, checking the European labels on his shirt, the American twang in his voice, and his Honduras passport—and she put the puzzle together without blinking an eye. She smiled sweetly and asked Minns for his date of birth, still holding his passport in her hot little hands. As it happened, Minns had half a dozen I.D.s in his bag, and for the life of him he couldn't remember which date of birth he'd used on which document. In other words, he couldn't remember which lie he'd told last time. In *other* words, he was sunk. Oh, what a tangled web. . . . The sweet little inspector pressed a button, called for assistance, and said "Book him, Danno," or the equivalent. Minns was then trotted off to a holding cell, where his fingerprints would reveal his true identity. Once his identity was known, he became a new resident of the Harris County, Texas jail.

Of course I'm not suggesting you're a heinous criminal of Minns' ilk, and I'm certainly not implying he didn't deserve to be caught—but there is a moral to his story nonetheless: *Live your new identity.* Eat it, breathe it, sleep it, and don't put yourself in the position where it will come under the bright light of day. Don't tug on Superman's cape, don't pee into the wind, don't gamble with United States Customs, and watch out for the little old lady in tennis shoes who is waiting to check you in.

Is Customs Watching *You*?

One of the secret weapons of United States Customs is their database of people who engage in frequent foreign travel. Once known as EPIC (El Paso Intelligence Center), and now re-tooled as TECS II (Treasury Enforcement Communications System), this database tracks all United States and many foreign citizens' re-entry into the United States from a foreign port. It also gives Uncle Sam a potent tool in the war against drugs and money laundering. And, oh, yes, the IRS uses this database too. Cozy, huh? (If you weren't paranoid when you started reading this book, you will be when you finish!)

Customs looks at this information to examine the frequency of your travel, targeting certain hot spots as suspicious entrance points. These hot spots are countries such as Colombia, Ecuador, Bolivia, and other nations known to be heavily involved in the drug trade. But the database also focuses on third-world financial centers such as Anguilla, Barbados, Granada, Grand Cayman, St. Maarten, Nauru, and the Turks and Caicos Islands.

You should also know that the Customs database is shared with other law enforcement agencies. Besides the aforementioned IRS, the database is accessed by others who are interested in travelers who may be involved in dirty deeds—for starters, the FBI and the DEA.

And then there's FinCEN, the Financial Crime Enforcement Network. Oh, you don't know about FinCEN, the government's little secret agency that digs up your financial dirt? I'll give you the gory details in Chapter 7.

How do you know if "they" might watching you? If you travel outside the United States four or more times a year, go through any of the suspicious or questionable entrance or exit points, spend too much money (i.e., you enjoy a lifestyle disproportionate to the income you report), and/or fit the profile[3] of people that the agencies are looking for at any point in time, you could very well be a target for investigation. The TECS computer can be made to focus on any given individual's activities. Remember this when you are filling out that little blue Customs declaration form.

Die and Let Live

Do you want out of the computer? Would you like all of your records deleted from Social Security, the IRS, and maybe even the FBI? Here's one way to do it: *Die—yes, die on paper!* Upon receipt of information regarding your death, most government agencies delete data about you, thereby exorcising you from their files.

So how do you die and still live? With the wonders of modern technology, and a little green, it's very easy to "die" in a foreign country. Countries such as Nigeria, Mexico, and the Philippines, in fact, specialize in deaths and funerals, offering a package deal of a death certificate, a funeral, and a newspaper article about your death—and all for a very reasonable fee. These aren't the only countries that provide such service, but they are certainly the most well-known. Other places offer such death-defying services on a local level; all it takes is one friendly official who has a basic understanding of his greed and your

---

3 There's a good possibility you fit "the profile" if three or more of the following apply to you: (a) you own a car worth $60,000 or more; (b) you conduct real estate transactions in excess of $250,000 in any one year; (c) you cause four or more currency transaction reports (CTRs) in a year; and (d) as mentioned above, you travel outside of the United States four or more times a year. Those are some of the parameters as of this printing; needless to say, they are subject to change.

need, and you are on your way to being deceased. And it won't hurt a bit. Once you have "died," see that a friend reprints the newspaper article in your hometown paper.

Just be sure that all of your bank accounts are already closed too, and that your personal estate is in order, because the banks, upon learning of your death, will close your accounts and freeze your assets until a proper distribution of them can be made in probate court.

Oh, and one other admonition: This ploy, like many others, has been used before—so if you're really "wanted," or even just a little bit notorious, there may be some suspicion over the verity of your "death." You probably remember the recent news stories about the expiration of the infamous Mexican drug trafficker Amado Carrillo Fuentes, the "Lord of the Skies." Carrillo used a fleet of airplanes in his billion-dollar operation, smuggling cocaine, methamphetamines, and marijuana into the United States. Supposedly, he died of complications from anesthesia given during extensive plastic surgery to alter his appearance. But once the death was reported, rumors began flying, on

both sides of the border, that Carrillo had faked his demise. After all, it was known that he was making plans to flee Mexico, fearing he was on the verge of being arrested and extradited to the United States Even though in this situation there was actually a body (which, of course, we hope will not be the case if you decide to take this route), the rumors persisted. Mexican authorities were loath to say for certain if the body was Carrillo's; after all, they'd been fooled before by similar situations. Finally the DEA even got in on the act, offering to perform post-mortem tests on the cadaver. Their conclusion was that it was indeed the Lord of the Skies' remains.

My point, of course, is that the fake-your-death ploy isn't fool-proof. But if you're a fairly low-profile sort, and not one of the world's most wanted, you can probably pull it off, with a minimum of fuss.

Creating a Whole New Appearance

Along with fabricating a new identity on paper, one step you may want to consider is creating a new appearance, one that is consistent with and accentuates your lifestyle. Within those parameters, you can change as little or as much as you wish. Just make sure that if you are planning to change your appearance, you do so before you get pictures taken for those new I.D.'s.

Hair and Now

The simplest thing to do, of course, is to change your hair length and style, and perhaps the color. A little lemon juice or perox-ide can do the trick if you are, or want to be, a blonde, or you can buy the commercially available hair dyes that will give you any color you want. But be sure to choose a shade that mutes your appearance and helps you blend in; don't do a Dennis Rodman or go for a flam-ing red or any other color that makes you stand out in a crowd. Look at the other people in the neighborhood, and try to blend in with them.

What if you don't *have* hair? Try growing some. If hair transplants or hair weaving aren't your style (or aren't within your budget), con-sider minoxidil, marketed under the trade name Rogaine and available without a prescription. This is a topical preparation that works for about 30 percent to 40 percent of the men who use it. The downside: it has to be applied twice a day, and once it's discontinued, the hair you've gained usually falls out. Even so, it might be worth a shot. Disclaimers aside, many folks swear by minoxidil, and my personal opinion is that under the right conditions, this stuff could grow hair on a billiard ball.

Also there is the anti-baldness pill, Propecia (finasteride), which is a weaker version of Proscar, a drug now used to treat enlarged prostate. Besides, if you can grow new hair, solidify your new identity, *and* keep your prostate from swelling up to boot, you've got a real win-win-win.

If all else fails, invest in a good rug; yes, they do exist. Let's face it—having hair, whether it's yours or not, makes you look years younger. More importantly, it will also confound those who remember you as a Yul Brynner look-alike. And that's what you want, isn't it?

Life's a Beach: Live It

Now is also a good time for you to lose a little weight. After all, as the motivational gurus like to say, "If not now, when?" Many of these expatriate resorts have beautiful beaches, so take advantage of them by going for long strolls on the beach at sunrise or sunset. Go snorkeling, fishing, or swimming in the surf. Not only will these activities improve your appearance, but they will probably add a few years to your life. At the very least they will make you feel better about yourself and may do you some good.

An early morning constitutional will not only get your heart, lungs, and blood moving, but may even help your libido. Speaking of which, the view on these beaches can be spectacular, and not just because of the sand, surf, and sky, if you know what I mean. These places are known to be frequented by attractive people looking for a fellow expatriate with whom to live and share a little piece of Paradise for awhile.

The Care and Feeding of Your New Body

While regular, vigorous exercise is perhaps the most important step to getting in shape, it's only part of the formula. A healthier diet is a must too. Cut down on your fat and cholesterol intake, include whole grains and other complex carbohydrates in your diet, and indulge shamelessly in all of the fresh fruits, vegetables, and seafood delights your new paradise has to offer. You'll discover that it is possible to eat healthily without depriving yourself. You may even find that you prefer a succulent swordfish steak with slices of juicy mango to a Big Mac and fries (hey, it could happen).

And why not take advantage of the exciting longevity research that has produced "designer" drugs and other anti-aging supplements? Though the miraculous Fountain of Youth has yet to be discovered, researchers are coming pretty darn close. Of course, it's best to try to get your vitamins, minerals, and anti-aging nutrients from fruits, vegetables, and other foods before you begin popping pills. But it's not always possible to get an optimum diet, even in paradise. At the very least, consider *a good antioxidant vitamin supplement*, which includes vitamins C, E, and carotenes.

If you feel that you've somehow lost your "edge" over the years, try ginkgo biloba. This herb has been proven to restore memory and increase alertness. It is an antioxidant that also helps maintain natural blood and oxygen flow to the brain by supporting stable, flexible red blood cells. You can take gingko as a pill or drink it in an herb tea. (Oh, yes, green tea has been rediscovered as a cure-all for many of man's worst ailments, particularly cancer, so drink up, my friend!)

Today, we even have a new shot at sex through the wonder of Viagra. Be careful though, the newspaper says that there have been more than a dozen deaths attributed to overindulgence brought on by the benefits of Viagra. If you are going to be a *Romeo Erectus*, just take it a little easy at first.

Two substances that have received a lot of attention in the media lately are DHEA (dehydroepiandrosterone) and melatonin. These have been hailed as miracle potions, but are they really? Well, yes and no.

Proponents of DHEA, a steroid hormone, claim that it lowers cholesterol levels, reverses diabetes, inhibits cancer, helps in weight loss, alleviates stress, restores virility, increases life span, lowers risk of heart disease, and restores memory. And indeed, it's been proven to do all of the above, at least in white mice. Limited human trials to date have shown it does bolster the immune system, helps older people sleep better, and alleviates joint pain. But scientists are reluctant to say that all benefits shown in rodents will translate to humans. Some rats have also developed liver cancer after receiving DHEA, but again, there are no long-term human studies. So DHEA may indeed be helpful, but take it judiciously.

If DHEA causes problems for you, perhaps you'll want to consider a newer hormone supplement called pregnenolone, or "preg" for short. No, it's not a fertility drug; it's another anti-aging substance. Dr. Ray Sahelian, a family practice physician and editor of the quarterly newsletter *Longevity Research Update*, believes that preg can be helpful in small amounts. Dr. Sahelian has written several books on the new supplements, and he states that if DHEA is the mother of all hormones, then preg is the grandmother. Preg, he explains, is the hormone from which the body makes DHEA, which is then converted into estrogen, testosterone, and other vital hormones. Proponents claim it offers the same benefits as DHEA but has fewer potential side effects, as the body will utilize only what it needs. As with DHEA, the scientific and medical communities are skeptical about these claims, urging that consumers exercise caution.

Melatonin is a naturally occurring hormone that regulates the body's internal clock. The older you get, the less melatonin there is in your blood. This is probably why many elderly people have problems with insomnia. Though melatonin by itself will not reverse aging, it has definitely been proven to aid in sleep and to ward off jet lag. However, some users have experienced moodiness, depression, rashes, impotence, and disturbing "virtual-reality" dreams, so use melatonin with caution, too. If you have any of the unpleasant effects listed here, consider that the melatonin may be the culprit, and find another way to solicit the sandman.

There is also some promising research on human growth hormone, or HGH, replacement therapy. Studies suggest many positive effects from synthetic HGH—including increased muscle mass, higher energy levels, enhanced sexual performance, stronger bones, lower blood pressure, faster healing of wounds, smoother skin, regrowth of hair, sharper vision, and elevated mood. Wow. Excuse me while I go get me some of that miracle potion.

Actually, the FDA has not quite approved HGH for general use as an anti-aging pill, but keep an eye open for new developments. If you want HGH now, be aware of its limitations and dangers. In the United States, HGH therapy is now being used mainly in children who cannot grow because of health problems. But it is expensive—about $800 a month for twice-daily injections—and it can have unwanted side effects, such as swollen, achy joints, hypertension, clogged arteries, and stiff hands. In more extreme cases, gigantism results, which can lead to premature death. HGH is nothing to play around with; I'd wait until the general-use pill is perfected. Again, that may be just around the corner. Meanwhile, the good news is that you can get many of the benefits of HGH by stimulating your own hormonal levels naturally through diet, exercise, and supplements.

So now that I've gotten the disclaimers out of the way, here's my personal take on some of these new drugs and supplements: after losing twenty pounds in two years in all the right places, and getting that "under 40" feeling back, I swear by DHEA and melatonin.

At any rate, even though there's really no single wonder potion yet (darn it all), you still have a host of options to consider, and you have many allies in the battle against aging. The 1,500-plus doctors and scientists at the American Academy of Anti-Aging Medicine in Chicago share one fundamental belief: *Age is inevitable; aging is not.* That's a "thought for the day" to carry with you as you begin your new life.

Dress for Less Stress

Not for nothing do they say that clothes make the man (or woman). Wardrobe should definitely be considered in your quest for a new identity. The simple solution, of course, is to go native. Do as the locals do, which in most places means to dress in a casual, simple style. Leave most of your old stuff at home with your old identity, and buy locally. The clothes in your new home will probably look and feel better than your starched shirts, suits, and ties, anyway. And mentally, the local duds will make you feel more like a native, because you'll look like one. The best way to do this is to observe the locals for awhile. Nothing will make you stand out more than dressing like a foreigner who's trying to look native. Think "aloha" shirts, and recall the image of Japanese tourists getting all decked out in western wear . . . you get the picture.

Be a Savvy Sun Worshipper

First, buy a couple of good pairs of polarized sunglasses. By the way, be sure you've acquired any needed prescription glasses; hopefully you'll have done this before you left home. Bring at least two or three pairs with you so you'll have extras for emergencies. Whatever you do, don't send back to the United States for your prescription glasses. That's a dead giveaway.

Next, learn to love hats (this fits in quite nicely with the go-native wardrobe advice above). Wearing a hat with a brim will keep the sun off your face and will also serve as a further disguise.

Work on gradually getting yourself a beachfront tan, but be sure you start with a good suntan lotion that has a high SPF (sun protection factor), so you don't fry your new body the first time out, or dry your skin to the consistency of leather. Make sure that the formulation you choose contains a UVA ray protector such as titanium dioxide, zinc oxide, dioxybenzone, or oxybenzone, which are four of the more common ones. Unfortunately, most sunscreen products place the emphasis on blockage of UVB rays, but provide inadequate protection against UVA. That's because UVA was once thought to be less damaging than UVB. However, recent research shows that UVA causes wrinkling and perhaps skin cancer, so you really need protection from both types of rays.

Also stock up on Skin-so-Soft or a similar product. It keeps your skin moist and helps repel those nasty little "no-see-ums" and sand fleas that make you itch like crazy at the beach.

Erase the Past

If you have any tattoos, it's best to get rid of them before you leave. A good stateside plastic surgeon can make even the largest and most prominent tattoos disappear without blotching your skin or your pocketbook. The advances made in laser surgery in recent years will also take out wrinkles, facial creases, and other identifying marks, to help you look and feel more youthful and, most importantly, less obtrusive. And you might be amazed at the mental lift resulting from even a small improvement in your appearance. Even if the procedures outlined above don't change your physical appearance that drastically, they will help you feel like the new person you are trying to become. Believing in your new self is probably the best disguise of all.

Going All the Way

If you feel the need to go first class and *really* alter your appearance, full-fledged plastic surgery might be an option. This can be rather costly, but in recent years new sources for reasonably priced plastic surgery has appeared.

Dozens of clinics have opened just across the Mexican border, and also in Guatemala, Honduras, and especially Costa Rica, catering to people wanting face-lifts, peels, tucks, sucks, and body sculpting of all kinds. The clinics ask no questions, keep no records (if you so request), and could perform such a transformation that even your own mother wouldn't recognize you—if that's what you want, of course.

Some of these clinics are perhaps best avoided; recent horror stories have surfaced about cut-rate south-of-the-border plastic surgery. But don't be so quick to dismiss this option. The clinics in some areas, in particular Costa Rica, have excellent reputations and are certainly worth considering (see Chapter 3). If you're a bit wary about trusting your face or body to a surgeon south of the border, that's certainly understandable, but don't rule out the possibility entirely. Get a recommendation from a friend or a state-side plastic surgeon; I can almost guarantee the surgeon will know exactly where to direct you.

A little shortening of the nose, tightening of the facial skin, and moderation of the hairline will change your visage sufficiently to pass even the closest scrutiny. Even your old friends won't recognize you, if you don't let them—as a certain shady businessman named Johnny could testify.

Fly the Friendly Guise

While flying first-class from Miami to Buenos Aires on business, three IBM executives spied a man, sitting two rows ahead of them, who they thought was an old friend and colleague. Said friend had left the firm under very questionable circumstances, relating to the theft of the company's intellectual property, and hadn't been seen since.

One of the IBM execs approached the man, took a long hard look at him, and said, "Hi, Johnny, it's been a long time since IBM, hasn't it?"

The traveler lowered his glasses, gave the suit the once-over head to toe, and said, "I'm sorry, Señor, but you must be mistaken. I am Adolpho Rocha, a buyer for Petroleos Mexicanos. I am not your friend."

Feeling a little sheepish, the suit stepped back to his chair and told his friends, "You know, that guy looked just like Johnny. Talk about a coincidence. I'd swear that was him when I got on the plane."

Little did they know that it really *was* their friend Johnny, and that Johnny had three other identities he'd used over the years under similar circumstances. Working for different companies, Johnny claimed

Latin, Italian, and other Mediterranean descents. Furthermore, he'd been a vice-president at many of the Fortune 500 companies, stealing every one of them blind by taking their technology to resell to the highest bidder. You never know, Johnny might come out of retirement and work for your company someday.

If Johnny can do it, so can you (I'm talking about re-creating your appearance, of course, not defrauding Fortune 500 companies). With a new tan, a new identity, and a new mental outlook, you'd be amazed at how good you feel and how easy it can be to create a new you. Even your old pals won't know it's you—and that, my friend, is exactly what you want.

6

How to Travel in and out of Your New Country, the U.S., and Anywhere Else—Without Getting Caught

Still More Reasons to Be Paranoid

Your passport provides the U.S. government with its chief method of tracing you through your foreign travel. This document was created in the first place specifically to identify a person's country of residence, but there are other purposes as well. The passport creates a means by which governments can tell where else their citizens have traveled—and, not incidentally, offers a handy means to keep tabs on said citizens' financial dealings abroad.

As we've discussed in earlier chapters, the wonders of modern technology allow not only the government to keep track of you, but also the credit bureaus, credit card companies, and banks—and, of course, the airlines. Remember, you can run (or fly), but it's getting harder and harder to hide.

You must realize that when you purchase an airline ticket, you are not only doing business with TWA, Delta, United, America, or Continental, but you are also entering a universal airline database. This database is maintained by a prospering Virginia-based firm known as the Airline Reporting Company, or ARC. This company, and its foreign counterpart, the International Air Transport Association (IATA), provide the ticket stock and computer support for all of the world's major airlines. ARC and IATA collate, bend, fold, and mutilate all of your airline tickets and their flight segments, properly crediting each airline that you flew on, and ensuring that each gets appropriate financial credit.

Let's say you left New York on Delta, changed plans in Miami to Cayman Air and went on to the Grand Caymans, and returned to the United States via Continental Airlines. The ARC and IATA would credit the proper airlines for each portion of your flight, and in so doing would create a database that tells who you are, when you flew, and, more importantly, what travel agency you used to book your flight.

What's so important about the travel agency? With the name of your agency, investigators can determine not only where you flew, but where you booked a hotel, rented a car, how far you drove, and even which tours you took. Any travel arrangement made through that agency is fair game for the snoops. Armed with this information, they'd be able to know your every step in a foreign country, and they could investigate every movement you made—including the phone calls you made to a local lawyer or banker to set up an appointment to open your new account. (Gotcha, O.J.!)

Roberto and Friends Leave a Trail

If you don't believe how easy it is to leave a trail that will lead investigators right to your door, then consider what happened to Roberto, a minor official in the finance ministry of one of the "Banana Republic" countries of South America. Roberto found a way to embezzle more than twelve million dollars of his nation's funds by creating false invoices for weapons purchased on the country's behalf. He did this by making up phony purchase orders that allowed sight drafts to be issued, just like cashier's checks on foreign banks in Switzerland.

Roberto contracted with a U.S. mercenary wannabe, who traveled to Zurich, obtained the signed drafts, cashed the checks, and brought the money to an agreed-upon meeting point. There Roberto, the mercenary, and a third conspirator divided up the loot. After each man filled a suitcase with cash, they scattered in different directions, expecting to live a life of luxury for many years to come.

Alas, it was not to be. Once the fraud was discovered by the governments auditors, investigators focused on the banks where the drafts were cashed. They knew, as the conspirators unfortunately did not, that most European banks photograph every single person who comes in the door.

This is because European banks have a much higher robbery rate than U.S. banks, and therefore take far more elaborate means to identify everyone on the premises from the moment they walk in the door.

Because this was an international bank scam, and a powerful world bank was involved in the loss, the Swiss bank provided investigators with photos of everyone who came into the bank on the day in question. And guess who the photos revealed? That's right: Roberto, the mercenary wannabe, and the heretofore unknown co-conspirator, who turned out to be the army general responsible for ordering weapons for the country's militia. They were all three walking in the bank together, literally hand-in-hand.

Armed with the photo of Roberto and the mercenary, plus the name of a business entity used by co-conspirator number three, shrewd investigators were soon able to get the travel records of the conspirators through IATA—which revealed not only the destinations, but the credit card number that was used to verify the travel plans and to make the reservations for the airline tickets.

It's that credit card that can really trip you up. Do you know how difficult it is to travel anywhere today if you want to pay in cash? You can't rent a car without a credit card. Hotels require one to check in, even if you pay cash! You can't even make airline reservations without that piece of plastic.

With the telltale credit card number, and the conspirators' flight plan, it was a simple matter then for the investigators to figure out the hotels they'd registered in, as well as where they ate breakfast, lunch, and dinner. It was all charged to the trusty American Express card. From there it was reported daily to their gigantic Cray computer in Phoenix, Arizona, that collates all of the credit histories of the customers of American Express records. Even though the card happened to be in a fictitious name, it was still traceable to our guys whenever and wherever they used it. The moral is: Don't leave home *with* one; it will catch you every time.

The Stealth Traveler's Guide

If you want to travel safely and quietly, then *get that foreign passport and use it wisely*. See the previous chapter for more details on acquiring a second passport. Beyond that, here are some tips to remember:

- Pick your travel times so that you move during high traffic periods, when Customs officials don't have time to give you the attention you truly deserve. If they've seen thousands of others just like you that day, they've lost their edge (if they ever had one to start with).

- When traveling to places that are known third-world financial centers, *don't travel there directly to or from the United States.* This will raise a red flag for the Customs computer; it is geared to check for such things.

  Let's say you are traveling from the United States to Grand Cayman. You already know, I hope, not to go directly from Point A to Point B. So, first you take a flight from the United States to Mexico City, Mexico. Once you've arrived in Mexico City, go to another travel agency or ticket agent, and purchase a round-trip ticket from Mexico City to Grand Cayman. When you return to Mexico City, go back on that round-trip ticket you purchased there, or buy yet another ticket from a third travel agency so there is no paper trail through the Customs computer showing that you traveled to Grand Cayman from the United States.

  Remember, the possibility exists that you could still be traced through the ARC or IATA, so be sure you buy the second ticket (the round-trip ticket from Mexico City to Grand Cayman), *in the other passport or in another name.* This way you will trick all of the government's computer resources, and will avoid all of their traps.

- Be sure that you don't charge any of your foreign tickets to one of the credit cards in your name. If you do, then all of your scheming is for naught, because the credit card companies have the biggest computers in the world. These companies can trace any credit transactions if they are given sufficient information—and incentive.

A Note on Air Travel Privacy

As I mentioned early on in this book, I think our rights are eroding daily in this country, and that definitely includes our right to privacy. Within this broad issue is the matter of air travel privacy. This is worthy of a whole separate book, but I want to touch upon it here.

As of this printing, there are several proposals being considered that would allow more intrusive security methods at U.S. airports. Most of these measures were suggested after the tragic explosion of TWA Flight 800 in July 1996. One suggested measure: Cameras that will "see" and project the image of a person's naked body under their clothes—surely a voyeur's dream (and a smuggler's nightmare, which is the whole point). Also on the proposal list is the building of a comprehensive "profile" database to fight terrorism and drug smuggling. There's even talk of creating a massive data base of all potential air passengers that would include identifying information (a picture, description, fingerprint, DNA sample, or PIN number), as well as address, flying patterns with a particular airline, bill paying history, criminal records, and other information. Such a database would put the ARC and IATA to shame.

Furthermore, as terrorism mounts throughout the world, airports all over the globe may be gearing up for more intrusive measures as well. Israel already has some of the most radical procedures in place. Every traveler is profiled; arriving visitors may be subject to prolonged questioning, detailed searches of their personal effects, and, in some cases, body searches. (If you have an Arab surname, count on experiencing extra delays.) Persons leaving Israel by air are also subjected to detailed and lengthy security questioning.

Extreme as these measures are, they may seem logical for an area where terrorism is so widespread—but they may very well be the wave of the future everywhere else as well. Although various civil liberties and privacy groups are fighting intrusive proposals in the U.S., the sad fact is that Americans seem to be more and more willing to give up their rights in order to make their world "safer." (Well, whaddaya want, Vern? Privacy or protection? You can't have both. Pick one, only one, and don't make a mistake!) And, of course, U.S. activists have little say about what goes on in other nations.

All this is by way of letting you know that it's imperative to do a little research before you travel. Be aware of the security measures at your airports of origin and destination. Ask your travel agent, or look at the travel advisories available on the Internet (such as those issued by the State Department).

You can keep up with the latest information on air travel by accessing the very useful website for Air Security International, at www.airsecurity.com. These folks are experts on travel security for corporations, governments, and individuals. They maintain current data on virtually everything the wary traveler needs to know, including detailed information on airports all over the world.

You can also monitor air-travel and other privacy issues at EPIC—no, not the El Paso Intelligence Center, but the Electronic Privacy Information Center. Their Internet address is www.epic.org.

You'll find other privacy publications and organizations in the Resource List at the back of this book.

Where You Go Is Who You Are

You need to be aware that if you travel to certain countries, this gives investigators a clue as to your intentions and the possible source of your funds. If they trace you to London and suspect you of hiding money, for example, they will conclude that it's a good bet that your money went to the Isle of Man, or the Jersey Islands off the coast of England. In fact, that's how investigators knew where to look for O. J. Simpson's hidden assets, which were alleged to be hidden in the Isle of Man. (You do remember his trip to London to speak at Oxford, don't you? And how many of you really believe that was the real reason for his trip?)

If you travel to France, Holland, or Germany, it would suggest the funds were secreted in Liechtenstein, Belgium, or Luxembourg, which have some of the strongest bank secrecy laws in the world, and offer comprehensive trust services and facilities for laundering money far from peering eyes.

A trip to the Far East would point to Singapore or Hong Kong as your money center, with the new smart money seriously considering Malaysia as its alternate source. An Asian Pacific sojourn might even suggest a look into dealings in Nairu, a small but interesting island in Micronesia, smack in the middle of the Pacific. This little island, which is best know for its guano exporting, specializes in making money and financial records disappear.

Trick or Treaty

Years ago, anyone with money to hide went to Switzerland or possibly the Cayman Islands and knew that their money was safe from prying eyes. Today, however, these countries have signed Mutual Legal Assistance Treaties (MLATs) with the U.S and other members of world banking nations. MLATs provide, among other things, the release of financial information on any individual and their bank accounts if they can be shown to be involved in organized or drug-related crime. So, if you even smoked one marijuana cigarette, and inhaled—and someone besides you knows about it—your bank account could be subject to the MLAT and made available to the United States Attorney General. The records could then be used to prosecute you for money laundering or tax evasion.

As of 1996, MLATs were in force with nineteen governments:

- Argentina
- The Bahamas
- Canada
- Italy
- Jamaica
- Mexico
- The Netherlands
- Panama
- Switzerland
- Turkey

United Kingdom-dependent Caribbean territories:

- The Cayman Islands
- Anguilla
- British Virgin Islands
- The Turks and Caicos Islands
- Montserrat
- Uruguay
- Morocco
- Spain
- Thailand

But wait, there's more. Any day now (if not already), the following will be added to the roster:

- Belgium
- Colombia
- United Kingdom
- Korea
- Hungary
- The Philippines
- Austria
- Nigeria

And there's still more. Similar treaties are in various stages of negotiation elsewhere, according to the U.S. Department of State's International Narcotic Control Strategy Report. This is to be expected as more nations strive to enter the world banking community. It seems that no country now wants to be identified as a shelter for drug dealers and drug money, so there is a rush to cooperate—at least on this specific issue—at many of the foreign financial centers.

Information on MLATs is available in several sites on the Internet and in government publications, such as the State Department's International Narcotics Control Strategy Report. (See the Resource List at the back of this book.)

Another banking tool being developed and used by our government is the Annunzio-Wylie Act, a law that basically turns your banker into a snitch. This is commonly known as the "know your customer" rule which requires that a bank know both the sender and receiver of money in a foreign wire transfer transaction. (See Chapter 7 for more of the gruesome details.)

The Smart Money Gets Around

The new hot money, the money, or money that wishes to remain undetected, is now appearing in countries that are in political or financial turmoil. The events in Eastern Europe since the late 1980s have given rise to a frenzy of activity. Poland and Bulgaria, for example, have seen a tremendous upsurge in financial activity, particularly at their casinos and banks. Many extremely large transactions have gone undetected through these countries, because of the poor financial controls provided by emerging governments, and the offered ability to wash or launder millions of dollars from the foreign government investigators' prying eyes by pumping it through their casinos.

The same circumstances can be found in some of the smaller Caribbean countries such as Anguilla or Grenada, the latter of which was once "liberated" by our own government. These countries, and others with limited resources and a need for hard currency, have attracted casinos and other businesses with financial relationships that want a quiet, safe place in which to conduct their business. Of course, since many of these nations are now involved in MLATs with Uncle Sam, the *really* smart money will be treading more carefully these days.

Next year, who knows where the smart money will be? The world is an ever-changing place; it pays to keep tabs on what's going on where. You can be sure that savvy investigators are doing just that. It's amazing what can be found out by "following the money trail."

A Man, a Plan, and a Scam: Panama

During his years as dictator of Panama, Manuel Noriega provided the ultimate service to many of the world's largest drug dealers. He is alleged to have offered, through his Panamanian National Bank, a government-sanctioned depository with means to transfer money in and out of his country's banks—for a fee.

Government investigators and world banking sources have found information that indicates that Noriega got one cent of every drug-deposit dollar passing through his country, which accounted for the tremendous rise of financial activity of Panamanian banks throughout the 1980s. Hindsight is 20/20, but an astute world bank examiner could have traced the rise in drug money by watching the clearing records of the Panamanian banks rise from five million to over fifty million a day during the time that Noriega was allowing free rein of said drug money in his country.

And if the federal drug agents had been really smart, they probably could have taken note of how the activities in many of the world's banks altered dramatically the day after the U.S. invaded Panama. They would have seen large transactions appear in brand new places, in amounts big enough to show them the new trails of the drug money that were forged once Panama and Noriega were no longer players in the game.

NOTE: One way that government investigators snoop out dirty banks (and the bankers) is by monitoring the number of $100 bills bought by the bank. You see, the big bill is the "coin of the realm" of the drug trade and banks that all of a sudden buy large amounts of $100 bills from the Federal Reserve are quite likely to be targeted for an audit of just why they need all those big bills.

All of this talk of money has gotten me excited; how about you? Now that I've given you tips on how to travel safely and keep *yourself* hidden; it's time to learn how to move your money securely, and keep it hidden from prying eyes. We'll go into detail about that in the next chapter.

Moving Your Money Safely

7

Head 'Em Up and Move 'Em Out

There are many ways to move your money outside the boundaries of your host country and many reasons to want to get your assets and money offshore. In fact, there are probably more ways than reasons if you look at it closely. There are many ways to hide your assets and disappear and they range from very simple to stealthy, sneaky, and devious.

The simplest way to move your assets out of home base is simply to bag it yourself. By law, you can take up to $10,000 per person out of the country each time you depart. If you feel brave, you can carry even more, but remember, when they play that recording in the airport warning that it is a crime to carry more than $10,000 outside the U.S. without reporting it on a U.S. Customs form, then they might be playing it for you. (Whenever Customs get an anonymous "tip" that someone is moving cash out of the country, they play a recording of the law over the loudspeaker to be sure that they have evidence in court.)

If you take $10,000 for yourself and a traveling companion (they don't even have to know that you are carrying it for them, unless you want them to), then you can legally lower your U.S.-based assets every time you travel, with no one being the wiser. You see, cash makes no enemies and leaves very few trails, especially if you stay under the $10,000 currency transaction requirement imposed by the banking regulators.

Most people buy one of the little belly bags, available wherever briefcases are sold. These little pouches wrap around your waist and very easily hold $20,000 to $30,000, just below your beltline.

If you don't want to carry cash, then another time-tested way to make money disappear is to purchase cashier's checks or money orders and tuck them inside a money belt made for just this purpose. Most leather shops (and airline magazines) sell money belts that open up their seams so that you can tuck a dozen or more negotiable instruments into your belt and walk it right through the inspection process. With no metal in the belt, other than the buckle, you won't set off any alarms or generate any curious inspection. Once at your destination, just unload the belt and make your deposit in the bank. One note, though. Don't buy these cashier's checks, money orders, or other negotiable instruments where you have previously held an account. If you take money directly from your account and use that money to buy negotiable instruments, it leaves a trail on your bank statement, one that can be traced back to the financial instrument, and ultimately to its new home in a foreign land.

One way that financial investigators find out your best-laid plans is by subpoenaing your bank statement and searching for large, even number withdrawals ($7,000, $8,000, $9,999) under the CTR (Currency Transaction Report) reporting requirements. If they see such withdrawals, they will then go to the bank and ask for the records documenting the purchase of cashier's checks and money orders in the same amount on the same day. *Sooooooo*, don't use the same place for both sides of your transaction or you just might get nailed.

The Offshore Order Gambit

There are many countries that allow their citizens to travel, but don't let them carry their cash out of the country. Several countries in South Africa and others around the globe keep their citizens in check by holding their capital and assets hostage.

The Reicherts had a thriving business in South Africa selling farming and industrial equipment to many of the country's small farmers and ranchers. Their problem, like many others, was that they did not fear for their own lives, but those of their children. The Reicherts firmly believed that a revolution was going to take place in their homeland, a very bloody revolution that would leave millions dead in its path and destroy everything they had built for their families.

To get around their own country's laws and to preserve their piece of the rock, the Reicherts made a deal with their favorite U.S. suppliers to buy millions of dollars worth of products that would be paid for from by the Reicharts family business South African account, but would never be delivered to South Africa. The deal they cut was that the Reicherts would open up their own dealership, in the U.S., with money paid out of their homeland account.

When they arrived in the Western World, their new business was all setup and waiting for them, signed, sealed and delivered. A company franchise granting them exclusive rights to a trade area and enough inventory to repatriate their assets in their new home.

I have seen the same set-up work from the United States to a foreign country as well. A certain U.S. builder, placed in bankruptcy because of increased competition and increased costs, found that he could order his building materials from Guatemala and have half of them sent to another building site in Costa Rica. The U.S. business continued to downsize and lose money but the Costa Rican venture, with little expense and material costs, made enough profit to pay for the owners retirement.

The bankruptcy trustee, unsophisticated in such matters and not wanting to spend the money to audit his equipment or supplies, let the company fold in bankruptcy, thus wiping out all of the debts and creditors of the U.S. entity.

The builder? Well, he walked away from all of his U.S. debts and built a row of seaside condos in Costa Rica. You can find him there now, living in one of his villas with a beautiful view of the harbor and coast. How does he live? The other nine rental units provide more than enough income to pay all of his expenses and supports a lifestyle that any one of us would be jealous of—if we only knew!

Covering Your Ass–ets

One way to get your money out of the country, without making a lot of trips carrying $10,000 each time and without leaving a trail through wire transfers or checks, it to drive it down yourself.

Rumor has it that in many major cities, particularly in the south or southwest, there are people who make a living running caravans down into Mexico, Guatemala, Honduras, and Costa Rica. These people make a living by buying second hand and repaired appliances, vehicles and commercial equipment, making a few repairs and selling them in the Central American countries. You see, American cars, appliances, and construction equipment are in such short supply and are taxed so prohibitively in these countries, that there is a lot of room for an entrepreneur to bring in affordable merchandise on the gray (if not black) market.

These same "south of the border" entrepreneurs not only bring in trade goods, but escort individuals and families that wish to make their way down through Mexico into Central and South America looking for a new home. Since they have a regular route, know all of the stops, and regularly grease all of the right border guards, they make traveling a snap if you have a dependable car, preferably a Jeep or a truck. (Don't try this trip in a clunker!)

Every six weeks, Ted Barbour takes three or four cars that he has bought that month and a good supply of small hand tools from Houston to Honduras. He also advertises, through word of mouth, the opportunity to discretely transport individuals (or families) and their worldly goods with him and his caravan, for a small fee.

Ted's route is a six-day trip with stopovers in quaint little villages known to be safe and secure. (They are not the caliber of the Ritz Carlton Hotel but all of the places are clean and provide a comfortable and cozy stay with a trace of adventure, to say the least.) No one asks you any questions as long as you are not transporting guns or drugs.

If you are ready to leave without a trace, without lighting up any of the computers, leaving any footprints in a financial institution or leaving a ticket trail with one of the airlines, a travel agency, or the ARC, then this method just might be to your liking.

WARNING! This is not a trip to be engaged upon, carrying all of your worldly goods alone, as a virgin experience. If you make this trip, remember that there is safety in numbers. Making this trip alone is not recommended for several reasons. First, it is very easy to get lost and wander into an area that is in turmoil or worse. Second, just like a sheep wandering from the flock, you could become easy pickings for the occasional group of brigands, bandits, or robbers that make a living robbing unsuspecting sheep who have wondered too far from home.

Another method of moving moola (used by many of our biggest banks and wealthiest corporations) is simply wire it to a foreign account or corporation set up by you, or your agent, in advance of your flight. Oh, you didn't know that the big boys send their money offshore every Friday night to gain a chunk of interest over the weekend? U.S. banks don't pay interest on the weekends and holidays, so they slip it back into their U.S. bank Monday morning without missing a beat or losing a penny of interest. These types of financial transactions may be monitored at any time, but thousands of these transfers take place every day.

Once you arrive in your new destination, however you arrive, your first step is to find a friendly lawyer and banker. Almost all of the Caribbean Islands and most of the Central American communities have a very strong banking infrastructure, both of local and international extraction. In Belize, Honduras, Costa Rica, and Panama, you will find such luminaries as Barclay's Bank, CIBC, and the Bank of Nova Scotia, each extremely knowledgeable and competent in the ways of the financial world and more than willing to help you "learn the ropes" in your new community. In addition to the large international banks, each of these countries has a number of local financial institutions that offer higher interest than the U.S. and interesting exchange rates and investments if you want to gamble on the local economy.

When my good friend "Bob" made his first trip to Honduras and placed his life savings with the bank of his choice, he was offered the ability to keep his money in dollars or lempiras, the local currency. The friendly neighborhood banker explained that they paid only 8 percent on dollar accounts, but up to 27 percent on lempira or local accounts and up to 37 percent on investments in the Bolsa (investments are made on commercial notes to local industries like consturction and building financing), the local stock exchange.

Why the dramatic difference in interest? It is all in the exchange rate. As long as the currency doesn't devalue, you can make a killing by investing in a local currency or investment. Just watch out for political or financial troubles. When they loom on the horizon, you would turn your money into the safer dollar accounts.

Bob decided to put half of his money in dollars and the other half in the Bolsa where it was used on new construction loans (the hottest growing industry in Central America). Over the last four years, he has more than doubled his money in the Bolsa and didn't lose more than a small percentage to devaluation, as the currency has remained very stable. His dollar account, well, that has made him 25 percent but with the Bolsa paying better than four to one over the U.S. interest rate, Bob may put more of his money there next year. Currently there is a tremendous building boom and the construction industry is desperate for working capital to meet the housing needs of the growing population.

In addition to bank accounts and trust, a good banker, like Bob's, can steer you to local investment opportunities and set up a brokerage account so that you can invest anywhere in the world, even in the United States if you want to. Through the creation of an anonymous International Business Corporation (IBC), you can issue yourself bearers stock and "run silent" and "run deep" by investing through the IBC instead of your "real" name.

If you like the return and the stability of U.S. mutual funds (and who hasn't over the past few years?), but don't want to have an account in your name in the U.S., your banker can set up an account for you in your new home and invest your money in the U.S. with no one the wiser. The way it is done is to buy the stocks in the bank's name, as your trustee, so that your name doesn't appear as a shareholder in the good old U.S.A. or to utilize the IBC (and still remain invisible as a buyer or seller).

In many of the Caribbean and Central American countries, the law permits and welcomes the establishment of an IBC by individuals with stocks held in bearer names. In fact, it is my understanding that most real estate transactions and almost all of new business development is done through vehicles of this type.

Now the juicy part . . . to establish an IBC, your friendly neighborhood lawyer (preferably a nephew of the local governor) incorporates a business entity for you that is allowed to conduct any business legal under the prevailing government's law. This entity will then open bank accounts and conduct its business, such as purchasing real estate, making investments and acting out your fondest desires (on paper).

The lawyer will request that someone be appointed as trustee (frequently himself) who will administer the actions of the IBC and will distribute or hold the bearers shares of the corporation as you desire. With a vehicle of this type, you can then have bank accounts, credit cards and access to investment sin a name other than your own and no one will even get a whiff of the name of the real owner—unless they can trace the money going *into* the IBC, from an account that can be associated with you.

When in Rome, Watch Out for the Romans

One word of warning, the fastest way to have a million dollars in some of these countries is to come in with two or three. The learning curve can very easily cost you half of your hard-earned wealth, especially if you don't know the player or the territory and you invest with the wrong people.

You are not the first and only one to find the benefits of these countries that offer financial privacy and a lack of extradition. Every con man from Canada to Colombia has come as well, usually just one stop ahead of the law.

One of my oil-drilling clients got a little short of cash during the last banking crunch and sought outside help in getting a loan from the international banking community. Somehow, they heard of, and met with, a Costa Rican businessman named Paul Noe who promised them that he could get a $10 million business loan by pledging Noe's stocks to guarantee it. But first, he wanted $100,000 up front (as a fee) and another two points (2 percent) when the deal closed.

My client, a little hesitant to just fork over the $100,000, sight unseen, asked me to look into the credentials of the learned Mr. Noe to see if he really could do the deal and if the money was drug money or legitimate.

Assuming that Mr. Noe was not a native of Costa Rica (no one there with a high net worth is), I ran his name through the wonderful worlds of computer information and found that in the 1950s, "Dr. Noe" was the biggest financial crook in America. Paul Noe was legendary in the world of financial fraud, to a point where he was the subject of a book on fraud named *The Fountain Pen Conspiracy.* Looking further, I found several articles in the *New York Times* and *Wall Street Journal* documenting Dr. Noe's escapades and mention of his arrest in New Orleans when the FBI lured him back into the U.S. to close and sign a supposed multi-million dollar financing deal in New Orleans, Louisiana. When Dr. Noe got off the plane, guess what happened! He got bagged! This is a good idea for you to keep in mind once you leave the country. Don't look (or come) back.

Warning: There are more than a few Dr. Noes lurking about in Paradise. Some sell real estate, others do exotic investment, and others run a variety of businesses that will dip you if they can. When in doubt, check them out through a knowledgeable local banker or gumshoe.

With the wonders of modern computer technology and a few local reputable business sources, you too should be able to keep from making the mistake of doing business with the local barracuda, at least on a big scale.

Now, How to Keep Your Money from Disappearing

Once you have gotten your money offshore and done it in such a way that there is no direct link to an account in your name, the next issue is how to manage, invest and direct your money, to your best benefit.

If you are just hiding your assets from civil litigation or the ex-spouse from hell, then the steps are much easier. A little known vehicle called the Offshore Asset Protection Trust (OAPT) was made just for you.

An OAPT or Foreign Security Trust, is a trust wherein you, as a settlor or grantor, create a trust by placing your assets within its welcome arms. You then establish individuals who become beneficiaries, who are named by you, the grantor, to benefit from the assets of the property. To distance yourself even further from the ownership or management of this trust, you then appoint a trustee to manage the assets of the property on behalf of the beneficiaries. All of this is stated in a drawn-out trust document that appoints the various parties and sets out the arrangement for the distribution of the assets.

The advantage of an offshore OAPT over a trust set up in the U.S. is that the trust operates under the laws of a foreign country whose laws favor the trust participants and make pursuit of the trust and it assets almost impossible for future litigants and lawyers to penetrate.

One word of caution, the OAPT does not protect you against criminal charges of the U.S. government and the Internal Revenue

Service. While the trust will protect you from almost any type of civil circumstances, many governments have signed legal treaties knows as MLATS (Mutual Legal Assistance Treaties) with the United States. This agreement allows the U.S. to penetrate bank accounts and trusts of certain individuals, particularly those who have smoked at least one marijuana cigarette—and inhaled.

The only problem for the common Joe is that setting up trusts of this type can take a deep whack out of your bank account. If you use a lawyer in the U.S. to set up these accounts, then the possibility exists that their records can be subpoenaed, seized, terrorized, or bought off by the other side via the "long arm of the law."

Another problem with OAPT's is that they have to be set up well in advance of any knowledge of financial liabilities or problems that would indicate a foreknowledge of potential problems on your part.

Ted Canton was a smooth operator, a real estate "wheeler-dealer" who made $85 million developing a downtown slum into a vibrant urban park and recreation center. Ted took his money made from the real estate deal and invested in high-stakes oil and gas project in a number of foreign countries, some of which were on the U.S.-proscribed business list (such as Libya and Iran).

As the foreign business deals started coming together and the money started pouring in, Ted's dirt-bag lawyer, his sweetheart, and his two trusted vice presidents decided to get greedy. While Ted was out of town, they embezzled more than $12 million of the company's money and turned Ted's business records over to the IRS so that the government would go after Ted instead of them. (They also asked for the informant reward of 10 percent of the recovered funds.) Et tu, Brutus!

Upon returning home from his travels and finding his company stripped naked and his cupboards bare, Ted went after his employees with a vengeance, but was, in turn, chased by Uncle Sam (and he had a bigger gas tank). The IRS seized all of the foreign bank accounts it could find claiming that the money in them was the result of a violation of the Foreign Trading with the Enemy Act. They also alleged that it was a fraudulent conveyance, and was made with the knowledge that the assets were made from ill-gotten gains in violation of various Racketeering Influenced Corrupt Practices (RICO) Acts and the Foreign

Corrupt Practices Act. They also claimed that the trusts set up to protect these assets were set up while Ted was scheming with foreign countries and therefore, trusts were set up with the specific intent of keeping the ill-gotten gains from the long arm of the law.

As usual, the government won. They seized all of Ted's U.S. bank accounts, foreign bank accounts and the real estate that he transferred into his ex-wife's name. The only thing that Ted got away with was a few million dollars worth of bearer bonds that, fortunately, were never put in his name and never appeared in the U.S. The moral of this story is that you can beat almost everyone but the government. You can float like a butterfly and sting like a bee, but if the big rhino sees you, your ass is grass and he is the lawnmower.

As long as you don't get tagged with a criminal charge and you don't lie to the IRS about having a foreign trust (See it? It's right there on your tax return. That little box that you have to check to admit to your foreign trust), you should be in good hands with an OAPT.

If you want to be really cautious, then I would suggest moving the location of the trust, several times, when and if its security is ever breached. How could that happen? Well, if you fire that life-long assistant or trade in that spouse that you took on a vacation to the island paradise that houses your trust, then it's time for a change. The French were right to coin the phrase, "Cherchez la femme."

If it were mine to do, I would find an American attorney that has a foreign affiliation in the country of choice for the OAPT and have them work together in setting up the plan. I would then request that all of my records be sent to the custody of the foreign attorney so that the U.S. mouthpiece has no records or documents that could find their way to court or to Uncle Sam. I would also require the local mouthpiece to sign a confidentiality agreement and tell him to invoke every attorney/client privilege available.

Checklists for Setting Up a Foreign Trust

1. Itemize all of your assets, listing their value and equity.
2. Pick a home for you OAPT, some place politically and socially stable (one with strong financial privacy laws) with a good infrastructure and the place that you cold retire, if you wanted to.

3. Find a lawyer who specializes in trusts and estates and has proven experience in the offshore arena (don't look in the Yellow Pages, get a referral from someone who knows).

4. Visit the future home of you financial future and see for yourself if you like it (while you are there, interview the potential trustee recommended by your U.S. mouthpiece).

5. Select a trust beneficiary, one who is not going to turn around and bite you someday and will do what you wish, as you wish, when you wish.

6. Execute the trust by funding it through one of the methods we have detailed in this book.

7. Drain all of the equity from your real estate and tangible assets by establishing second mortgages on them, with the proceeds payable to the trust.

8. *Remember,* three can keep a secret if two of them are dead. Don't share this information with your family or your friends.

Success Stories

Unfortunately, this book is littered with people who tried to hide and failed, people who were not knowledgeable enough or dedicated enough to protecting their wealth and themselves. So, to show that it can be done, that you can hide and disappear, I would like to share a few favorite success stories with you.

Harry was a very successful insurance broker—in fact, maybe too successful. Harry built up a thriving business insuring small businesses, boats, and aircraft through offshore carriers that beat the pants off of the big boys in the insurance business in the States. Due to his ability to outsell his competition, or really because of it, the State Department of Insurance dropped into his office one day and seized all of Harry's books and records. The next thing Harry knew, investigators were offering immunity to anyone who would roll over on his operation, whether they were guilty or not. (Could you afford to defend yourself from a state agency with unlimited funds and the power of the badge behind them?)

Knowing that he had not broken the law, and wanting to stay in the States, Harry hired two high-powered law firms to talk to the Department of Insurance and resolve the problem. Six months later, with his legal bills mounting astronomically and still shut down by the Insurance Department, our friend found himself facing criminal and civil charges for insurance fraud and a warrant for his arrest, based on a plea bargain by one of his former associates.

Faced with the State charges and clients wanting him to write new insurance for them, Harry went to the old pro for some advice on how to solve his problems. After a few hours of scheming and planning, we decided on Costa Rica as his new base of operations and his future home. His reasons for choosing Costa Rica included the following: a growing business community, favorable tax laws, no extradition, a pleasant and inexpensive lifestyle and access to the international business community provided by an excellent telecommunications infrastructure and tax free zone.

While Harry built his business in Costa Rica, the Stateside Insurance Department screamed, yelled, and tried every trick in the world to shut down his business and lock him up. But, sitting in his hillside estate overlooking San Jose, Harry and his business thrives today in a country that is pleased to have him and will bend over backward to help him prosper, because it is in their best interest as well.

Eventually, the government was found wrong and settled out of court, dropping all charges, rather than be embarrassed by the exposure of their dirty deeds and their expenditure of big bucks on a worthless case. Harry could come home again, but, what do you think he chose?

In his new home, Harry actually has a higher standard of living than he had in the States (for a much lower price), a whole lot less stress, and the security of a relationship with a government that wants to see business grow, and employ their own citizens in meaningful jobs. Yep, he stayed in Costa Rica and has never looked back!

Skippy, my mentor and best friend in Mexico, beat the system and, hopefully is now enjoying himself in the ultimate Paradise. Twenty years ago, he bugged out on a tax debt in the neighborhood of $2 million, and settled in Manzanillo with all of his worldly possessions packed in a truck he bought to haul it with. Skippy rented a house overlooking the water (Americans couldn't own property that close to the ocean in Mexico, and probably wouldn't want to) with a great view of the harbor and a nice breeze in from the Pacific. To keep his mind active, and to pick up a little pocket change, Skippy ran a little cash and carry pawn

and jewelry business, lending money to locals and buying gold and silver for cash.

Every few months, Skippy would send his girlfriend across the border, wearing and carrying the jewelry that Skippy pawned and bought.
June sold the jewelry, collected enough cash to pay all of their bills for
the next six months (and then some) and returned to Manzanillo to start
all over again.

Instead of losing everything and possibly doing time in Club Fed,
Skippy lived the life that many of us would envy. When he died last
year, I'll bet it was with a smile on his face, both for beating the system
and for the many years he and June lived like Jimmy Buffett in
Margaritaville.

8

Keeping It Hidden Once It's Gone!

All right. You've made the decision to move out of the country and you've chosen the exotic locale where you want to establish your new life. You've decided who you want to be, and you know how to travel safely, but how are you going to get your money out of the U.S. and into your new home? And how are you going to protect your assets once you've moved them? That's what we are going discuss in this chapter. Though it's not within the scope of this book to delve into all of the technicalities of overseas financial transactions, we will cover the basic information, and I'll refer you to specific resources for further reading.

The $70,000 Question

Before I get into the sneakier stuff, I want to deliver on a promise I made at the end of Chapter 3. I mentioned that there's a loophole for folks who are not trying to bug out entirely—people who want to retain their American citizenship but just want to keep Uncle Sam from taking such a vicious bite out of their hard-earned bread. If you fall into this category, then you'll probably be interested in the "$70,000 exclusion." Also known as the *foreign-earned-income-exclusion*, this loophole is one of the clearest provisions in the U.S. tax code. It's actually broader, and allows you to earn far more tax-free income, than even most expats realize. However, like most loopholes, this one can be a noose around your neck if you're not careful.

Very simply, the provision allows for U.S. citizens who live and work outside the U.S. to exclude from gross income up to $70,000 of foreign-earned income. Besides that, an employer-provided housing allowance can be excluded from income. Other tax breaks are available too; for example, each member of a married couple working overseas can exclude salary of $70,000 (as of this writing), for a total of $140,000 plus housing allowances. Note that this is not a deduction, credit, or deferral, but an outright exclusion of the income from gross income.

To get these benefits, of course, you must meet certain requirements. Most of the information I obtained in this section was from an excellent site on the World Wide Web, "The Offshore Entrepreneur."[1] The report cited in the footnote was taken from various books and special reports by Adam Starchild, whose many titles include *Reviving the American Dream: Stop "Just Getting By" and Build Real Wealth* (Paladin Press). See the Resource List at the back.

Here are the requirements you must meet for the $70k exclusion:

1. ***You must establish a tax home in a foreign country.*** To the IRS, your tax home is the location of your regular or principal place of business. It's where you work, not where you live. A flight engineer found this out the hard way. He lived in the Bahamas, but all his flights originated from Kennedy Airport in New York, rather than from the Bahamas. The tax court ruled that his tax home was in New York, so he did not qualify for the $70,000 exclusion.

   However, the definition of "home" goes even further for the foreign-earned-income exclusion. You have to pay attention to the rules, or you'll get caught in a trap that snares many overseas Americans who think they are earning tax-free income, but really aren't. *You see, if you work overseas but are still maintaining a place of residence in the United States, your tax home is not outside the U.S.* What it all boils down to is that if you want to qualify for the foreign-earned-income exclusion, you must establish both your principal place of business *and* your actual residence outside the United States. If you want to be certain of getting this tax break, sell or rent your U.S. abode and establish a primary residence outside of the States.

---

1 "Moving Your Offshore Residence" by Adam Starchild; www.au.com/offshore/sample/movingyourreside.html.

2. *After establishing your tax home, you must pass either the "foreign-residence test" or the "physical-presence test."* The *physical-presence test* is the most straightforward; you simply have to be out of the U.S. for 330 days out of any 12 consecutive months. The days themselves do not have to be consecutive. Sounds simple, doesn't it? Well, a number of picky little rules can complicate it. Few people begin their foreign assignments on January 1st and end them on December 31st, so for most people, their 12-month period will occupy two tax years—making it necessary for them to prorate their income and the $70,000 exclusion for those tax years. Oh, and there's more: to count a day as one spent outside the U.S., you must be out of the States for the entire day. There are exceptions for traveling days, and for days you spend flying over the U.S. if your flight did not originate there. The IRS has a number of rules on counting days. Frankly, I think it would just be less of a hassle just to bug out entirely and let them soak.

Well, no, wait a moment; there is, alternatively, the *foreign-residence test*, which is probably easier for most taxpayers to pass. What you have to do is establish yourself as a bona fide resident of a foreign country, or countries, for an uninterrupted period that includes an entire taxable year, and you must intend to stay there indefinitely. If you fail to pass this test, the IRS will consider you a "transient" or a "sojourner" rather than a foreign resident, and you will not qualify as a foreign resident.

In the eyes of the tax law, residency is a state of mind. It is where you *intend* to be domiciled indefinitely. To determine your state of mind and your intentions, the IRS plants electrodes in your brain and tracks your thought processes via sophisticated technology that they stole from extraterrestrial beings. No, just kidding—but they do the next best thing; they take a close look at just how "attached" you are to the country in question. A number of factors are considered, including:

- **Sleeping quarters:** do you sleep in a hotel, or have you signed a one-year lease for a house or apartment?
- **Personal belongings:** The more you take to a foreign country, the more you "seem" to be establishing a foreign residence.
- **U.S. property:** Owning a U.S. residence that you leave vacant is considered a sign that you don't intend to establish a foreign residence. Selling or renting your U.S. home signals the opposite.
- **Local documents:** It behooves you to obtain a foreign driver's license and foreign credit (however, maintaining your U.S. license and registration won't kill your chances).

- **Local involvement:** Show involvement in your local social and community activities, at least to the same extent that you were involved in same in the U.S. Of course, if you were a recluse and a couch potato in the States, you don't have anything to worry about.
- **Foreign taxes:** Foreign countries tax on the basis of residence. If you claim exemption from local taxes because you're not a resident of that country, the IRS will conclude that you are a U.S. resident and do not qualify for the foreign-earned-income exclusion under the foreign-residence test, so pay the local taxes.

Now, here's one reason you might prefer to qualify under the physical-presence test rather than the foreign-residence test. With the physical presence test, *you might be able to claim that you are not a resident of the foreign country, and are thereby exempt from their laws. At the same time, you can claim exemption from U.S. taxes.* This could be worth a shot, particularly if the tax rates in your new home are outrageous.

- **Bank accounts:** They do not seem to greatly affect residence status, but if your case is borderline, it's a good idea to open at least a local checking account in your host country, even if you're still maintaining a U.S. account. (Many U.S. expatriates maintain U.S. accounts because it is easier to have their U.S. employers deposit paychecks directly into the U.S. account.)
- **Permanent address:** Again, intention is everything here. Once your foreign residence is established, you must show that it is for an indefinite duration. To determine this, the IRS generally looks at your employment contract. If your contract is for one year or less, that is an indication that you have a definite intent to return to the U.S. after a short period of time—in which case you would not meet the foreign-residency requirement. But if the contract is indefinite, open-ended, or renewable, or if it is likely to lead to a new job, you can probably qualify as a foreign resident.
- After establishing your **foreign residence**, you can make occasional trips to the U.S. for business or vacations without losing your foreign-residence status. Be certain, however, that the trips are temporary and that you don't do anything to disturb any of the factors qualifying you as a foreign resident.

3. *And, finally, you must have earned income that qualifies for the $70,000 exclusion.* Not all income qualifies for this exclusion—only foreign-earned income. Very simply, foreign-earned income is income paid for services you have performed in a foreign country. This includes salaries, professional fees, tips, and similar compensation. Interest, dividends, and capital gains do not apply.

Self-employed people must adhere to additional rules. Professionals who do not make material use of capital in performing their services can qualify all of their net income for the loophole; however, when both personal services and capital are used to generate income, no more than 30 percent of net profits are eligible for the exclusion. For self-employed individuals and for partners, the net income (rather than the gross income) is the amount that is applied toward the exclusion limit.

There are other types of income that do not qualify for the loophole, such as employer-provided meals and lodging on the business premises, pension and annuity payments, and income paid to employees of the U.S. government or its agencies. However, some of these payments—such as employer-provided meals and lodging on the business premises—are tax-free under regular U.S. tax rules, and they retain that status. *This is one way you can earn more than $70,000 tax-free.*

The $70,000 limit on the offshore loophole applies to individual taxpayers, so if you're married, you and your spouse potentially can exclude up to $140,000 of foreign-earned income. The catch is that you cannot share each other's limit. Let's say one of you earns $80,000 and the other earns $30,000. In that case, you can exclude only $100,000 on the return ($70,000 plus $30,000).

If you're not careful, you can easily close this loophole. Here are a few points to remember:

1. **Make sure you meet the provisions.** Many Americans assume that because they are living overseas, everything they do is free from U.S. tax. As you can see by the requirements we just listed, nothing could be further from the truth. You should discuss your situation with a tax attorney or accountant who thoroughly understands the offshore loophole—and you should do this *before* you leave the United States. That way, you'll be sure that you qualify for and make maximum use of this loophole.

2. **File your tax returns.** In order to get the exemption, you must file a tax return and claim the exemption on Form 2555. Even if you meet all of

the requirements, you lose the loophole if you don't file. Remember, the loophole exempts your foreign-earned income from tax, but it doesn't exempt you from the filing requirement.

3. **Beware of those other taxes.** This is the disappointing part of the $70,000 exclusion; it applies only to federal income taxes. The social security tax might still apply to salaried employees, and the self-employment tax might still apply to self-employed individuals. Again, you'd be wise to consult a professional who can discuss any exemptions that could possibly apply to you here.

I mentioned earlier that savvy taxpayers can expand the loophole and exempt more than the $70,000 per individual. In many situations, you can exclude or deduct foreign housing costs. You have a choice; you may either deduct your housing costs to the extent that they exceed a base amount, or, if your employer reimburses you for the excess, the reimbursement can be excluded from income. To get the write-off or exclusion, you must meet the same tests as for the foreign-earned income exclusion—which means either establishing a foreign residence or meeting the physical-presence test, as well as establishing a foreign tax home.

Here again, I'd advise you to consult a professional to help you maneuver through the details, particularly since tax laws are always changing. To get a head start, however, I do suggest you refer to Mr. Starchild's complete report on the World Wide Web. Not only will you find information about still more loopholes, but the author discusses the benefits of several overseas tax havens. (The Web address for this report is listed in the footnote at the beginning of this section.)

Don't Take Foolish Chances

While the $70k exclusion plan is a great help for many people, it's obviously not for everyone. What if you want to—shall we say—keep a lower financial profile? Which brings us back to our original question: How do you move your money safely, and keep it hidden once it's moved?

Okay, first things first. There are a lot of wrong ways to move your money—in other words, ways that might get you caught, in which case your cash will be seized and you may be fined or put in jail. The first rule is: *Don't take any foolish chances.*

Let's say you're in an airport, and you hear an announcement over the airport's PA system about the illegality of carrying more than $10,000 in cash outside of the United States without declaring this money. Wake up and smell the coffee, pal. If you hear the bell toll, and it tolls for you, turn around and go home, and find some other way and some other day to move your money and yourself. Don't push your luck and hope they are looking for someone else on that day.

Here's a secret: Everyone thinks that their ideas are original and that they have figured out the ultimate way to hide their money. They don't realize that with millions of people trying to do the same thing, investigators have pretty much figured out every single possible way to smuggle money or valuables out of the country.

To give you a little global perspective, in my life in the business, I have seen at least a hundred different ways people try to get money out of their home countries. People fleeing South Africa, for example, convert their worldly possessions to jewels and take them out through their children's teddy bears. East Indians place their faith in gold and smuggle it out inside the life preservers worn aboard ships, taking them to foreign ports. Americans tend to do it with a little more technology, sending cash and negotiable financial instruments overseas through Federal Express envelopes and wire transfers.

My point is this: be aware that investigators who have been around awhile have seen and know every trick in the book. Charles learned this lesson the hard way.

Tanks for Nothing

Charles was an accountant with a small but prosperous CPA practice in a small but prosperous bedroom community, taking care of the financial affairs of attorneys, doctors, and other self-employed professionals. His clients saw their businesses and profits expand as the community grew, but they went ballistic when they saw that their taxes grew faster than their income as the years went by.

Charles, seeing their predicament and recognizing an opportunity, went to his clients with a brilliant idea. "When you take in cash in your business, as you do on occasion," said Charles, "put it in an envelope and give it to me. I'll take the money to the Cayman Islands and deposit it in an account for you that will grow and provide a substantial nest-egg when you're ready to sell your practice and retire." As you might imagine, he had a lot of takers. Each month, Charles collected his clients' cash, gave them a receipt, disappeared for a few days, and returned with a smile.

Charles' modus operandi was to pack up his scuba tanks and take his wife and children on a diving trip to the Cayman Islands every month after the money was collected from his clients. Like a good accountant, and just like clockwork, Charles followed his plan and deposited hundreds of thousands of dollars in the bank for his clients, taking a modest ten percent for himself.

Little did Charles know, however, that the U.S. Customs computer spotted his travel pattern and provided the clues the government needed to piece together his plan. Figuring out what he was up to wasn't exactly rocket science. If you were an investigator, and records showed that a certain individual went on a scuba diving trip to the same island every month, that he was employed in an industry handling other people's money, and that his income did not continue to rise as the general income of his community grew—well, wouldn't you be a bit suspicious?

So where was Charles hiding the money? You got it, in the scuba tanks. Customs officials knew that divers normally do not bring scuba tanks with them on flights because tanks are pressurized, and besides that, they are too bulky and heavy to lug around. Most divers rent their tanks at their ultimate diving destination. The fact that Charles always brought his with him was a big red flag and was his undoing.

A little judicious sawing on the tanks revealed the envelopes of money with each of the client's names and amounts of cash written on the envelope. Charles was then given the government's version of the Mafia's offer—you know, the deal you shouldn't refuse. He had the choice of being a witness or a co-defendant in a RICO (Racketeering Influenced and Corrupt Organizations) case. Which deal do you think he took, and who did the time in the slammer?

Dealing for Dollars

Now, before we get into the specifics about your money, I want to talk a little about money in general—specifically, United States currency. An ever-increasing proportion of U.S. currency is being held outside the country by people who are uncertain about the future value of their own currency. Not all of these people are participants of the underground economy—drug dealers and the like—not by a long shot.

Overall, the good old U.S. dollar is a refuge during times of political and economic insecurity. It is a relatively stable source of purchasing power, it's widely accepted, and it is at least reasonably secure from counterfeiting. And unlike some other currencies, which may be re-called with little notice or limited opportunities for exchange, Federal Reserve Notes are ultimately exchangeable at full face value, regardless of when they were issued. Furthermore, currency is much more portable and less cumbersome than, say gold. This provides many advantages, for example, in countries with unstable political climates. The dollar offers a form of wealth that can be stashed in a suitcase and carried if the resident needs to flee. And currency affords at least a degree of anonymity for its holder, because shipments of less than $10,000 do not have to be reported to Customs. (The anonymity factor may not survive Big Brother's devious plans, however, as we'll see in a moment.)

While it is impossible to know the exact figures, it's estimated that since 1988, about 30 percent of U.S. currency sent overseas has gone to the Middle East and Far East, and around 20 percent has gone to Central and South America, with a substantial amount appearing in Argentina.[2] And nearly half has gone to Europe, with Russia the most likely destination.

Russia has an especially large demand for U.S. currency—particularly the newly designed hundred-dollar bill—because it is such a solid hedge against the enormous inflation of rubles. In addition, counterfeiting and bank fraud are so prevalent in the former USSR right now that the one-hundred-dollar bill is the only medium of exchange many people will take.

One of my clients has leased a space exhibit from officials of the former Russian government, and twice yearly he has to bring them the proceeds of their income. So twice a year, he and I go to the bank and draw out $500,000 to one million in brand new C-notes. The money

---

2 See Richard D. Porter and Ruth A. Judson, "The Location of U.S. Currency: How Much Is Abroad?" Board of Governors of the Federal Reserve System, manuscript, June 1995. Note: The figures from the Porter and Judson manuscript, as well as much of the information in this section, are from an article entitled, "Where Is All the U.S. Currency Hiding?" by John B. Carlson and Benjamin D. Keen, April 15, 1996.

is then split into equal carrying bags for each of the three or four commissars, and taken aboard the next jet to Moscow, where it is hand-delivered to its ultimate recipients. They don't want cashier's checks, they don't want credit cards, they just want those brand new hundred dollar bills.

Cash a Falling Star

Despite its many advantages, currency still has its drawbacks. Drug dealers who smuggle cocaine into the United States are finding this out, as they're having an increasing problem trying to get their cash out of the country. (You see, one kilo of cocaine generates at least five pounds of cash, even in one hundred dollar bills.) Dealers are learning that the more successful you are—the more money you make—the harder it is to hide and launder those ill-gotten gains.

For one thing, bank regulators are on the lookout for banks that suddenly increase their purchases of brand new hundred dollar bills. The regulators in the FDIC know that this is a clear warning sign that drug money has come into the neighborhood, especially when those quaint little country banks suddenly buy big stacks of new C-notes.

There's a real possibility that currency may ultimately lose most of its anonymity appeal too. Let's begin with the ongoing art project by the U.S. Treasury and Federal Reserve: the re-design of U.S. greenbacks. The overhaul has already begun with the new one-hundred-dollar bills, since these bills are most in demand world-wide, and therefore a favorite target among counterfeiters. The plan is to introduce new designs for each denomination at the rate of one denomination per year.

In many countries, the old currency becomes worthless when new currency is issued. Therefore, one has to exchange all the old bills for new by a certain deadline. However, the government has announced that there is no plan to do this with U.S. currency. The rationale is twofold: to avoid disturbing foreign economies, and to protect the special anonymity feature of the dollar. (Wait a minute. Uncle Sam wants to help preserve the privacy of ordinary folks like you and me? Something doesn't compute here.) Anyway, for now, let's say "old money" is still relatively anonymous.

But what about the new stuff that will gradually replace it? Many changes have been incorporated with the new currency designs, some obvious and some quite subtle—but what really scares a lot of people is the little Mylar strip in the new hundred-dollar bills. The alleged purpose of this strip is to aid in the detection of counterfeiting, but unless you believe in Mother Goose and the Tooth Fairy, I don't think you are going to buy the story that this is all the little Mylar strip is going to do. It's alleged that this strip is encoded to provide for more information than just the identification of the currency. If that doesn't make you jumpy, read on.

Remember what we just said about there being no plans for mandatory currency exchange in the United States? Well, despite our benevolent Uncle's promises, there may very well be an exchange plan in the future anyway. Since the early seventies, various proposals have been made by different agencies for a two-tiered U.S. currency.[3] When such a proposal was first rumored, around 1970 or so, it was dismissed as a paranoid fantasy.

Paranoid or not, it was one of those ideas that just wouldn't die, and in 1994 the *Washington Post* reported a plan suggested by an "expert on terrorism" for two separate U.S. currencies: new "greenbacks" for domestic use, and new "redbacks" for overseas use. The International Counterfeit Deterrence Strike Force, informally known as "The Super-Bill Committee," supports a revived 1989 DEA scheme for the forced conversion of "domestic" dollars into "international" bucks by U.S. travelers at the border. These would then be re-exchanged upon their return. Senator Patrick Leahy (D.VT) has introduced bills to enact such a plan.

It's possible that the newly designed U.S. currency, with all its added security measures, will quell the two-tiered advocates for the time being, but keep your eye on this issue anyway. There seems to be no end to what the powers-that-be are willing to do under the guise of the battle against counterfeiting and, of course, the ever-popular war on drugs.

Welcome to the Future

So what do you do when cash is no longer king? Well, in the world of the future, which began yesterday, we will have virtual bank-

---

3 "The End of Ordinary Money" by J. Orlin Grabbe, Liberty, Vol. 8, Number 6, July 1995, pp. 32–42. This article is also available on the Internet at www.vanbc.wimsey.com/~sage/snn/ z-files/zmoney1.html

ing. For starters, there's an international debit card that lets you maintain a bank account in a protected third-world financial center. With this deal you get a credit card giving you access to your money anywhere in the world—without leaving a "financial footprint" or record anywhere but at the point of sale and the home of the host bank.

Imagine my surprise one day when I opened an airline magazine and saw that American Airlines and Barclays Bank were teaming up to offer American's "high flyers" a deal they couldn't refuse. The offer was for an international debit card based on a London bank that provided a depository account in the Channel Islands, giving withdrawal privileges at any Visa or MasterCard center in the world. With this account and card, anyone could withdraw money at an ATM, make any charge purchases at a retail store, or access their money in one of a dozen other ways without creating any records except at the point of sale and at the host banking company in the Channel Islands.

With an account of this type, which is now freely available through many of the world's entrepreneurial banks, you can have instant access to your money without providing a direct trail to your banking records. Unless the investigative agency was able to document an MLAT[4] request, your money, your records, and your financial privacy would be assured.

A word of warning, though: there may be trouble in paradise, at least in the Isle of Man, the Channel Islands and other British financial havens. Lately the U.S. government has been putting increasing pressure on institutions such as Barclays and Lloyds.[5] Why? Simple: these banks are subject to British banking laws with their attendant secrecy requirements. This is driving Uncle Sam to distraction because he can't get his hands on the hundreds of millions of dollars held in these institutions by U.S. citizens. In a recent edition of the *PrivacyInc Newsletter,* Bill Hill writes about the presence of "plants" in the banks—tellers and clerks that are in fact spies for the U.S. government. These spies

---

4 MLAT, as you may recall from the previous chapter, stands for Mutual Legal Assistance Treaty, which says your banker has to show your records to the government if the government thinks there's a chance your money is drug-related.

5 "A Warning from Bill Hill," in The *PrivacyInc Newsletter,* April 1997. See Resource List at back of this book for subscription information.

allegedly go through account details and transfers in the dead of night, and report their findings back to their bosses at the IRS.

Up till now, however, Big Brother hasn't been able to do much except stew about the situation. However, U.K. banks must use the U.S. banking system to clear the dollar transactions through, and this, according to Hill, is where the U.S. government is making its latest stand. Uncle Sam is now trying to pressure British banks into adopting American banking laws, or they can't use the American banking system. Basically what this means is that the British bankers have to become tattletales or be left holding large dollar values on their books that they cannot clear. Since their laws forbid revealing information on their customers, their only other alternative, if the pressure continues, will be to close out the dollar accounts. The money will be sent back to the citizens' accounts in the United States, just where the IRS wants it. If the accountholder doesn't have a valid explanation for the origin of that cash, then all of his or her U.S. accounts will be frozen. It's all in the name of fighting money laundering, of course.

Though this hasn't happened yet, it may happen soon. What can the holders of the targeted offshore dollar checking accounts do? PrivacyInc suggests diversifying into Swiss Franc and assorted EU currencies (e.g., Spain and Portugal). Of course, in the next few years even this advice may have to be revised, as Europe moves towards a common currency. . . . Oh, but that's a whole separate topic. We'll talk more about world currency markets in a little while.

The good news is that despite this little snag, it is still possible to obtain a secure international debit card. Find yourself a good international tax attorney who keeps current on these matters. There are also several websites that can point you in the right direction (see the appendices of this book), such as Universal Corporate Services' "Offshore Banking Options" web page at www.skysurf.com/ucs/bank.htm.

Caveat Expat

Moving money clandestinely has become more tricky since the mid-1980s, ever since the government decided to get tough on money laundering. But just what is money laundering? In an October 1984 report from the President's Commission on Organized Crime, money laundering was defined as the "process by which one conceals the existence, illegal source, or illegal application of income, and then disguises that income to make it appear "legitimate." J. Orlin Grabbe wrote, "Note the word 'existence.' The sentence could be construed to mean that simply disguising the existence of income is money laundering."[6]

By that definition, if you've ever under-reported on your tax return at all, even by a couple of dollars, you're a money launderer. Shame on you. Well, whatever money laundering is in theory—and we could argue semantics all day—in practice, U.S. law attempts to detect it through the mandatory reporting of cash transactions of $10,000 US or more (with a new exception for wire-transfer services such as Western Union; see below). For countries in Europe, the figure ranges from ECU 7,200 to 16,000.

Here's the bottom line, according to Grabbe: "Anyone who has studied the evolution of money-laundering statutes in the U.S. and elsewhere will realize that the 'crime' of money laundering boils down to a single, basic prohibited act. *Doing something and not telling the government about it.*"[7] While the money-laundering laws supposedly exist to fight drugs and terrorism, many insiders say that it's really all about revenue gathering. In other words, governments want money, and they're going to grab all they can, by force if necessary. We'll harp on that some more in a little while, when we discuss FinCEN.

As you might imagine, Uncle Sam is on the front line of the war against money laundering, and accordingly, there's a formidable array of laws on the U.S. books. Consider, for example, Title XV of the Housing and Community Development Act of 1992. Title XV contains the *Annunzio-Wylie Anti-Money-Laundering Act*, a law whose many provisions include a stipulation that all financial institutions—including banks, savings and loans, credit unions, and even stockbrokers—must implement a "know-your-customer" policy. In his book, *Vendetta: American Express and the Smearing of Edmond Safra* (HarperCollins, 1992), Bryan Burrough writes that what this really means is that "banks must know not only their customers, but their customers' customers, and in many cases their customers' customers' customers." Whew.

The Annunzio-Wylie Act and related acts have effectively gutted legislation such as the Right to Financial Privacy Act of 1978. Now banks

---

6 "The End of Ordinary Money," Part II by J. Orlin Grabbe. Available on the Internet at www.vanbc.wimsey.com/~sage/snn/z-files/zmoney2.html.
7 *Ibid.*

are required to document both sides of financial transactions that involve money leaving the country. The financial institution must require identifying information on the sender of the funds, and also on the recipient if the transaction is $10,000 or more, or if it is any way "suspicious."

The Annunzio-Wylie Act also contains a number of significant amendments to the ironically named Bank Secrecy Act (can you say, "doublespeak," boys and girls?), which—and here I quote from Federal Reserve System Docket NO. R–0888—"authorizes the Secretary of the Treasury to require financial institutions to keep records and file reports that the Secretary determines have a high degree of usefulness in criminal, tax, or regulatory investigations or proceedings." I could go on for pages and pages (*they* sure do), but let me just say now that one of the provisions of this Act is the requirement for a Currency Transaction Report, or CTR, to be filed each time you enact any cash-related transaction of $10,000 or more in a financial institution since the institution of this Act.

In other words, to quote J. Orlin Grabbe, "Beware of your banker; by law he's a snitch."[8] Regulators have been given the authority to require the reporting of any transaction of $3000 or more (on a regional basis), just to catch those people who try to skate under the $10,000 transaction guideline by hiding their ill-gotten gains through a process called "smurfing."

A Few Words About FinCEN

In Chapter 4, I promised I'd tell you about FinCEN, the Financial Crime Enforcement Network. FinCEN was established by the U.S. Department of Treasury as the result of an Executive Order dated April 25, 1990. Though FinCEN was born in the midst of President Bush's War on Drugs (okay, stop snickering), its work is not limited to narcotics intelligence. FinCEN's mission is to provide "a government-wide, multi-source intelligence and analytical network to support law enforcement and regulatory agencies in the detection, investigation, and prosecution of financial crimes."[9]

Why was FinCEN *really* created? Let's look at this from two perspectives. First, the Gospel According to the Treasury Department.

---

8 "The End of Ordinary Money" by J. Orlin Grabbe.
9 *Asset Forfeiture News*, Nov./Dec. 1991

"In order to fully comprehend the important role FinCEN plays in law enforcement, it is first necessary to understand the significance of financial crimes and, in particular, the process by which illegal proceeds are laundered. With the possible exception of crimes of passion and certain violent crimes, all criminal acts are committed for one reason—profit.

Since the profit motive is the driving force behind most criminal activity, the identification, seizure, and forfeiture of the profits or proceeds generated by the criminal activity is one of the keys to the disruption and ultimate cessation of a particular criminal activity.

Normally, the greater the profit, the more sophisticated the financial manipulations necessary to conceal the roots of the profit. Therefore, the profit, usually in the form of currency, becomes a vulnerable point for law enforcement agencies to focus upon."[10]

And now here's a viewpoint—not necessarily contradictory to the one you just read—quoted from the opinionated J. Orlin Grabbe:

Since the governmental powers that be can't do much about drug dealing or terrorism—if only because they themselves are the chief drug dealers and the chief terrorists—they have transferred these and other (often alleged) sins to the money supply. And since every dollar is a potential "narco" dollar or "terror" dollar, they must track each one as best they can. The fact that monetary monitoring has done nothing to diminish either drug dealing or terrorism is treated of no importance, because it's all part of a larger game. All the players can easily see that this same financial tracking yields political side benefits in the form of social control and government revenue enhancement.[11]

Hmmm. Who do you believe? Gives you something to think about, doesn't it?

FinCEN is everywhere. Though FinCEN uses information from many databases in its analytical work, the most significant is the Financial Database. The information in this data base is taken from reports that are required to be filed in accordance with the Bank Secrecy Act, such as:

---

10 *Ibid.*
11 J. Orlin Grabbe, "The End of Ordinary Money," Part II.

- Currency Transaction Reports (CTRs) (IRS form 4789)
- Reports of International Transportation of Currency or Monetary Instruments (CMIR) (Customs form 4790)
- Currency Transaction Reports by Casinos (CTRC) (IRS form 8362)
- Reports of Foreign Bank and Financial Accounts (FBAR) (Treasury form TDR 90–22–1)
- IRS form 8300, reporting business transactions involving more than $10,000 cash

FinCEN uses a multitude of other databases, with more being added to the system all the time. It also maintains its own database to log, profile and track inquiries made to FinCEN. This database was specifically designed to be shared with other agencies (like the FBI, IRS, and the DEA). As I've said before, there's an incestuous relationship among government agencies. And the reason why I have gone, and will continue to go, into so much detail on these matters is to reinforce my caveat: You can't be too careful, because even if Big Brother isn't specifically watching you, more than likely, he's on the lookout for you and your profile.

The Future That's Not Quite Here: Anonymous Digital Cash

It is very easy to get dismayed about the Orwellian nightmare that seems to be unfolding before our very eyes. Technology is, indeed, a two-edged sword. There's just too much information out there to keep in a bottle, and too many ways that information can be used against a person.

But information technology doesn't necessarily have to be our enemy. All of the Big Brotherly doings—the legal reporting, the spying mechanisms, and myriad activities of agencies such as FinCEN—fly in the face of a contrary technological and social development: *anonymous digital cash made possible by advances in cryptology.* The line in the sand has been drawn. Grabbe says, "The edicts against money-laundering represent a broader attempt to make all financial transactions transparent, while the aim of anonymous digital cash is to keep financial activities private."[12]

---

12 J. Orlin Grabbe, "The End of Ordinary Money," Part II.

Perhaps Grabbe is overly optimistic, but he believes that in the end, we'll win out over Big Brother. At least in theory, advances in the technology of anonymity are putting financial privacy within the reach of everybody. Add to this the growing awareness by the citizenry that existing laundering laws are having little or no effect on terrorism or drug dealing, and we just might have ourselves the makings of a peaceful revolution.

In "The End of Ordinary Money," Part II, Grabbe goes into some detail about the logistics of a digital cash system. There's no room to go into all of it here (and some of the information is both boring and technical)—but in a nutshell, the system he envisions is based on the use of *smart cards*, which contain microprocessors capable of retaining huge amounts of information. Of course there has been some controversy about smart cards too, as they could easily be used for general surveillance and social control—but again, the technology doesn't *have* to be used like that but it just works out that way, every time.

After all, there is nothing intrinsically evil or Orwellian about storing large amounts of information about ourselves. Isn't that why some of us carry around portable computers or have grocery store smart cards that tell what we eat and drink and give us airline point for the privilege? The key is that the use of these computer systems is *voluntary*. We ourselves allow or control the access to, and the content of, the information (though of course there is the danger that the information can be hacked, or stolen). Grabbe believes that smart cards can truly allow financial privacy through cryptology. It's simply a matter of our taking control of the technology and using it to enhance personal liberty rather than giving it to the government and the mega credit bureaus.

Now, this is not to say that Big Brother and other governments won't be rushing to make amendments to existing statutes, in order to apply the same reporting requirements to anonymous transactions as to normal ones. But such laws will probably generate little compliance, and since the transactions in question will be unconditionally untraceable, there won't be evidence of any wrongdoing.

Oh, and just in case you're curious, the anonymous cash system would not replace, but would exist parallel to, the present monetary system. Therefore a floating exchange rate would be created by market transactions between ordinary money and anonymous money.

In the best of all possible worlds, anonymous digital cash would be untraceable, yet at the same time would enable you to prove unequivocally whether or not you made a particular payment. Does this all sound to good to be true? Hey, it could happen. The technology is there, or almost there. Keep an eye on this development. But meanwhile, back to the present. . . .

The wonders of the Internet combined with the advent of new encryption algorithms makes it possible to conduct virtual banking outside the nine dots. I have recently run into several of my old cohorts who have moved to Grand Cayman and set up a trading company that allows its customers to buy, sell and trade stocks, bonds and futures over the Internet, without clearing through a U.S. brokerage house or appearing on the scope of the SEC and NASD.

Is There a Safe Way *Now* to Take the Money and Run?

I may have been sounding like a broken record as I've repeated what has become the theme song of the justifiably paranoid. *You can run, but it's getting harder and harder to hide.* So now that you have a few dozen more reasons to be paranoid—and since we've not quite entered the era of anonymous digital cash—you are no doubt wondering: How *do* you protect or move your money safely and secretly, in or out of the country?

Getting your money out of the country is always the hardest part. Once this is done, the rest is easy, that is, unless you slip up in some other way and get caught by bringing it back into the United States In fact, that is how most criminals get caught through the process of bringing the money home, usually through wire transfers, money laundering or smuggling.

At one time it was very common for sophisticated businessmen, especially those who often were trying to hide their assets from spouses rather than from the government, to send money out of the country through a system of wire transfers into personal accounts or foreign business entities that they controlled. Every Friday they would tally up their proceeds and send the profits out of town through the purchase of cashiers' checks, money orders, or by a wire transfer to a foreign account. That way they knew their spouse or a shyster lawyer couldn't get the foreign bank records that documented the recipient of the funds or the name on the account in a foreign country.

The Annunzio-Wylie act (see above) put an end to that. But even with the eagle eye of Big Brother, it is, in fact, still possible to hide it all and keep it hidden. On the next few pages we'll take a look at what savvy money movers can do while they're waiting for virtual banking and the anonymous digital cash revolution.

Banking on the Run

For the Perpetual Traveler (P.T.) on the go, there is literally a world of banking and financial resources available. Today's online, offshore banks offer depository services, checking accounts, credit cards, brokerage services, and trust facilities to meet your every whim and desire.

Not only do these companies offer a wide array of professional services (for a small fee); they have situated their branch offices in all of the financial privacy centers of the modern world, many of which are just the places that we have been talking about.

Tax Havens

Many of the world's private safes and tax havens are located on islands. Why, because they need to bring in money to support their country and its residents, and there is no better way to bring in capital than to offer it protection from the money grubbing big governments of the world.

When countries like Great Britain, Germany, and the United States tax their citizens and businesses to the point where its impossible to get ahead, the smart money and its owners get the hell out of Dodge! (We talked about this earlier.) If we followed through with the tax reform, especially with the idea of the 10 percent flat tax propounded by several of our forward thinking senators, much of the money now going out the door would stay at home. But, since we refuse to face the prospect of less government spending and a balanced budget, the money will continue to pour into these little island paradises that open their arms to everyone and anyone with a buck.

The list of these wonderful little tax havens spans the globe. Here is a few of them for your future deliberation.

Switzerland: After all the bad press, still one of the safe and secure places to stash wealth. Their only problems are that they signed the

MLAT and their passport stamp is a dead giveaway for financial investigators, plus, they don't pay interest.

Luxembourg: A well known tax free European Union (EU) member that has been stealing depositors from Switzerland. A possible problem is if the EU moves to limit banking secrecy and coordinates taxation.

Channel Islands: (Guernsey and Jersey) *The* financial center of Western Europe, but its getting too popular. The minimum required to open an account here has been raised to $100,000.

Isle of Man: Another U.K. financial center offering bank secrecy, tax protection and you can even vacation there! My best choice for doing business in the European theater.

Bermuda: The home of choice for the Hong Kong and Far East expats. They have voted to stay under British rule and stiffened privacy laws to bring in the money from people like our own Carl Ichan.

Cayman Islands: With over 460 banks and more money than Croesus ($412 billion at last count) combined with no taxation, this has been the star of the west for years. The only drawback is that this is where the Feds will look for you first, particularly if you are into white collar crime or drugs.

Netherland Antilles: An alternative to the Caymans, many of the big German and Dutch banks have branch offices here. And when the government comes, "We know nothing, we know nothing."

Turks and Caicos: The true gem of the Bahamas, both for vacationing and depositing your nest egg. And, it hasn't really been discovered yet!

Macao: This legendary island of intrigue is updating its facilities and image, hoping to become *the* pearl of the Orient. It comes under Chinese rule in a year, so think about this one, hmmmmm!

Mauritius: Another island Paradise, in the middle of the Indian Ocean, yet! Great vacationing and world class fishing add to the developing international banking community growing there.

Nauru: A rock in the middle of the Pacific, covered with bird doo! Every phony business deal in the world seems to use this as its banking cover. Forget it!

For the newly anointed P.T., I would highly recommend the more well established and secure banks, such as Barclays, ScotiaBank, Canadian Imperial Bank of Commerce, Credit Suiss, and Standard

Bank as your bank of choice, at least until you learn a little more about the local banking scene.

The Brits have long been known for their banking savvy and their protection of their clients information. Not having enough business in their homelands, the bankers of Britain, Scotland, and Canada have expanded into the Channel Islands, the Caymans, the Turks and Caicos, Latin America, and the Pacific Rim with their full range of well known private banking operations.

When you are ready to venture out on your own, you can find all the information you want, right at your fingertips. If you go to the friendly, neighborhood Internet, you will find a world of banks, trust companies, and service providers willing to help you make your money disappear into thin air. The only problem is that some of them will make it disappear *too* well, either by making off with your deposits or charging you fees ranging from $300 to $3,000, just to set up a bank account and secure credit card and that doesn't include the minimum $5,000 deposit required by most financial institutions.

Until you learn the ropes a little, stick to the big boys who have been doing this for years. Once you get to know the territory a little and make personal contact with a banker that fits your plans, then you can make the switch to a quieter, less well known depository of the golden egg. Go ahead, read all of that cryptic stuff on the Internet, but take most of it with a grain of salt, at least until you have a chance to get a little experience under your belt with the banking community.

For many years, one of the best known and respected bankers in the Caymans has been Clive Munyard, the manager of Barclays Bank, Grand Cayman. Clive not only takes care of his clients' money, but lines them up with a full range of recreational services, including the use of a 54-foot fishing yacht that has caught more marlin than God allows. Clive's clients include many of the former Savings and Loan bandits as well as a host of attorneys who make a living making their client's money vanish into thin air.

Wire Transfers

In May 1997 the Clinton administration announced new rules on wire transfer reporting. Under these new rules, street-corner check-cashing services, as well as large money-transmittal services such as Western Union and American Express, would be required to file reports with the Treasury Department on *wire transfers outside the U.S. of more than $750*. The reports would—you guessed it—include basic information about the sender. This is a dramatic change from the previous requirements, which demanded a report only if the transfer was for more than $10,000.

Full-service banks are exempted from this new requirement, although of course they still must file reports of international transactions exceeding $10,000.

As you might expect, the stated purpose of the revised rules is to make it far more difficult for drug cartels to move their profits from the United States to Colombia and other drug centers in Latin America. There's no denying that drug profits are huge. According to a *New York Times* story, intelligence reports suggested that in New York City alone, wire-transmittal services moved more than $1 billion in drug money a year to Latin America, chiefly to Colombia. The money was moved in increments of just under $10,000 to skirt the reporting requirements. However, law enforcement officials say that after New York City implemented a $750 limit, the cartel's money-wiring business in the city virtually dried up. This makes sense; after all, it's much more of a burden to divide a $1 million payment into $750 chunks than to divvy it up in increments of $10,000.

Organized crime and drug cartels aren't the only organizations who will be inconvenienced by this new rule, however. The wire services themselves, as well as government staffers who process the reports, face a paperwork nightmare. And yet, in the classic pattern of reaction to government intimidation, the members of the Non-Bank Funds Transmitters Group which includes Western Union, American Express, Thomas Cook Inc., and the like—are complying with a minimum of protest. It seems they are *very* eager to show Uncle Sam that they are not laundering drug money.

So what do the new rules on wire-transferring mean for you? Well, my friend, it means that you have to report all financial transactions that involve the transfer of funds or other financial instruments and transactions that go out of the country, based on the reporting act requirements for those transactions, if you want to stay in the good graces of the law.

9

How the Pros Will Look For You: To Beat Them, Think Like a Detective

How badly does someone want you back? Do they want your carcass or your money? Are you avoiding the law, a spouse, or creditors or do you just want to get the hell out of Dodge? In Chapter 2 we asked you to consider this issue in order to help you decide where you want to go. But it's also a factor to think about after you've bugged out, so you can determine if someone is going to look for you and how hard they are going to try. That way, you can take appropriate measures to make sure they don't succeed.

Obviously, if you have done something that has serious criminal implications, the victim's family and possibly even the government will want to track you down to the ends of the earth. If you make it easy for them, they just might catch you. The solution is simple: don't make it easy for them.

But that's easier said than done. In this chapter, I'll give you information that I hope will help you learn to think like an investigator. This will make it easier for you to stay one step (or more) ahead of those who may be looking for you. Who knows, one of them might even be me!

Don't Get Careless Now

First of all, at the risk of sounding like a nag, I'm going to throw some more caveats your way regarding the many mistakes you can make; mistakes that can prove fatal to your carefully crafted new life. We've discussed some of these items in previous chapters, but I'm repeating them here—not just to stress their importance, but to place them in the context of the investigative process. Investigators thrive on information, and this is some of the information they can and will use to hunt you down.

The Telephone.

Don't be like E.T.; *don't* phone home. If you call your parents on their birthdays, Mother's Day, Father's Day, Thanksgiving, Christmas, Hanukkah, etc., their telephone traffic may well be monitored to reveal your whereabouts. We investigators live for holidays such as these, because we know the power of family ties. We know that even the most hard-nosed fugitive has a sentimental streak and will keep in touch with his or her family. My advice is to keep the sentiment to yourself. If you call your girlfriend on Valentine's Day or your daughter on her birthday (and rest assured that a savvy investigator will know the birth dates of all those near and dear to you), your ass is grass if someone really wants you.

Oh, and don't think you're safe if you phone home when you're *away* from home. A lot of things can give you away, but none more thoroughly than your hotel long distance phone bill. These things can get you in more trouble than you can ever imagine.

Think about it. What do you do when you check into a hotel? You eat dinner in a restaurant, have a few drinks in the bar, go up to your room, watch a little television, and then make a few phone calls. Investigators know this drill well; in fact, you may be interested in knowing that more cheating spouses get caught through a little judicious investigation of their hotel phone bills than by any other method.[1] Consider, for example, this typical phone-call sequence for the traveling business person who's engaged in extramarital activities:

Call number one: *"Hello, baby . . . I love you, I need you, I want you, I miss you. I'll see you tomorrow night. God, I can't wait!"*

---

1 Well, with the possible exception of the cellular phone. Those car phones can get you in a heap of trouble too; they're an eavesdropper's wet dream. In the case of the cheating spouse, guess who the first call is made to on the way to work, and the last one made on the way home every single day?

Call number two: *"Hello, honey. I'm beat, I'm whipped, I'm tired. I'll be home in three days. Give the kids a hug for me."*

It's pretty easy to guess who those calls were made to: first the lover, and then the spouse.

When you travel out of the country, it gets even worse. Not only do you make phone calls to your secret lover if you have one, but if you're like most people, you'll use the phone to set up business appointments with attorneys, bankers, and other financial contacts. Your Cayman Island or Swiss phone bill is the surest way for investigators to track down bank accounts and business contacts in a foreign port and it lets them zero in on your most private moments; without you ever knowing that they were there.

A perfect example of how your hotel phone bills can trip you up is found in the case of a man we'll call Roger.

Roger was a brilliant businessman who recognized the savings and loan debacle as a way to make millions of dollars through OPM (Other People's Money). He purchased two S&Ls in the southwestern United States, placing his high school friends on the boards as presidents and filling the directorships with his cronies and borrowers. Over the years, he looted $25 million from his own institutions, as well as from other lenders who participated in real estate deals with his savings and loans. These deals were designed to fail and to make money only for their borrowers.

When the gravy train got derailed and the regulators moved in, Roger moved the money from his 90-plus corporations to Switzerland and the Cayman Islands, thinking that his convoluted trail of financial transactions could not be discovered. What he didn't realize is that he had left a paper trail through his corporations, bank accounts, and credit cards, which identified his travel to Switzerland and his stay at the Hotel Beau Rivage, one of Geneva's finest hotels. And while his financial information was still private in Switzerland, his hotel records were not.

Interpol investigators obtained copies of the hotel bills, which showed phone calls to both his lawyer and the bank that was the recipient of his $25 million. These bills created a clear paper trail that the jury ultimately was able to follow both to the money and to Roger's conspiracy—which led to a fraud conviction and an all-expense-paid trip to Club Fed.

The moral of the story is, don't make phone calls from your hotel room. If you have to make calls, use the lobby pay phones and bring lots of quarters or pre-paid phone cards, which can be bought at your friendly neighborhood Wal-Mart or grocery store. Don't make the mistake of charging them to your personal telephone credit card, because that can be traced as well.

Of course, if you're really trying to hide, if you've truly left your old life behind and are serious about starting anew, here's the bottom line. Don't call your parents, kids, sweethearts, or anyone else who was part of your old life. Whether it's a major holiday or not, and whether you're calling from your new home or a luxury hotel on some remote island paradise, calling *anyone at any time* to let them know you're alive and well in Costa Rica (or wherever you are) is just asking for trouble.

Subscriptions and Mail Orders

If you subscribe to catalogues and magazines, or if you're in the habit of making purchases via mail order, end your subscriptions and stop the mail orders before you bug out, and then subscribe or order later through your new identity. Even then, however, you should exercise caution, at least if the subscriptions or orders reflect a fairly uncommon or highly specialized interest. If you happen to be one of seven people in the world who are avid collectors of pre-Colombian transistor radios, you are strongly advised against subscribing to newsletters and catalogs which cater to that specialized interest, because you'd better believe that someone like me will be watching!

Robb Report

It is a little known fact that the IRS winkles out many a money launderer or dope dealer by finding their subscriptions to the Robb Report. By comparing the names of the IRS most wanted to the marketing list of this magazine made for the cash and carry trade, the service has sneaked up on several big time bad boys.

Years ago, one of my assistants opened her big mouth one day and said that she had learned all of my tricks about ferreting out those who try to hide it all and disappear. "If I ever leave you," she said, "you'll never be able to find me." *Hah!!!*

She neglected to consider her Achilles heel, which happened to be the Franklin Mint and other such purveyors of "collectibles." This woman has probably ordered every Elvis plate, heartwarming baby-animal sculpture, and special-edition Barbie doll ever made. And even though she's no longer working for me, word has it that she's still ordering those kitschy heirlooms. I could easily trace her whereabouts just by following the mailing labels or the credit card trail. Unless she radically changed her purchasing habits, finding her if she chose to bug out would be as easy as finding a velvet Elvis painting in the souvenir shop at Graceland. Gotcha!

Sports and Hobbies

These two can really blow your cover, particularly if you belong to a league or association of any kind. Consider the tale of Georgie, who wasn't exactly trying to hide himself, but he *was* hiding some pertinent information.

Georgie was a professional plaintiff; perhaps you know somebody like him. These folks make their living by having accidents, and collecting from insurance companies, on a regular basis. They'll work at a company for a few weeks or months, fall down the stairs when no one is looking, and milk the insurance company for all it is worth.

Georgie had gotten away with this for years, but, as most overly-successful people do, he got sloppy in his old age. He pulled an insurance scam on one of Hartford's finest, claiming that his latest injury had ruptured a disk in his back, and had torn ligaments in his groin to a point that it was impossible for him to work or play.

His performance before the jury was magnificent. He told them all about how he could no longer be the father his son needed, how they couldn't go camping, couldn't build fires in the moonlight, and couldn't bond as father and son in the great outdoors. The jury cried with Georgie as he told them about his fears for his son's future in a world where men were men.

What Georgie didn't tell the jury was that he was a bowling addict, and he liked to sneak out every Thursday night to bowl in a league 40 miles from his home. Imagine, then, the surprise on Georgie's face—and the thud in the heart of his lawyer—when the insurance company put the custodian of records for the American Bowling Congress on the stand. Said custodian had in his hand a print-out of every league game in which Georgie had bowled since the date of his injury; complete with his scores. And, oh, yes, once we'd learned what he was doing, we got a video, too. Oops!

Whatever your hobby or interest, you can be pretty sure that there's a related association, league or other organization that keeps score, and that they're not too secretive about the information they keep. Why should they be? It's not a matter of national security, after all. Don't be like Georgie and let those records give away your secrets.

Licenses

You name it, they've got a license for it these days. If you are a hunter, fisherman, scuba diver, or pilot, you have to have a license, which means your movements and activities can be traced quite easily by those who know where to look. Remember the hapless hunter in Chapter 1, whose scorned wife tracked him down via his elk hunting license? Well, rest assured that investigators with far bigger fish to fry than a runaway husband have used the license ploy to hunt down their quarry.

Charles Keating was one of the stars of the Great Savings and Loan disaster. As the FBI was scouring the land for Keating's pilot, in order to find the flight log showing that Senators John, Paul, George, and Ringo had made trips with Keating, one brilliant investigator (myself, of course!) contacted the FAA in Oklahoma City, Oklahoma. The question was simple: "When is this pilot scheduled to have his next flight physical?" You see, every pilot must have a regular physical; private pilots once every two years, and commercial pilots annually without fail, or they lose their license.

The FAA records showed that Keating's pilot was due for a physical in thirty days at a certain flight physical clinic in Kansas City, Missouri. He showed up at the physical as expected, but he didn't expect the proctologic once-over that awaited him, courtesy of Uncle Sam.

Have Computer, Will Track

Who has the power to track you down to the ends of the earth? Is it the super-secret law enforcement agencies like the CIA, FBI, and IRS, or the not so well known, but highly computerized, agencies such as FinCEN and Interpol? The answer is that anybody with a computer, a little imagination, and the energy or desire to track you down, can do so. And in today's electronic world, a professional private investigator or computer savvy citizen can do many things as well as, and sometimes far better and faster than a law enforcement agency.

The government has the authority and the law behind it, and therefore can get documents and cooperation unavailable to private investigators, but most good P.I.s have their own sources and tricks. With the right incentives (such as pictures of Ben Franklin), a P.I. can entice rabbits out of hats that the government may not even know exist.

This is not to sell the government's resources short. Just consider our friend FinCEN, for example. As I mentioned in the last chapter, FinCEN was established back in 1990 for the sole purpose of searching out fraudulently obtained hidden assets. FinCEN can and does access banking records, the National Crime Information Center, public record filings, travel records, and all the newspaper articles in the world. They are one of the very few sectors of the government having right of entry to so many diverse databases, and they're one of the few agencies possessing the motivation and savvy to use that access. FinCEN's operators spend their days not only searching out individuals' actions, but trends which point the way to suspicious financial and banking activities.

If your activities match their profiles, you may well come under much closer scrutiny than you are aware of (or comfortable with). We mentioned these parameters in Chapter 4, but for convenience I'll include them here too. You may be on "their" short list if you fit three or more of the following parameters (current as of this printing, but always subject to revision):

- You own a car worth $60,000 or more, especially paid for in cash.
- You conduct real estate transactions, the cumulative value of which exceeds $250,000 in any one year.
- You cause four or more Currency Transaction Reports (CTRs) in a year through the purchase of financial instruments.

- You travel outside of the U.S. four or more times a year.

Always remember, to paraphrase a famous (if ludicrous) statement of legal beagle Johnny Cochran, "If the profiles fit, you're in deep sh—. . . er, yogurt."

Naturally, not everybody who fits these profiles is a criminal. You'd be surprised at how many shady characters turn up in the profile checks, and even how many "law-abiding" citizens get caught doing something they're not supposed to. To make a long point short, unless you're the Pope or Mother Teresa, there's probably something in your lifestyle or history that you'd rather not be required to explain. So play it safe. Make yourself more interesting to that sweet young thing at the bar and not to some obsessive investigator looking for a promotion to GS-13.

What most government agencies lack in investigative skills and motivation, they make up for in equipment. When I consider how much information I can access with my little desktop computer, plugged into the databases available to me, it fairly amazes me what these government investigators can do with one of their CRAY supercomputers, tied into the most massive data files in the world. They can, with these phenomenal resources, create parameters to identify any kind of person in any kind of occupation, and pinpoint, with frightening accuracy, just who is most likely to break the rules.

The IRS routinely uses this procedure to select targets for TCMP (Taxpayer Compliance and Maintenance) audits, which are the equivalent of a financial enema. TCMP audits are your accountant's worst nightmare, and, should you be one of the "chosen" to receive such a reaming, it will quickly become your worst nightmare, too. In a TCMP audit, the auditor requests documentation in support of every item on the return, and, upon receiving it, verifies each item back to its source. Any item which lacks a clear trail back to its source is disallowed, and you are put in the position of proving that you weren't attempting to cheat Uncle Sam out of his money.

If you find yourself selected for one of these audits, you might want to give some real thought to hiding it all and disappearing, especially if you know that your heretofore brilliant financial wheelings and dealings can't stand up to this type of intense scrutiny.

On the upside, however, is the fact that the government is seriously considering shutting down the TCMP program altogether, due to its extremely high operations cost and the backlash against overly aggressive audits as exemplified by recent congressional hearings on IRS abuses against taxpayers.

They're Making a List, and Checking It Twice . . . Gonna Find Out Who's Naughty and Nice

Just to give you some idea of how the government structures its attempts to root out perpetrators of financial fraud, I'm going to share a copy of the June 1992 edition of the *Financial Investigations Guide*. Now, I know we've been talking about the IRS and FinCEN, which are under the jurisdiction of the Treasury Department, whereas this particular document is published by the U.S. Department of Justice (Executive Office for Asset Forfeiture). But what the heck; as we've noted before, they're all in cahoots.

By the way, I find it worthy of note that most of these documents are not available via the inherently anonymous source that is the Internet. You can, however, request selected FinCEN (Dept. of Treasury) publications by writing to Financial Crimes Enforcement Network, Office of Communications, 2070 Chain Bridge Road, Suite 200, Vienna, VA 22182. Or you may fax them at (703) 905-3885.

Remember, though, that by making such requests, you are acknowledging to the government that you have at least a passing interest in money laundering. It doesn't take too severe a case of paranoia to figure out that this may not be the wisest course for someone who wants to hide it all and disappear.

Anyway, I have included this Financial Investigations Check List (Table 9.01) in its entirety, even though it is several years old, because I believe it will help you "learn to think like an investigator." More to the point, you can use portions of this document as a checklist to aid you in covering your tracks.

TABLE 9.01

Financial Investigations Check List

DATABASES—Government Law Enforcement
A. Bureau of Alcohol, Tobacco, & Firearms (BATF)
B. Drug Enforcement Administration (DEA)
  1. Case Status Subsystem
  2. Computerized Asset Program System

3. Controlled Substances Act File
4. Controlled Substances Information System
5. El Paso Intelligence Center *(author's note: since this list was compiled, the EPIC database has been replaced by TECS II, the Treasury Enforcement Communications System)*
6. Events System
7. NADDIS
8. Precursor Chemical Information System
9. Tolls System
C. Financial Crimes Enforcement Network (FinCEN)
D. Internal Revenue Service (IRS)
E. Interpol
F. National Crime Information Center (NCIC)
G. National Law Enforcement Telecommunications System (NLETS)
H. Treasury Enforcement Communications System (TECS II)
I. United States Customs Service (USCS)

DATA BASES—Commercial
A. Financial data
B. News reports and articles
C. Legal
D. Bibliographies
E. Financial ratios, averages, and norms

PUBLIC RECORDS
A. Bankruptcy records
B. Civil & criminal court records
C. Divorce and legal separation records
D. Judgment index
E. Libraries
   1. Financial data
   2. News reports and articles
   3. Legal
   4. Biographical information and bibliographies
   5. Financial ratios, averages, and norms
F. Licensing Bureau
   1. Automobile License Bureau
   2. Drivers License Bureau
   3. Marriage licenses

    4. Professional licenses

    5. Liquor licenses

    6. Notary licenses

G. Probate and death records

H. Real estate records

    1. Building Permit Register

    2. Grantor/grantee records

    3. Maps and plats

    4. Mechanics Liens Register

    5. Real estate nation-wide computer databases

    6. Tax Assessor's records

    7. Utility filings

I. Secretary of State records

J. State Gaming Commission

K. State Vital Statistics Bureau

L. Trade Name Index

M. Uniform Commercial Code Index

OTHER RECORDS

A. Bank examination reports

B. Bureau of Public Debt

C. U.S. Coast Guard

D. Credit card companies

E. Department of Defense (DOD)

F. Department of State

G. Federal Aviation Administration (FAA)

H. Federal Reserve System

I. Financial Institutions – Other or Non-Traditional

J. Immigration and Naturalization Service (INS)

K. Office of the Comptroller of Currency (OCC)

L. Parole and probation departments

M. Police files

N. U.S. Postal Service

O. Securities & Exchange Commission (SEC)

P. Tax files

Q. Telephone company

R. Trash searches

S. Utility companies

T. Veterans Administration (VA)

BANKS AND FINANCIAL INSTITUTIONS

A. The Right to Financial Privacy Act
B. Account records
   1. Signature cards
   2. Corporate/partnership resolutions
   3. Bank statements
   4. Canceled checks
   5. Deposit tickets
   6. Items deposited
   7. Credit and debit memos
   8. Forms 1099, 1089, or back-up withholding
C. Bank checks
   1. Items used to purchase checks
   2. Items purchased with checks
   3. Applications for purchase of bank checks
   4. Retained copies of negotiated bank checks
D. Certificates of Deposit (CDs—open and closed)
   1. Copies of certificates
   2. Corporate / partnership resolutions.
   3. Items used to purchase CDs
   4. Items purchased with cashed in CDs
   5. Records reflecting interest
   6. Records reflecting roll-overs
   7. Forms 1099, 1089 or back-up withholding
E. Correspondence (between the bank and government)
F. Credit cards (open or closed)
   1. Applications for credit
   2. Corporate/partnership resolutions
   3. Credit reports
   4. Monthly statements
   5. Financial statements
   6. Charge tickets
   7. Items used to make payments on the account
   8. Correspondence files
G. Criminal Referral Forms (CRFs)
H. CTRs and CMIRs
I. Customer correspondence files
J. Exemption lists
K. Loan records (open and closed loans)

1. Loan applications
2. Financial statements
3. Corporate/partnership resolutions
4. Loan ledger sheets
5. Loan amortization schedules
6. Evidence of loan disbursement
7. Items used for loan repayments
8. Loan correspondence files
9. Real estate/chattel mortgages
10. Collateral agreements
11. Credit reports
12. Notes
13. Forms 1099, 1089, or back-up withholding

L. Safe deposit box records (open and closed)
  1. Contracts
  2. Corporate/partnership resolutions
  3. Entry records
M. Security or investment custodian accounts
  1. Items used to purchase securities
  2. Items purchased with cashed in securities
  3. Confirmation slips
  4. Monthly statements
  5. Payment receipts
  6. Safekeeping records and logs
  7. Securities receipts/delivery receipts
  8. Forms 1099, 1089, or back-up withholding
N. Teller tapes
O. Wire transfers
  1. CHIPS, Fed Wires, SWIFT documents
  2. Items used to buy wires
  3. Items purchased with wires received
  4. Notes/memoranda re wire transfers

SECURITIES & COMMODITIES BROKERAGE FIRMS

A. Account statements
B. Applications to open accounts
C. Applications to open margin accounts
D. Cash Management Account statements
E. Cash received and delivered blotters

F. Confirmation slips
G. Corporate/partnership resolutions
H. CTR's and CMIR's
I. Customer correspondence files
J. Dividend disbursing agent records
K. Payment receipts (currency/check/wire)
L. Payment receipts (securities)
M. Security depository form records
N. Securities position records
O. Stock certificates or bonds
P. Stock delivery receipts
Q. Stock transfer agent records

NET WORTH

A. ASSETS – LIABILITIES = NET WORTH
B. Net worth increase represents income
C. Expenditures represent additional income
D. Increase in NET WORTH + EXPENDITURES = INCOME
E. Reduce income by legitimate sources of income
F. INCOME – LEGIT INCOME = UNEXPLAINED INCOME
G. Document beginning cash on hand
H. Consider using net worth when:
    1. No direct link with alleged illegal activity
    2. Subject has acquired many assets
    3. Subject is a High Roller
    4. Records are unavailable or unreliable
    5. Case in chief needs corroboration
    6. Case hinges on a weak confidential source
    7. Case involves small quantity of drugs
I. Prove each asset/liability/expenditure
J. Prove beneficial ownership of assets held by others
K. Prove expenditures made for defendant by others
L. Prove assets still owned on each net worth date
M. Expert witness summarizes case

DEBRIEFING INFORMANTS

A. Who are the members of the group?
B. What are all the criminal enterprises of the group?

C. What are the receipts of the criminal enterprises?

D. What front companies are used?

E. What records do the companies or principals maintain?

F. What assets do the subjects or their companies own?

G. What are the favorite places of entertainment?

Info "R" Us

In most cases, it's not the government that's going to get you, however. It's probably not even us private investigators. No, it's probably going to be the *real* powerhouses of the financial super society: the credit bureaus. You'll remember from Chapter 1 that the three monster credit bureaus—Equifax, TransUnion, and TRW (now Experian)—have the largest data collection system in the world for gathering information on individuals. These super-bureaus collect information from credit card companies, banks, insurance carriers, small businesses, *and* the government. They compile data from all these sources into files on specific individuals, then sell the information in these files to their members for as little as pennies per transaction.

If you've ever wondered how that pesky collection agency found you, it's most likely through information provided to them by the credit bureaus. Virtually every financial transaction that you or your family members conduct is fed back into credit bureau files, and those files are updated on a daily basis. The credit bureaus receive data from their members, as well as from government files not available to you and me, courtesy of the Postal Service, Social Security Administration, and the Department of Health and Human Services. As I lamented in Chapter 1, you and I can no longer obtain information on address changes by plunking down a dollar at the Post Office, but be assured that the government still sells this data to the credit bureaus on huge magnetic tapes holding hundreds of thousands of these records, at a cost of a few cents per record.

All of this information is compiled into gargantuan credit bureau computers, and sold through an assortment of products that may or may not be protected under the Fair Credit Reporting Act. Just a few examples of the goods on the table at this Information Bazaar are:

• **Social Security Trace:** By entering a social security number, the purchaser of the data can determine every name and address which has used the social security number for a period of five or ten years. This information can easily lead to employer information, P.O. boxes used, credit information and assumed identity. So what can you do to prevent being snared in this kind of trace? Don't use your social security number at all if you can help it. (In many instances, such as voter registration applications, the use of your Social Security number is voluntary anyway.) Rent your place of residence from an individual who doesn't require identification instead of from a large leasing and management company that insists on knowing your life history. Rent P.O. boxes under your new identity, or under a false identity from a storefront mail drop.

- **Atlas Search**: This search keys on your address, and provides the addresses and telephone numbers of five to ten of your closest neighbors. Using this information, collectors or investigators can contact your neighbors and inquire as to your last known or current whereabouts. If you even casually mentioned to one of your neighbors that you were going someplace where the sun always shines and the booze always flows, a good investigator would have enough direction to narrow their search for your current whereabouts dramatically. So keep your plans to yourself unless you want to be found. Remember: *Three can keep a secret if two of them are dead.* (Yeah, I know you're probably sick of hearing this, but if you really want to hide it all and disappear, you need to imprint it on your mind until you say it in your sleep.) Follow the instructions in the paragraph above when renting a house or apartment. And stay away from nosy landlords, because they'll give you up every time.

- **Credit Report**: This provides addresses, employment information, and financial transactions that include banking, credit, and insurance, as well as other transactions so common in everyday human existence. Not only does a credit report list the companies with which you have had financial dealings, but also lists all parties that have inquired about you for one purpose or another.

By searching the credit inquiries on an individual, a smooth investigator can often figure out the location of their quarry's safety deposit box, bank account, or their new location, through even the most innocuous transaction by an unknowing spouse. You may have brilliantly covered your tracks, but if you take your spouse with you, your chances of being caught are more than doubled, because your spouse may quite innocently (and unintentionally) sign papers and conduct transactions that lead right back to you.

As I've said before, you should also be aware that the credit bureaus are the largest private investigative agencies in the world. Each credit bureau has its own investigative arms that conduct various types of investigations for insurance companies and other customers trying to reach out and touch someone.

- **Private Investigators:** If they have a paying client, or become personally involved in a case, they can focus their attention and experience on a target long after the government has given up. We investigators can be as infuriating as pit bulls, refusing to let up until we have found what we're looking for. This tenacity doesn't lead to large fan clubs, but it does pay the bills, and winning the game, especially against a crafty quarry, is more than half the fun of playing.

The Snoop with Something Extra

Consider the infamous Culture Farms consumer fraud scam of the mid-1980s, a get-rich-quick scheme that bilked 28,000 unsuspecting investors out of $80 million. These folks were suckered into buying kits to grow milk cultures in their homes, lured by the promise of a committed buyer for the smelly goo. The buyers, it turned out, simply didn't exist.[2] By the time the government finished with their investigations, eleven of the perpetrators had gone to jail, but very little of the money was discovered or returned.

Enter one Wichita, Kansas attorney named Christopher Redmond, who was appointed Culture Farms' bankruptcy trustee after the first trustee concluded that there were no funds to be recovered.

In his role as trustee over a bankruptcy proceeding, Redmond was able to circumvent many of the most stringent international banking privacy laws and gain access to the bankrupt company's account information. Though his investigation spanned many months, and necessitated extensive travel to Switzerland, the Isle of Man, the Netherlands Antilles, and the Cayman Islands (hey, tough job, but somebody's gotta do it), the end result was the recovery of roughly $15 million. That's all that was left after the principals spent a chunk and used the rest to run the operation.

It just goes to show to what lengths your pursuers will go if there's

---

2 "Closing In" by Dana Wechsler Linden, *Forbes*, June 7, 1993.

money in the till for them and/or if there's a principle involved. As a matter of fact Redmond seems to have been motivated far more by principle than by big bucks. "I know it sounds corny," he said. "But for me it's a question of whether the system really works. Can people do this and really get away with it?" Now I ask you, Do you want somebody like this coming after you?

For himself and his firm, Redmond netted only about $450,000 after expenses, hardly equal to his normal billing rate of $150 per hour. But the important point for him is that he got his guys, and the important point for you is that he blazed new trails for other investigators to follow when looking for hidden assets . . . such as *yours*.

Bound and Determined to Lose

Some people are very smart about bugging out, some are stupid, and there are some who are smart enough, but let their emotions foul them up. Take the case of Noel. At the conclusion of a contentious custody hearing, when the judge banged his gavel and ruled in favor of his wife, Noel vowed that it wasn't over, and that no one, not even a judge, would keep him from his children. As far as he was concerned, those children were *his*, and that was all was to it.

Six days after the hearing, Noel got his first weekend visitation, whereupon he left town with the children. Not satisfied with just having the children, he called his ex and taunted her, telling her she would never see them again unless she played ball with him and did things his way. It wasn't about the children at all; Noel was obsessive about continuing to exercise control over his ex-wife. He knew her well enough to know that the only way he could force his will on her was to take control of the children, who meant everything to her.

Noel called her several times that day, leaving hints as to his (and the children's) whereabouts. He was probably enjoying his taunts immensely. What he didn't consider was that the caller I.D. on his wife's telephone was plotting his location at every call. By simply tracing the addresses of the calls, Noel's ex and her investigator could see that Noel was heading west on Interstate 10, toward beautiful downtown Houston. When Noel stopped for the night at the friendly neighborhood Holiday Inn, investigators canvassing the parking lot spotted his car and bagged him and the children.

Spending several days in jail for his little escapade apparently didn't teach Noel anything. As soon as he got out, he grabbed the children from their day care center by jumping a fence and dragging them to his waiting car. This time, he was smarter(?), and didn't make any phone calls to give himself away, but still persisted in his plan to terrorize his ex. Finally, he forced her to meet him at the airport, figuring he could just disappear into the crowds after having his say. When she got off the plane, Noel reached out to grab her, but was instead pinned to the wall by her investigators, who were eagerly awaiting him with the airport security force. This time, Noel wound up in jail for thirty days.

Think he learned his lesson? Hell, no! Several weeks later, he stole the children again and *really* disappeared. This time, he had planned his escape, and made no attempt to contact his ex.

For several years, the ex, along with her private investigator and the FBI, conducted a thorough manhunt for Noel and the children. They traced his family's calls, credit cards, and financial transactions, as well as watching all his—and his family's—known hangouts, as it seemed obvious that his family was helping him. For years, investigators searched for that one break in the case, with no result. It was as if the earth had swallowed Noel and the children and driven them deep underground.

Seven years later, the first break in the case came when that big FBI computer in the sky, the NCIC (National Crime Information Center), reported that a set of fingerprints matching Noel's appeared on an application for a California real estate license. Noel's fingerprints had made their way to the database from both his military service and his short stay in a county jail after his second kidnapping episode. He never dreamed that information from his real estate license application would go to the FBI, and that his fugitive status would raise red flags.

When federal agents and the children's mother showed up at Noel's home, his world turned upside down, as did his new wife's. She knew him as Richard, the loving father of two beautiful children whose mother had died tragically in an auto accident seven years earlier. Noel's foolproof identity and carefully laid plans all fell apart because of one little slip, his own fingertips having given him away. And this time, he would spend considerably longer than thirty days in the slammer (and ultimately, a court awarded his sweet wife a $4 million judgment for his stupidity). Hee! Hee! Hee!

The One and Only You

The regulated industries—those that require proof of identity, fingerprints, and social security number verification—are the nemesis of people with something to hide. The computers that collate and store this identifying information never forget a face or a fact, often reaching far back in time or far out in miles to provide clues to your identity and location.

Fingerprints are one of the best examples of identification. Fingerprint information is stored and identified in computers, not only in the United States by the F.B.I. and local agencies, but by Interpol offices throughout the world. Interpol serves as a clearinghouse for law enforcement agencies worldwide. It provides the international law enforcement community with the same services provided by the FBI to domestic law enforcement agencies, such as the collection and dissemination of data and intelligence about criminals and suspects outside of the jurisdiction of the local agencies.

In addition to basic information such as fingerprints, social security, military service, national identity numbers, and date of birth, other identifying characteristics are documented in your file, such as identifying physical characteristics like physical deformities, birthmarks, scars, and tattoos. Anything that marks your individuality and separates you from the faceless masses is a means for the computer to sort information and narrow its field while searching the databases for you. The fewer identifying characteristics you possess the lesser the likelihood of information being compiled about you. If you haven't done so already, now would be a good time to consider removing those scars, tattoos, and birthmarks, and correcting any physical trait that makes you stand out of a faceless crowd. Go back to Chapter 4 if you need some inspiration.

The Eyes of Taxes Are upon You

The agency that is most near and dear to our hearts, and strikes fear in taxpayers everywhere, is the IRS. Our friendly neighborhood tax collectors gather financial information from employers and anybody else who has a reason to pay you money—whether it be in the form of wages, interest, contract fees, tips, and even winnings from gambling—anywhere in the world. This agency, more than any other law enforcement or regulatory body, holds the keys to your financial family jewels. From information which you have voluntarily submitted on previous years' tax returns, the IRS can create not only a financial profile on you and your family, but a frighteningly accurate prediction of what you will do in the future.

Think about it: each year, you provide the IRS with a signed confession of all your financial dealings, a detailed description of your family structure, and even the names of people (e.g., an ex-spouse) whose financial activities are in any way tied to your own. If you and your ex share tax liability, say, from earnings on an investment, and the IRS claims you owe more tax on those earnings, who do you think your ex is going to blame? You even provide the IRS with a detailed list of the things you own through your depreciation schedules, thus giving them a wonderful insight into what you're likely to purchase in the future. And if you think they don't use this information, then I have a warehouse full of malodorous milk culture I'd like to sell to you.

Apart from the Taxpayer Compliance and Maintenance audit program we talked about earlier, the IRS from time to time conducts a program known as "selective enforcement," targeting a specific industry, trade group, or occupation for extensive and merciless audits. This program is intended to send a message to taxpayers within the targeted groups, to literally scare these individuals into reporting—and paying taxes on—every cent of their income. What makes this program so effective is the IRS's tactic of auditing a few high-profile members of the groups within an inch of their lives, then prosecuting them to the full extent of the law.

In years past, the IRS has targeted horse jockeys, coin-operated machine vendors, and most recently, sports figures. Several of the most revered baseball players were investigated, charged, and convicted by the IRS on failing to report additional income derived from sales of autographed baseball cards and appearances at sports memorabilia conventions. And, lest you doubt the power and tenacity of the IRS, you should remember the case of gangster Al Capone. When all other law enforcement agencies had failed to get a conviction on this individual's well-documented criminal activities, the IRS was able to successfully prosecute him for income tax evasion, and to plant him securely in prison for the rest of his life.

The only way to avoid the IRS is to cut off the flow of information about yourself to them. Once this agency stops getting information from its sources, they have to assume that you have died, retired, left the country, or been beamed up to the mother ship. If you retire, they fully expect to maintain an interest in your future through your retirement income, dividends, and interest, even if you no longer have any tax liability. If you die, they still linger like vultures for their piece of whatever you have left to your heirs and beneficiaries.

Once the information flow stops entirely, the service is far too busy to nose around for your scent unless another law enforcement or regulatory agency comes to them for information about you. Then, the IRS adds the other agency's information to their database, and the chase resumes.

So How Do I Get Them Off My Back?

Well, you could fake your own death, as we discussed in Chapter 4. If you're not willing to go that far, you can still cover your tracks. The bottom line is, if you are going to bug out, you need to make sure that you have cleaned up your financial act. Leave nothing behind for the snitches and the snoops. Check the list below, and make sure that none of these entities are left with any information that could trace you to your new location:

- Employers
- Stockbrokers and agencies
- Banks and savings associations
- Credit unions
- Individual Retirement Accounts (IRAs)
- 401(k) plans
- Separate Employment Plans (SEPs)
- Insurance policies (dividend, interest, or income producing)
- Annuities, investments (remember those K-1 partnership returns)
- Business entities (corporations, partnerships, joint ventures, and proprietorships that throw money your way)
- Credit cards (if you pay them more than you owe, they pay interest and report it to the IRS)

Remember, *anyone* who provides information to the government about your financial activities is a potential information source for the IRS. If you truly want to hide it all and disappear, this is one area where you certainly don't want to leave any footprints they can use to track you.

"Wait a minute!" you may be protesting. "What about my retirement? I paid in money, year after year, to that gigantic pool called the Social Security Administration. I'm due something in return, aren't I?"

Yes, you are. However, if you receive and cash these checks, you will leave a clear trail back to your new life. While this information isn't generally available, any law enforcement agency, many regulatory agencies, and even some credit bureaus can access it. If you are entitled to this money, and don't choose to donate it to the general well-being of American humankind, be sure that the checks are direct-deposited into an interest-bearing account where it can grow.

If you haven't run afoul of the government, this money will be there for you if you have any emergencies. If, however, you have left the government the impression that you owe them money, or if you have left creditors with a similar impression, the money is theirs if they find it.

Your choices are to let the money sit until you really need it, or take it out as it is received. While you can designate someone to withdraw funds for you, this, too, adds a variable to the equation, another source of information as to your whereabouts. Obviously, none of these options is truly optimal for the invisible man (or woman). You may ultimately have to choose between getting what is due you, or getting away.

And don't forget: as we mentioned earlier, there are certain things that make you stand out as a likely target for scrutiny when traveling abroad. If you meet any of the criteria in the TECS database parameters, you will likely be looked at as a potential drug smuggler or money launderer, even if you are engaging in no such activities. And yes, the IRS does utilize this database, too.

In the end, it really doesn't matter if you are in fact innocent of the civil wrong or criminal activity this tangled system was implemented to stop. If you're caught, you're caught, and you can spend a long time moaning and bitching about the inequity of it all—but you won't be spending it anywhere you want to be. (They don't call jail "the pokey" for nothing!) It's all about priorities. You can complain about unjust tax laws or the intrusive government all you want, but you are the one who ultimately controls your fate. It's all about choices *you* get to make, and that you have to live with. Choose well!

10

Maintaining Your Lifestyle

It's been said that "getting there is half the fun." That may be true of lovemaking or going to Disney World, but it's not necessarily the case when you're radically reinventing your life. As you've seen, bugging out involves a lot of hard work, careful planning, and more than a few hazards. That's why most of this book has been devoted to "getting there." Well, in this chapter we're going to talk about what to do once you're "there"—in other words, how to maintain your lifestyle and be happy in your new home.

The good news is that many of the foreign countries where you might go to hide and disappear cost a lot less than the good old United States of America. If you've read the earlier chapters, particularly Chapter 3, you know that in many countries, you can quite easily maintain your lifestyle for a considerably smaller outlay of cash than in the U.S. An additional benefit is that in many of these places the pace of life is generally far slower, meaning that your heart won't take as much of a pounding, and your stress levels as well as your blood pressure should go way down.

Getting There Without Getting Caught

If your objective is to hide and stay hidden, it goes without saying that the first principle to maintaining your lifestyle is safeguarding your secrecy. Probably the most important point is to be sure you haven't given away the identity of your new home to Uncle Sam. If the

U.S. Customs computer (TECS II) shows that you have re-entered the United States from your new country twice in the last three years, you better believe that this is the first place someone is going to look for you after you're gone.

Remember, then, to plan in advance. Even if you need to travel to your new country several times before the "final bug-out," if you travel wisely you can stay a few steps ahead of the Customs computer.

As we admonished in Chapter 5, *never travel directly from the U.S. to your new country.* For your convenience, I'll take a moment to recap the stealth-traveler's strategy we talked about in that chapter. Assuming you now live in the U.S., let's say you've decided to settle in Costa Rica. You should purchase a round-trip ticket, not to Costa Rica, but to another destination altogether—say, Belize City, Belize. (Even if you're not planning on coming back to the U.S., I recommend a round-trip ticket; a one way ticket is an announcement—to anybody who might be looking—that you're bugging out.)

Once you've arrived in Belize City, go down the street to another travel agency, and buy a second round-trip ticket from Belize City to Costa Rica, your "real" destination. If you need to return to the United States, you'll fly back to Belize City on that second round-trip ticket, and then travel back to the States on the original round-trip ticket you purchased before you left. That way, your airline ticket and your Customs declaration only show Belize City, and not your future home in Costa Rica.

You Don't Have to Go It Alone

Once you've arrived in your new country, seek out a guide—someone who has already done what you're doing. In virtually all of the countries discussed in this book, there are other folks who have dropped out before you. Some even make a living helping other expatriates adjust to their new social, political, and financial climate. You certainly don't have to reinvent the wheel every time you do something new; there is always someone there to help you, perhaps for a price, perhaps not. In any case, just be sure you don't tell your mentor your whole life story (remember, three can keep a secret if . . . well, you know the rest). And don't expect them to tell you their entire history either. Ask no questions, tell no lies.

Unless you're truly the Lone Ranger type, you can benefit a great deal by seeking out the expatriate community in your new home. This is not a contradiction of the caveat issued towards the end of Chapter 3, when I cautioned against associating too openly with the American expat community. Of course you don't want to make yourself obvious to an investigator who might be nosing around in your business. But a little discreet networking can reap enormous dividends. Besides, completely avoiding *any* association with a peer group in a foreign land will make you stand out as well. You must find, and strike, a balance here. If nothing else, the company of other expats can take some of the strangeness out of being in a "strange land."

Home, Sweet . . . Houseboat?!?

One of your most important considerations upon arriving in your new country is finding just the right place to live. Again, this is an area where some of your fellow expats can provide valuable insight. I'd recommend that you rent at first, to give yourself time to look around for a permanent residence. Look for a rental property that offers a weekly or a monthly rate.

Shop around for bargains; you don't want to spend all your hard-earned savings on a squalid little cabana when you can get a decent villa for a reasonable price. And keep a low profile by paying cash; whatever you do, you don't want to get into any computers. This is not the time to use your frequent flyer points or hotel points or any other type of traveler's incentives. As we've said before, these have a way of leading back to credit card investigators, credit bureaus, and frequent flyer programs that are easily accessible to most investigators who know about such things.

In most countries it is a simple matter to rent an apartment, a house, or a boat that provides all of the comforts of home. "A boat?" you say. Well, yes, as a matter of fact. From my own personal experience, and that of many of my friends, I recommend that you consider a houseboat, if you are in a location that is conducive to them. Living on the water is very pleasant and restful. It's usually less expensive as well. Houseboats are usually very easy to maintain; for one thing, you don't have to worry about cutting the grass or scooping up doggie doo. An added bonus is that houseboat living introduces you to a liberal and outgoing social crowd. Living on a boat often provides a spectacular view—not just of the countryside, but of members of the opposite sex. Boy, does this bring back memories.

While staying in St. Maarten with friends one summer, I dragged my alcohol-befogged brain and body up to the deck early one morning, to get some fresh air and "pay the rent" on the previous night's margaritas. As I opened the hatch, I was met with a most wondrous vision of comeliness: a nubile, totally nude young European woman, anointing herself with suntan lotion on the front deck of the adjoining houseboat. Within a few seconds, she was joined by two of her equally attractive, equally undressed friends, and I watched in awe as the three of them coated each other with suntan lotion from head to toe. As long as I live, I don't think I'll ever see anything as sensual or naturally beautiful as those three seagoing nymphs, uninhibitedly cavorting on the deck that morning. It sure took the edge off my hangover and got my adrenaline pumping for the next few hours.

Whew. Excuse me while I go have a cigarette and a drink!

Don't Be a Fool with Your Money

Whether you live in a houseboat or a house in the hills, I can't advise strongly enough that you rent rather than buy, at least until you know the pluses and minuses of the local real estate market. You also need some time to get the feel of your new place, in order to know for sure whether or not you want this to be your home for a long time to come.

Please realize that in many of these countries, you cannot finance a home the way you can in the United States—you know, with only 10 percent down and a mortgage spanning three generations. Financial transactions in these countries often are in cash, and major purchases that *can* be financed generally require a much higher down payment than you may be used to at home. You certainly don't want to buy a home, put a serious chunk of money into a property—and then decide you really don't like the place after all, or, worse yet, find you have to leave in a hurry, just one step ahead of the heat.

As we discussed in Chapter 3, in many expatriate countries—particularly in Central America—real estate prices are rising steadily, and they're rising at an astounding rate. (Costa Rica, you may recall, has seen real estate prices rise 500 percent in five years.) Even so, you can still find some very good values, but you'd better hurry, because, as we've said before, the Europeans and Asians are closing in fast. As the political situation in Central and South America improves, more and more investors from all over the world will be flocking to these areas and buying up everything that's not nailed down.

Apart from your concern about finding a permanent residence, real estate can be a great investment if you want to make your money work for you in your new home. But, as in any other investment, this is one that should be carefully researched and investigated. There is a saying in Costa Rica about the real estate market: "The fastest way to have a million dollars in Costa Rica is to come here with two million dollars."

You see, Costa Rica is one of those places that is crawling with expat con men such as Paul Noe, white-collar crime masterminds who have fleeced thousands in the United States and Canada. These guys are certainly not above taking a new would-be real estate investor looking to make a killing in the "Little Switzerland of the Americas" out for a "ride."

Make Your Money Work So *You* Don't Have To

While we're on the subject of money and investing, there's one more point to remember. If you have money saved up—which I hope you do—you need to learn how to make it work for you. If you don't, then realize that you may be endangering your new life if you go out and get a job, because that brings you into the limelight and exposes you to unnecessary risks—particularly if you have done something that would make Uncle Sam want to bring you back to the United States.

The best way to make your money work for you is to invest it wisely. If real estate isn't your bag, there are many other options. A little ingenuity can carry you a long way. Take my good friend "Skippy," who retired in a little town in Mexico. He set himself up as a one-man pawnshop, who bought from the natives and sold to the gringos. By learning the language, and having ready cash available, Skippy soon became known as the "loan arranger of last resort" in his new home. He was able to capitalize on his entrepreneurial skill without creating a high profile for himself, and he had a ball doing it. Every month or two, Skippy would let his girlfriend go back to the States wearing the jewelry and gems that he'd purchased from local pickpockets and gigolos. She'd waltz right through Customs wearing the questionable goods, and would sell them in the local jewelry mart or to one of Skippy's old friends in the business. Their homemade "hock shop" more than paid Skippy's living expenses and made a little nest egg besides.

Don't Piss Off the Locals

Let's face it: You're really not going to be happy or successful in your new home unless you get along with the locals. You may not have a thriving business relationship with them the way my friend Skippy did, but at least don't make them your enemies. It's true that in some areas, you may have to watch out for the locals, and you may never be able to really consider them your friends. But in all cases, be sure that you don't piss them off. This is simply not the time and place to be the Ugly American.

Many of us born and raised in the United States have acquired a certain arrogance, a natural byproduct of being told all our lives that we live in the "greatest country in the world." This complacency can leave us vulnerable to a potentially nasty shock when we learn that throughout most of the world, a local citizen has more rights than *any* foreigner—that is, unless the foreigner has boatloads of money and influence. But common sense and decency should tell you that even if you do have the money and influence, you don't want to enrage the locals, because believe me, if you do, they will find a way to cause you grief.

If, on the other hand, you befriend the local populace and give them the opportunity to make a little money, or feel a little important, then they will become your eyes, ears, and mouthpiece. Your new countrymen and women will help you in ways you may not even be able to imagine. They can help you ferret out business opportunities, for example. They can report back to you when anyone starts asking questions about the new gringo in town. They can help you find a maid for a far more reasonable price than you could on your own. They can cut you a deal when you want to go on a fishing excursion or hunting trip at a reasonable rate. They can connect you with advantageous social circles that would otherwise be off-limits to you. And they can even introduce you to desirable members of the opposite sex who might otherwise be unavailable, or accessible only through strictly regulated social functions.

Here's a hint: Getting to know a local banker or real estate dealer is a sure way to get on the fast track to local information. Beyond that, a friendly smile or cordial greeting to your neighbors, and to people you pass on the street, is a fine way to get started off on the right foot with your new compatriots.

To maintain your lifestyle you want to do more than just get along with the locals; you want to blend in with them. If you haven't done so already, now is as good a time to tend to those details regarding your new identity. If you have any bad habits, or, for that matter, any identifying hobbies that would make you stick out, this is a good time to get rid of them, once and forever.

The longer you live in your new home, the more you will take on the color and flavor of your surroundings. It's a natural process. But you do need to take some initiative to ensure that this process flows smoothly. Pay attention to the people around you—their appearance, their habits, their mannerisms—so you can really learn to blend in. Learn to savor the local food, and really get into the local music. Make your new home as much a part of you as you strive to be a part of it.

Of course, you'll want to learn the local language, too, if you don't speak it already. If you can converse with the natives in the street, you'll certainly blend in a lot better. With a little bit of practice and a little bit of help—don't be afraid to ask your neighbors for assistance here—anyone can pick up enough of the local language within a couple of months to be both understood and accepted within the community. Once you have done this, you will find living a lot easier, and new opportunities will come to you because you've cleared an invisible but significant barrier. You'll no longer be an outsider. The locals will begin to treat you as one of them and not as a sheep ready to be fleeced.

Learn to live within reasonable means, in accordance with those around you. If you're wealthy, don't flaunt your wealth. (That may have been what got you into trouble in your old life.)

Maybe this can even be a time for you to focus on more profound values. Perhaps your new Paradise will be conducive to your reinventing yourself, not just on the surface, but on a deeper level as well. Or perhaps not; maybe you just want to concentrate on having fun. Whatever your priorities, it's important that you break away from your old bad habits and really *live* your new life.

And always remember the value of discretion. Resist the temptation to blab your true-life story to the bartender at Rick's or that nice English couple you see on the beach every day. Before you left home, you should have fabricated a plausible story about your background—based in reality, but distanced enough from the truth so that you can't be found out. I've said before and will say again that a big part of maintaining your lifestyle is being able to·stick to your story. The best way to do this is to keep things simple; don't build up such a complex web that you'll end up ensnaring yourself in your own lies.

"Say, Aren't You . . . ?"

What if, in spite of all your efforts to do as the natives do and blend in with your surroundings, someone recognizes you in your new home?

Well, here's where you really have to be prepared to lie, and lie convincingly. Actually it's not that difficult, when you think about it. After all, everyone has a double in the world, and besides, people change. You probably don't look the same way you did several years ago, so if this person is someone who hasn't seen you in quite awhile, it shouldn't be too hard to get away with your lie. If someone says, "Hey, aren't you Artie Johnson?" just reply, "You know, you're the third person who said I look like someone else. There must be a dozen people who look just like me running around the world. I'd sure like to meet one of them someday."

As long as you are convincing, and don't look as if you just got caught on "Candid Camera," you can almost always pull off your new identity without a hitch. Unless these people are family, or have known you all of your life—to the point that they recognize your mannerisms, scars, and personality traits—you shouldn't have any trouble convincing them that it's just a case of mistaken identity. (Of course, if you've really gone all out and reinvented your appearance in some of the ways we discussed in Chapter 4, you may never run into this problem.)

If you maintain a low profile, live within your means, and don't act the fool, your chances of being recognized, identified, or brought back to face the music are almost nil. Just don't be like "Mr. Spain."

The infamous "Mr. Spain" stole millions of dollars from his Savings and Loan Association. When his game was discovered, he fled the country and proceeded to live the high life in Madrid and Barcelona, thereby acquiring his nickname, Mr. Spain. Living in the best hotels, drinking the finest wines, and charging all of this to credit cards that were eventually discovered by federal agents, Mr. Spain thought he had it made. But his very conspicuous consumption was his own undoing.

Wanting to catch this high-living, high-rolling "hero" of the Savings and Loan debacle, the government made Mr. Spain a high priority. In the end, he was no match for officials who were determined to show that they could and would pursue and catch the looters who cleaned out our financial institutions. As Mr. Spain was such a blatant example of excess, he became the poster boy of the Savings and Loan scandal—a clear target for the government's wrath. He was singled out for prosecution over other, lesser-known and lower-profile individuals who stole their money and spent it quietly, without making any waves. Because of his conspicuous consumption, Mr. Spain is now in the slammer.

I suppose by now the lesson is pretty clear: When you're trying to hide it all and disappear, *you* are very often your own worst enemy. If you get caught, chances are the blame will lie not with the wicked IRS, nor with that thieving boss you used to work for, nor with your horrid ex-spouse, but with you. Whether through carelessness, indiscretion, an overly active ego or libido, or just plain arrogance, your actions can trip you up and land you straight in Club Fed.

Sometimes, however, no matter how careful you are, no matter how discreet your actions, no matter how well you blend in with your new surroundings, "they" will track you down anyway. Or there may be some other reason you need to get out of Paradise in a hurry. That's why you need to have an emergency back-up plan.

11

Always Have a Plan

No matter where you go, no matter what you do, always think through your circumstances and develop a worst-case scenario for having to leave your new home. What if you knew that the police were at your door, and that your local bank account had been frozen? What would you do? What *would* you do?

It is my hope, of course, that you'll never have to face this situation. But, as the saying goes, "stuff" happens, and if it happens to you, your best bet is to have a plan "B," a good emergency back-up plan. That way you'll be able to relax and truly enjoy your new life, secure in the knowledge that you have a way out in case things go wrong. You'll know that if "They" come pounding on your door, you can slip out the back window.

Of course, you have to know where the back window *is*. And that's why this idea is a very important one. It's not being melodramatic to compare your journey to your new life—and back out again—to a military operation. After all, you *are* fighting for your life here. That's why you need to plan your escape with the same care and precision as you would plan a covert mission.

In devising your escape plan, here are four important points to remember.

1. *Map out an escape route.* The first and perhaps most obvious part of any plan is to map out an escape route. By its very nature, your escape route should bear almost no resemblance to the route you took to get to your

new home. After all, if someone was able to track you once upon that route, they will certainly be watching it, waiting for you to re-trace your steps.

Know the strengths and weaknesses of the major transportation systems, and the reach of their computers, and find the best way to get the hell out of Dodge without raising any dust. Generally speaking, the best way to do this is by car, or, in the case of islands or coastlines, by boat.

While you're in the process of embracing your new home, learn how and where the locals travel. Befriend several of them who own boats or private planes, and it doesn't hurt to make a friend who has a guest house in the hills where you can camp out. That way, you'll greatly enhance your chances of successfully dealing with any "problems" that might come up. After all, that's what friends are for!

Tom and Maggie both came to Roatân to get away from their respective pasts. They each left their stateside problems and began anew on the pleasant island and found each other to be just what they were looking for. The only problem was that they continued their old ways in their new home. Within a year, they had gotten behind on their debts and pissed off enough locals that a warrant was issued for them with the island constabulary.

With the only official ways on and off the island being scrutinized (the airport and the island ferry), Tom and Maggie prevailed on one of their few remaining friends to sail them up to Belize, where they took a commercial flight to wherever they decided to start all over again.

2. *Know who your friends are—and aren't.* Speaking of friends, it pays to know who your friends really are. A little bit of suspicion is well advised when you encounter truly helpful people. Those who are real friends will understand and appreciate your caution. They know that an unwary traveler doesn't go very far or last very long.

The only folks who will resent it are people who, for one reason or another, have a great stake in gaining your trust. Whether they are minor scam artists, looking to benefit from association with a desperate gringo, or local operatives, paid to keep an eye open for suspicious behavior, they can mess up your life with equal aplomb. Always remember that beyond the above-board and legal techniques used to locate you, investigators and government agencies rely heavily upon informers and "plants" to be their eyes, ears, and bait for their quarry.

So how can you tell if someone is truly on your side or working to set you up for a fall? Ultimately, you can't. But utilizing a little caution, a little common sense, and your detective logic can go a long way toward protecting you from getting nailed. What you can do is to take the individual in question into your confidence on a very limited scale, to see how they react. Don't give them anything that could remotely lead back to you, of course. Feed them a rumor (false), and see if it comes back to you. Entrust them with an allegedly valuable piece of information or property (but which is, in reality, worth very little), and see how they handle it. In short, build friendships in your new home as if your very life depended upon them. It very well may.

3.   *Make sure all of your financial eggs are not in one basket.* You're not going to get very far without money, and if your local bank account is frozen you've got to have another source of ready cash. The most important principle is to diversify your wealth. Don't deposit the majority of your assets in the same place that you conduct most of your financial transactions. And for Christ's sake, don't have a safety deposit box in the same bank you use for your checking account, puh-*leeze!*

   Be sure that at least some of your money is in another place, another name, or another country that your friendly neighborhood banker is not aware of, and to which he or she has no records leading to. Don't tell anybody about that secret stash, not even that exotic, non-English speaking islander you picked up at the local disco. Oh, well, I just can't resist repeating it one more time: *Three can keep a secret if two of them are dead.* (Are you saying it in your sleep yet?)

4.   *Have another identity for traveling.* We discussed identification at length in Chapter 4, so you know it is relatively easy to get a passport and other I.D. in most countries if the price is right. You may already have a solid "second identity," but it might behoove you to have a third, just in case. If you entered your new home as John Doe, engineer, travelling by way of Belize, you should leave as someone entirely different, like Wilhelm Jorgensen, third generation woodcarver from Duluth, going to Stockholm by way of Netherlands Antilles to research your ancestors. Don't live up to the expectations of the people looking for you by treading upon familiar ground, either physically or administratively. Remember that you don't want to retrace *any* of the steps that got you here.

If you haven't broken any major laws, and have selected a country that welcomes tax dodgers and other expatriates who are unhappy with the rules back home, you may never need to worry about "Them" coming after you. Even so, the proverbial "stuff" does, indeed, happen. These are definitely interesting times, in the sense of the old Chinese proverb. Even if your ex-spouse never manages to convince Uncle Sam that you are a drug dealer and deserving of divine intervention, events can occur in the larger arena that have nothing to do with you or your past misdeeds. A coup, a government takeover by a junta, or even one of Mother Nature's more violent performances such as an earthquake or volcano, can quickly turn your erstwhile Paradise into the seventh circle of Hell.

If, however, you know how to get out of town safely, are you sure that you have access to enough money to tide you over? Do you have the "proper I.D"? Then, you can pour yourself another drink and sing along with the characters in the movie *The Lion King*: "Hakuna Matata" ("No worries").

There are few statements you can make which communicate stress as clearly as "What am I going to do?" and nothing that instills confidence as well as knowing the answer.

Well, this has been quite a trip, hasn't it? I sure hope it's been as good for you as it has for me. Hopefully the best is yet to come, and who knows, maybe I'll see you someday in some bar, in some tropical Paradise. I won't tell you my story if you won't tell me yours. Perhaps we'll just have a drink together, and talk over old times that never were.

Oh, but wait. Before we do that, there's one more order of business. Call me a sucker for technology, call me an infomaniac, but don't try to call me while I'm online. In my humble opinion, no expat guide these days would be complete without a look at that most amazing of entities: the wild and wooly Internet. The Net is a bounty of information for now and future expatriates. So let's log on for a few minutes, and *then* you can start packing your bags.

BON VOYAGE!

You and the Internet

12

Never in human history has there been as vast and comprehensive an information source as is now available via the Internet. If you have Internet access, you literally have the world at your fingertips (or at your keyboard), no matter how remote the location of your chosen Paradise. Even if you don't have a television, and the nearest newsstand is three islands away, the Internet can give you up-to-the-minute information on everything from the temperature in Bangkok to the climate on Wall Street. The Internet is the ultimate encyclopedia, the resource for information about anything or anyone in the world.

The catch is, you have to know where, and how, to look for this information, and let me tell you, it can be pretty bewildering until you get used to it. Hopefully this chapter will help clear up some of the confusion, and maybe even get you excited about the Internet (in case you're not already). I do believe that the Net, properly used, can be an expat's best friend and keep you up to date on the rest of the world.

Before we go any further, I want to make it clear that this is not going to be a comprehensive Internet primer. I'm assuming you know the basics—mainly, what the Internet *is*—and that you have a computer or have access to one. If, however, you grew up before color television or jet airplanes, the chances are that computers and the Internet are all Greek to you. But that's easily rectified. If you really need to begin at the beginning, there are almost as many books about computers and the Net as there are websites. I'm pretty fond of IDG Books' *Dummies* series, and highly recommend *The Internet For Dummies* if you're searching for a good basic reference that will tell you what the Net is all about.

What this chapter will do is give you a few pointers on how to navigate the Net without going nuts, and also on how to maintain your on-line privacy. I'll follow up with an Appendix listing some useful Web sites devoted to the topics we've discussed throughout this book.

So Many Sites to See, So Little Time

It is impossible to report an accurate count of available addresses, or websites, on the Internet, because the number fluctuates not just daily, but hourly. Some pages are removed due to the information they contain becoming dated, some are simply removed for lack of activity, and some because the owners simply didn't pay their bills. Much like the many-headed Hydra, however, for each page removed, many more arrive to take its place.

An important fact to keep in mind is that websites can be developed and posted by *anybody*, with no machinery in place to certify the accuracy, validity, or even reality of the information they contain—or the true identity of the person posting the information. For all you know, I could be just another nut-case, showering the world with my personal delusions, were it not for the ease with which the information I present can be verified. At any rate, before you take *any* significant action based upon information you get off the Internet—especially concerning your money and investments—you would be well advised to check it out! But that advice holds true for information you get anywhere.

In addition to websites, there are, at last count, some 15,000 Usenet groups, usually called *newsgroups*, which exist as an open (and sometimes moderated) forum for discussion of virtually any topic you can imagine, and then some. Think of these groups as being huge, global coffee shops, where anybody who is so inclined can wander in, voice their opinion, sell their wares, or even pick a virtual fight. While there's an abundance of good information available in these places, you have to sift through a lot of chaff before you get any wheat.

The moderated Usenet newsgroups tend to be somewhat more reliable, as they have a person (or persons) to screen entries before they're posted to weed out some of the useless, deceitful, and danger-ous chatter. Again, however, you don't usually know the moderators from Adam, and they might be as crazy as a peach orchard bore! So be cautious here, too.

The Gifts That Keep On Giving

Now that I've told you about the boogey-men (and women), let me add a little more gloom and doom before we go on to the good stuff. There's one more bugaboo you really need to be aware of even before you start: *viruses.*

If you spend much time on the Internet, you are going to encounter a virus. No, not the kind you get after having a good time with someone whose name eludes you, but scary, nonetheless. A virus is a mini-program that gets into your computer by hiding inside some-thing you download and open, something you get on disk from some-one else, or even (rarely) it can be hidden within commercial software. The virus may be relatively harmless, such as one that simply sticks the word "Wazoo" in your documents at random intervals. Or, it may be truly insidious, such as the newer ones that tell your hard drive to erase itself or to turn all your files into gibberish. You may never know what hit you until your system is rendered completely useless.

So how do you protect yourself? Simple. Just get hold of one of the better anti-virus, or AV, programs, install it, and keep it current. My personal favorite is McAfee's Viruscan. You can get a fully working demo of the newest version from McAfee's website, or from large shareware sites like File Pile at www.filepile.com. The download is free, but you'll need to register and pay for it within 30 days if you decide to keep it.

Once you've installed the AV program, you'll want to scan any file you introduce into your system, whether downloaded off the Net, obtained from friends, or anywhere else. It's easy to do; the AV pro-gram has a help function to walk you through it.

Furthermore, you'll need to check back at the AV program's web-site every week or two to see if they've updated their virus database, as new viruses are being written every day with the sole intent of sneaking past your AV software. You see, this is all a game for those sick little puppies who create the virus; I guess it's the only way they have to exert any influence on the world. Unfortunately, the anonymous nature of online communications allows these little cockroaches to hide quite effectively. However, with simple diligence, and the right weapons, you and your computer should be pretty safe.

Privacy and the Internet

While we're dancing around the notion of being inconspicuous, we might want to mention the issue of how private *your* actions on the Internet are—after all, this book *is* about hiding and disappearing. Did you know that every time you post a message to a newsgroup, you make that message available for the whole world to see? Neat, huh?

Well, you also are posting your return e-mail address for the whole world to see. Think about it. Say you post a message grousing about the virus-spreading monsters described above, and one of them reads it. You just might get an e-mail response, offering you something you simply can't resist. You open the attached file, and, instead of a picture of Pamela Anderson in the nude, you activate the newest, most destructive virus ever created.

Or, more likely, you've just entered your e-mail address on the mailing list for every multilevel marketing scheme created this decade. You're gonna get some mail, my friend. Lots of it. And not much that you'll want to read. In fact, there's even a name for Internet junk mail. It's called spam, but it doesn't taste as good. Note to the attorneys at Hormel: our generic use of the term "spam" is in keeping with accepted usage in Net culture, and is in no way intended to disparage the fine foodlike substance marketed by your firm, and distributed to the U.S. Army (blah!).[1]

How do you stop spam? In your e-mail "Preferences" settings, try putting an asterisk, or any other symbol, before your domain name in your real e-mail address (Example: yourname@yourdomain.com would become yourname@*yourdomain.com). Since most spamming

---

1 Most serious scholars of Internet culture (no, that's not an oxymoron!) agree that the term "spam" has its true origin in the famous Monty Python "Spam"® routine, which takes place in a restaurant where virtually the only available food choice is Spam®. For example, one of the specials is Spam®, Spam®, baked beans, and Spam®. The "lady" in the sketch finally says, in exasperation, "But I don't want any Spam® at all!" Which is pretty much the way most of us feel about junk e-mail.

programs simply grab e-mail addresses off the newsgroup headers without any human ever looking at them, the added symbol will make your address invalid. The spam will never get to you *or* your Internet Service Provider (at least until the spam programmers—who are almost as loathsome as the virus vermin—figure a way to filter such blocks).

Just be sure to make note of your clever little trick somewhere in your message, or the people you want to hear from will think it's a valid address, and they'll get their responses to your message back, marked "Return to Sender." Typically, you would add a line to your signature (or "sig") file which reads something like this: "My return address is intentionally invalid to minimize automated responses. Please remove the asterisk from the domain name when responding. My correct address is yourname@yourdomain.com."

Well, since we've been talking about food (sort of), there's one other devious little item you need to know about: *cookies*. No, I don't mean the kind you dunk in your scotch. Cookies are little strings of code that some websites plant in your computer when you visit. They don't do anything but announce, to anyone who has the right program, every place you've ever gone in cyber-space. Now, be honest: are you willing to proclaim, to the world, every website you've ever visited? Even that "just this once 'cause I'm curious" trip to Mistress Angelica's XXX-rated Dungeon? In essence, with cookies you are unwittingly providing information on all your interests and personal preferences to any number of marketing organizations, or worse, to your rabidly vindictive ex-spouse. Even if you never wander into those places that Mama wouldn't approve of, you're still telling an awful lot about yourself to people you don't even know. Think about it.

Luckily, the fix is easy. On my Windows-based computer, for example, I just search my hard drive for any files named *cookies.txt*. I then open the "Properties" dialog for that file, and change the attributes to Read Only. When a site accesses this file and tries to put its signature on it, my computer won't let them. They'll still be able to read it, but since I've erased all the entries, it'll be a pretty boring story, and they'll move on. No matter which operating system your computer uses, you no doubt have access to a means for tossing your cookies, too. If you're not sure, ask a computer guru who's familiar with your type of machine.

What about E-Mail Privacy?

Okay, let's say you're not in the habit of visiting racy sites on the Web, or any sites at all, for that matter, so you're not particularly worried about cookies. And you don't post to newsgroups, so you're not fretful about your anti-government sentiments being out there for "Them" to read. And maybe you don't even mind a little spam-o-gram once in awhile; after all, it's easy to hit the "delete" key, and besides— who knows?—some of those schemes for making millions in your spare time by stuffing e-mail boxes just might be legitimate.

But let's say that you *do* like to use your online time to post sweet e-nothings to your secret cyberlover. For months now you and this person have been burning up the bandwidths with your passionate declarations of undying lust for each other. Not to worry, though; it is just between the two of you, right?

Well, not necessarily. It comes as a shock to many people when they learn how notoriously *un*-private e-mail is. In fact, it's less secure, and in many ways more dangerous, than sending your personal or business messages on a postcard. Andre Bacard, author of *Computer Privacy Handbook*,[2] says that when he asked a Silicon Valley CEO if he uses e-mail, the man said, "Hell no. Half the nerds in my company can hack e-mail. E-mail is a party line!"

A *MacWorld* survey taken a couple of years ago found that roughly 25 percent of the businesses contacted admitted they eavesdrop on employee computer files, e-mail, or voice mail. In many firms this is simply considered legitimate company policy; the 25 percent reflected in the survey excludes *unauthorized* e-mail monitoring. Anyway, if you're using a computer at work, it's just plain foolish to assume that nobody is going to be reading your e-mail communications except you and the recipient.

Even if you're not e-mailing on a company computer but have your own machine at home, the truth is that e-mail is child's play for some people to intercept. The typical e-mail message travels through

---

2 Most of the information in this section is from Andre Bacard's "E-Mail Privacy FAQ" Also check out Bacard's book, *Computer Privacy Handbook: A Practical Guide to E-Mail Encryption, Data Protection, and PGP Privacy Software* (published by Peachpit Press).

many computers, and at each computer, people can access your personal and business correspondence. I'm not saying that they necessarily will, but the fact that they *can* is cause for concern.

"Well, doesn't my password protect me?" you may be asking. Not from astute hackers, it doesn't. As Bacard writes in his e-mail privacy FAQ, "Unix, DOS, and other software networks are . . . easy for administrators to manipulate. Who is to stop your Internet hook-up provider or any network supervisor from using or distributing your password?"

Okay, so I've gotten you properly paranoid, to the point that you've gone and deleted all those pulsating-modem mash notes. Well, aside from the fact that e-mail is "owned" by both the sender and the recipient—so your cyberhoney has carte blanche to exploit those sweet messages in any way she or he sees fit—there's another reason to be nervous. You see, even if you can persuade your love to follow your lead and get rid of all that incriminating correspondence, e-mail doesn't necessarily vanish after it's been "deleted." Many Internet providers and network administrators archive, or store, your incoming and outgoing mail on a computer disk for six months or more after you think you've deleted your mail—even though you may specify that all mail, once deleted, is to be deleted from the server. So if your spouse gets wind of your online affair and decides to sue you for divorce, he or she may be able to subpoena and read your previous correspondence. Or, some random unauthorized snoop might choose to read your archive for their own reasons.

What motivates these meddlers? Any number of things, according to Bacard. Apart from government busybodies, snoops come in all flavors and genders. An unauthorized snoop could be anybody from the office intriguer trying to play people against you, to a computer stalker like the one who shot actress Rebecca Schaffer to death, to a blackmailer, to an old-fashioned voyeur. As Bacard says, "Information is power. Snoops want power."

Well, then, let's say that you *don't* have a secret cyberlover, or any other dark secrets, and in fact you feel you really have nothing to hide. Why would you even be concerned about e-mail privacy? Bacard has an answer to that: "Show me an e-mail user who has no financial, sexual, social, political, or professional secrets to keep from his family, his neighbors, or his colleagues, and I'll show you someone who is either an extraordinary exhibitionist or an incredible dullard. Show me a corporation that has no trade secrets or confidential records, and I'll show you a business that is not very successful."

Robert Ellis Smith, who is the publisher of *Privacy Journal*, cracks both wise and profound when he says, "An employee with nothing to hide may very well be an employee with nothing to offer." Bacard goes so far as to declare that "privacy, discretion, confidentiality, and prudence are the hallmarks of civilization." I'd have to second that notion. We're talking principle here.

So what can you do to protect your e-mail privacy? Two things, suggests Bacard. First, use PGP (Pretty Good Privacy) software to encrypt your e-mail, and for that matter, all your computer files, so that snoops cannot read them. PGP is the de facto world standard software for e-mail security. You should be aware, however, that the government is busily working on regulating such programs, so they can decipher your messages if they deem necessary. Stay tuned for future developments in this matter.

Secondly, use anonymous remailers to send e-mail to network newsgroups or to individuals. That way, snoops can't tell your real name or e-mail address.

To find out more about e-mail privacy tools, check out the Usenet newsgroups (alt.security.pgp) and (alt.privacy.anon-server). Bacard also suggests you support groups such as the Electronic Frontier Foundation (for information e-mail info@eff.org), and the Electronic Privacy Information Center (EPIC), which I mentioned earlier in this book. Check out their website at www.epic.org or send them an e-mail to info@epic.org.

Bacard believes, as I do and have said several times throughout this book, that we live in an anti-privacy society with too much information technology and not enough safeguards. Computers can serve your personal data on a silver platter to virtually anybody: government snoops, office gossips, or criminals. Even if you're not trying to "hide your assets and disappear," you need to be aware of how vulnerable we all are to those who can't keep their noses out of other people's business.

Okay . . . So I'm Terrified Already. Tell Me Something *Good* About the Internet!

Even with the pitfalls noted above, the Internet is easily the world's richest source of current information on virtually any topic.

But, as I said earlier, finding the information you want can be frustrating. What begins as a focused search for answers can easily degenerate into aimless wandering from website to website. It can be fun, but it's not very efficient.

Imagine you're in the grocery store, shopping for your dinner. Well, to really get a proper analogy going, let's also imagine that some time before you left home, you ate a couple of herb-infused brownies. So now you're in the store, your mission being to purchase ingredients for an entrée and a salad. You pick out a couple of nice steaks and head for the produce section. While you're there, you eye some beautiful, juicy-looking strawberries, and remember about the delicious strawberry pie your mom used to make. Hungrily tripping down nostalgia lane, you wander over to the bakery to look for strawberry pies. Standing at the bakery, you notice a burned-out light bulb in the display case, which reminds you of the light in the closet you've been meaning to replace. Off you go to housewares. Passing the magazine rack on the way, you notice that one of the fanzines features an article about what your favorite movie star does with his pet sheep, so you naturally pick it up and read. You read for about 10 minutes when it occurs to you, "Damn, I'm hungry." You've been in the store for nearly an hour, and you're not any closer to dinner than when you arrived.

It sounds silly, but that's how many people "surf" the Net. The real art is in using efficient search techniques and tools, and *staying focused*. Whatever you do, don't eat any magic brownies before you log on; that's just asking for trouble.

So where does one begin an online search for information about beginning a new life in another country? (Remember? That's what you're reading this book for . . . unless you're still stuck in the produce aisle!) My advice is first to seek out the websites and Usenet groups referenced in the appendix of this book. In this appendix, I have listed a number of websites and newsgroups from which I have gathered valuable information, some of which appears in this book.

Within the sites and newsgroups, you will find innumerable "links" which will take you to even more sites, some featuring related information, and some offering more specialized data to answer specific questions you might have.

You may also want to start from scratch by accessing one of the *search engines* or Web page directories and typing in a keyword upon which your search is based. You'll find that the more specific you are in your query, the more closely the search results will come to answering your questions. If, however, you're too specific in selecting your search criteria, you might not get any information at all. For example, if you use the word "offshore" as your only keyword, you will get responses dealing with everything from the oil business to sport fishing, with a few references to the world of foreign finance thrown in for good measure. (As more and more sites are added to the World Wide Web, the ratios will shift, and a broader range of topic-specific sites will become available.)

On the other hand, let's say you type in "offshore investment Costa Rica," because that's what you really want to know about. Bingo! You will receive far fewer responses, but they will be much more pertinent to your query.

Surfing the Internet and developing effective search techniques are, as stated earlier, their own art forms. There are stores full of books and software to help you, but ultimately, you'll have to develop your own style.

When you find a site, a person, a business, or a location that catches your interest, one good way to check up on them is to query the Usenet newsgroups. Let's say you want to see if XYZ Corporation is a reputable firm. You could go to a search engine such as AltaVista or my favorite, Dogpile (www.altavista.com and www.dogpile.com), and type "XYZ Corporation" in the keyword block, then select "Usenet" in the "Search In" box. Click on the Search button, and within a few seconds, you'll have a list of references. Then simply click on the ones that seem to apply, and see what other folks have to say. Granted, you'll run into some crackpots and folks with axes to grind, but if an overwhelming majority of the entries express the same opinion, it's a pretty good bet that opinion is accurate. Use your judgment.

Beyond the basics, you're pretty much on your own to develop a search technique that works for you. Just remember to stay focused, stay wary, and sleep and eat every now and then. The Net can be very seductive, and easy to disappear into. Save that for your new home!

In Conclusion

I hope I have planted the seeds of your own fulfillment. The *choice* is yours to make. Don't be the one that someday says, "I wish I had done that" or " I could've started all over."

We all have the chance to do or to be whatever we want; it is what we do with it that makes the difference. My father once told me, "The only things you will ever regret in life are the ones that you've never done."

I think he was right.

APPENDICES

Appendix A
Resources on the World Wide Web

Topic	Sources	Website / E-Mail Addresses
Banking / Offshore Information	Offshore & Int'l. Taxation page	http://www.law.vill.edu/~mquarles/int_tax.html
Barbados Business Information	Fleethouse	http://www.fleethouse.com/barbados/barb-bus.htm
Belize Information	Belize First Magazine	http://207.136.90.57/belizefirst
Caribbean Information	CaribNet	http://www.caribnet.net/
Caribbean Information	Caribbean Online	http://www.caribbean-on-line.com
Consular Information Sheets	U.S. State Department	http://travel.state.gov
Costa Rica Information	Cinde	http://www.cinde.or.cr
Costa Rica Information	Costa Rica NetGuide	http://www.costaricainfo.com
Costa Rica Medical Information	Health Tourism Corp. of Costa Rica	http://www.cocori.com/healthtourcr/
Expat Admin. / Investment Information	Freebooter	http://www.freebooter.com/index.html
Expat Information	Expatriate Life	http://www.hiway.co.uk/expats/
Expat Information	Escape Artist	http://www.escapeartist.com
Foreign Investment Information	Taipan	http://taipanonline.com
Guatemala Information	Infoguate	http://www.infoguate.com
Guatemala Information	QuetzalNet	http://www.quetzalnet.com
Health Care in Costa Rica	Health Tourism Corporation of Costa Rica	http://www.cocori.com/healthtourcr/
Honduras Information	Honduras Online	http://www.turq.com/honduras.html
International Issues	Agora Publishing	http://agoralang.com
Investment Data	Infodat	http://www.infodat.com
Offshore Business Opportunities	Usenet newsgroup	Alt.business.offshore
Offshore Investment	DataOffshore Outlook Online	http://www.offshore-outlook.com
Offshore Investment Information	The Offshore Entrepreneur	http://www.au.com/offshore
Personal Privacy Issues	Eden Press	http://www.toplink.com/eden.htm
Political Commentary	Mother Jones Magazine	http://www.mojones.com
Privacy Issues	PrivacyInc Newsletter	PrivacyInc@compuserve.com
Privacy Issues & Advertisements	The Privacy Pages	http://www.2020tech.com/maildrop/privacy.htm
Privacy Issues & Advertisements	Usenet newsgroup	Alt.privacySpecific
Information (by country)	Usenet newsgroup(s)	soc.culture.[country name]
Travel Advisories	U.S. State Department	http://travel.state.gov
Travel Tips	Lonely Planet	http://www.lonelyplanet.com
Vietnam Information	Vietnam Business Journal	http://www.viam.com/
Visa Information Telephone numbers	U.S. State Department	http://travel.state.gov/phone_faq.html

Appendix B

What to Take with You
Passport ☐
Visa ☐
Other Identification (Driver's License, MedicAlert, etc) ☐
Traveler's Checks ☐
Cash (For local exchange and purchases) ☐
Legal Records ☐
Will ☐
Financial Documents (Trusts, letters of incorporation, etc.) ☐
Family Records ☐
Medical Records ☐
Prescriptions (Valid, signed by physician) ☐
Medications ☐
Pet Records ☐
School Records ☐
Suitable Clothing ☐
Address Book ☐
Photo Albums ☐
Electronics (VCR, Television, Radio, Stereo, Camcorder) ☐
Converters (Check voltage in destination country) ☐
Favorite Books ☐
Tools ☐
Photography Gear ☐
Sporting gear ☐

What NOT to Bring
Guns and Other Weapons
(Check applicable federal and local regulations first) ☐
Illegal Drugs ☐
Pets (Check quarantine requirements) ☐
Materials deemed offensive in your new home
    Religious materials contrary to majority standards ☐
    Pornography ☐
    Political materials and propaganda ☐

Appendix C

Before You Leave . . .

Are your finances in order?   ☐
Have you handled your forwarding address?   ☐
Are all your travel documents validated?   ☐
How are you explaining your departure?   ☐
Have you resolved necessary legal matters?   ☐
Have you left the government a reason to look for you?   ☐
How about your creditors?   ☐
Your ex?   ☐
Have you "covered your tracks"?   ☐
Have you said your good-byes?   ☐
Have you disposed of unneeded property and possessions?   ☐
Have you *really* decided to leave?   ☐

Real Answers to Real Questions

Since the initial publication of this book, I received letters, e-mails, and calls from thousands of readers wanting more information on how they could leave their old lives behind and create a new life of financial and personal freedom. Here are up-to-date answers to the top twenty reader questions:

1. **Is there work offshore?**

a. Yes, many third-world or emerging countries are in dire need of people who have technical, teaching, and sales skills. If you can operate, program, or repair a computer, you sit on the right hand of God. If you can fix appliances, machinery, or automobiles, you are a God! There is also a big demand for teachers who can teach children and those who can teach English to children and adults.

2. **Can I still open a numbered account in a foreign country?**

a. Sorry, no can do! The world banking powers that be have decreed that all new account holders be identified by a photo I.D. and must state the source of their funds. The reason for this is to screen out drug money and to ensure that heirs of the account holder can be identified if they become deceased.

3. **Is Switzerland still a good place for a secret account?**

a. Nope, Switzerland has signed the mutual legal assistance treaty (MLAT) that provides for the sharing of information in certain criminal cases. Besides, they don't pay interest in their bank accounts, so who would want one, especially in a place that is too well known for its secrecy in the past!

4. **Can I have dual citizenship, legally?**

a. Yes, you can have dual citizenship. Many people now do, many do so legally. The best way to do it is to repatriate in the land of your forefathers, which can be done through the assistance of the branch of their U.S. embassy!

5.   **What is the best retirement in the Caribbean?**

a.   Costa Rica has the best living conditions and highest standard of living (great views, schools, and medical care), but I think that Roatân in Honduras is the best value for the dollar, followed by the Honduran mainland, which is recovering from Hurricane Mitch through some major construction assistance from Uncle Sam.

6.   **How can I find out about or check out offshore people and their business connections?**

a.   The best way to check someone out is to make contact with a local banker, attorney, or embassy officer who knows the local politics and people. Another thing that you can do is to research these people on the Internet, looking for old newspaper articles about their past deeds and misdeeds.

7.   **Are any foreign bank accounts insured?**

a.   Foreign banks are not usually insured like the FDIC insures American banks. There is a scam floating around called the International Deposit Indemnity Corporation (IDIC) that purports to insure deposits of banks in Grenada, Nauru and other offshore areas. This is not the real thing, and does not afford any protection of your accounts.

8.   **Can I avoid U.S. taxes by moving out of the United States?**

a.   This is a qualified maybe. Uncle Sam has put the squeeze on his citizens by passing legislation making it more and more difficult to avoid taxes by moving offshore. It can be done if you show that you did not INTEND to avoid taxes and that you have followed the new IRS guidelines for the $70,000 tax exemption offered to U.S. citizens who work and have their primary residence outside the United States. (Of course, if you don't care to return at any time, who cares. Most other countries consider tax evasion a sport, not a crime, and will not extradite you for this most heinous of offenses.)

9.   **Is there good medical care in the third-world countries?**

a.   Many countries have excellent doctors and much lower charges because they don't have to pay for malpractice insurance, golf courses, and yachts. Besides, you can really get in to see one of them, and they even make house calls!

10.   **What is the best way to get money offshore into a foreign account?**

a.   If you want an account in any bank, do it yourself. Take a nice vacation to your place of choice and bring up to $10,000 per person (cash, cashier's checks, traveler's checks, or money orders) to open a savings account with a credit card that can be used to access your money anywhere in the world.

11. Can you safely buy property outside the United States?

a.   Real estate is a major investment, and one that should be done right the first time. Be sure that you have clear title, which usually entails all related family members signing off on the deed. Get a GOOD local attorney to do your due diligence and title work.

12. Do I have to show I.D. to open a foreign bank account?

a.   Sorry, that's the rules, if you open a BANK account. Now, if you are opening a trust or certain brokerage accounts, then personal identification may not be requested.

13. Are the "offshore opportunity seminars" offered by various groups legitimate, and can I be safe in investing with people offering products through them?

a.   The products offered at these seminars range from the good, to the bad and the UGLY. You have to be the one to look into these "opportunities" and really scope them out (that's one of the main things that I do in my day job). Remember, it's your money and no one will watch it like you.

14. Are foreign banks secure from seizure by government or creditors?

a.   In some third-world countries, there have been banking problems, but most of them relate to devaluation of the local currency or the failure of the institution due to mismanagement or fraud (same as in our good old home banks). There have been instances where governments have frozen or closed banks, especially during a financial crisis, but those circumstances are rare.

As Mae West would say, "It's best to do business with a well-established firm," meaning, in our terms, that if you do business with the international banks that have offices world-wide, then you can move your money around within their system and branches at the blink of a fax. If you smell a revolution or a devaluation in the works, "poof," the money gets transferred to the far Pacific or some neutral region of the world where peace is the word of the day.

As far as creditors go, most civil or credit matters end at the border. If a U.S. creditor wants money from your offshore account, it's very difficult (if not impossible) and VERY expensive to attempt to pierce the veil of your foreign affairs and attach your bank accounts or assets. First, they have to get jurisdiction of you, then they must make a legal claim in that country, and then they must get the approval of the courts to pursue their claims (while you transfer the money somewhere else). Most creditors give up far before they reach that point.

15.   Does my credit history follow me outside the United States?

a.   Fortunately, your credit history goes only as far as the computer databases reach, and that is mostly in the United States. Most foreign countries don't offer the kind of credit we are used to in the U.S. of A., and don't have the computer resources or interest to care. Third-world countries loan money on collateral, like land, buildings, or money in the bank. They don't issue credit cards (unless they are the secured debit cards), student loans, or consumer credit, and therefore don't subscribe to the mega-credit bureaus that proliferate in this country.

16.   Can I wipe out a student loan?

a.   If you can figure out how to do this, tell me and we can both become millionaires. The government, in its effort to sell these loans to banks, have make ironclad rules and laws that make it next to impossible to discharge student loans, even by bankruptcy.

17.   Can U.S. courts pierce foreign trusts or corporations (IBCs)?

a.   In general, it is very difficult for a U.S. court, especially a civil court, to pierce a corporate veil and to determine the owners, beneficiaries, or nominees of a foreign entity. It has been done in the United States in some criminal cases, especially those involving drugs or organized crime, but the great majority of civil courts have found that they cannot get jurisdiction of the parties in foreign countries or agreements to provide information (the Mutual Legal Assistance Treaty or MLAT and the process called a Letter Rogatory, is one of the possible means of obtaining such assistance) from foreign courts or their governments.

18.   How can I travel invisibly and return without the U.S. government knowing where I have been?

a.   You can travel invisibly by either avoiding U.S. entry points or by having a second passport. U.S. Customs rarely checks private airports or marinas. Many people slip in and out of the country on boats with no one the wiser of their travel plans or destinations.

Now, if you have a second passport, then it's an easy matter to go in and out on a second passport rather than your own.

A third way to mask your travel is to stop off at some country along the way to your ultimate destination, as a cutout. For example, if you really wanted to go to Panama and didn't want anyone else to know, then you could buy a round-trip ticket from your U.S. home to Mexico City, get off the plane in Mexico City, and then walk down the street to another travel agency or ticket counter and buy another ticket to your final destination, Panama, with a return to Mexico City. When you come back home, your re-entry point will list your travel destination as Mexico City. *N'est pas?*

19. Do foreign banks report interest to the U.S. government?

a.   You are in luck! Few, if any (I don't know of any) foreign banks, brokerage houses, or foreign employers report their dealings with you back to Uncle Sam. They are certainly trying to make this happen, but it hasn't happened yet.

20. What countries grant citizenship and how?

a.   There are several ways to obtain the citizenship of a foreign country. One is to be a descendant of a family member of that country (Most foreign countries—especially Ireland, Germany, and Italy—are happy to welcome you home.) You can contact the nearest embassy of that country and ask them their policy and procedure for repatriating your citizenship to your native land.

If you would rather have a new native land, then you can pick one of several countries that offer *residencia* or citizenship to financially solvent people who deposit $50,000 to $100,000 in their high interest bearing bank accounts, or show the ability to financially support themselves and create opportunities for less fortunate natives.

ABOUT THE AUTHOR

EDMUND J. PANKAU, rated one of the nation's top 10 private investigators, is a world-renowned professional speaker and author of numerous articles and several award winning books on privacy and investigation. His published books include *Check It Out: Everyone's Guide to Investigation* (Contemporary, 1992), *How to Make $100,000 a Year as a Private Investigator* (Paladin, 1993) and *The P.I. Portfolio* (Inphomation, 1994).

He is the associate editor of *PI Magazine* and a contributing writer to *International Living* and many financial and investigative trade journals and magazines.

His experiences and cases have been featured in such publications as *Time*, *BusinessWeek*, *People*, *USA Today* and the *New York Times*. He has appeared as a guest on radio and TV on *ABC 20/20*, *Larry King Live*, *BBC London*, *Geraldo Rivera*, *CNBC Moneyline* and *America's Most Wanted* as an authority on privacy issues.

Ed is a graduate of Florida State University and is the director of Pankau Consulting, an investigative agency headquartered in Houston, Texas. If you *really* want to find him, it has been rumored that he was last sighted on the island of Roatân off the coast of Honduras. (P.S. Try to find him at Hideyourassets.com.)